WITHDRAWN

Author
Andy Seto

Translators
Kathy Lee
Wayne Moyung
Ken Li

Editors
Shawn Sanders
Mark Fujita
Duncan Cameron
Angel Cheng

Production Artist
Ying-Hsiang Lin

US Cover Design
Calvin Choi

Production Manager
Janice Chang

Art Director
Yuki Chung

Marketing
Nicole Curry

VP Operations
Thomas Kuo

English translation by
ComicsOne Corporation 2002

Publisher
ComicsOne Corp.
48531 Warm Springs Blvd., Suite 408
Fremont, CA 94539
www.ComicsOne.com

First Edition: January 2003
ISBN 1-58899-212-8

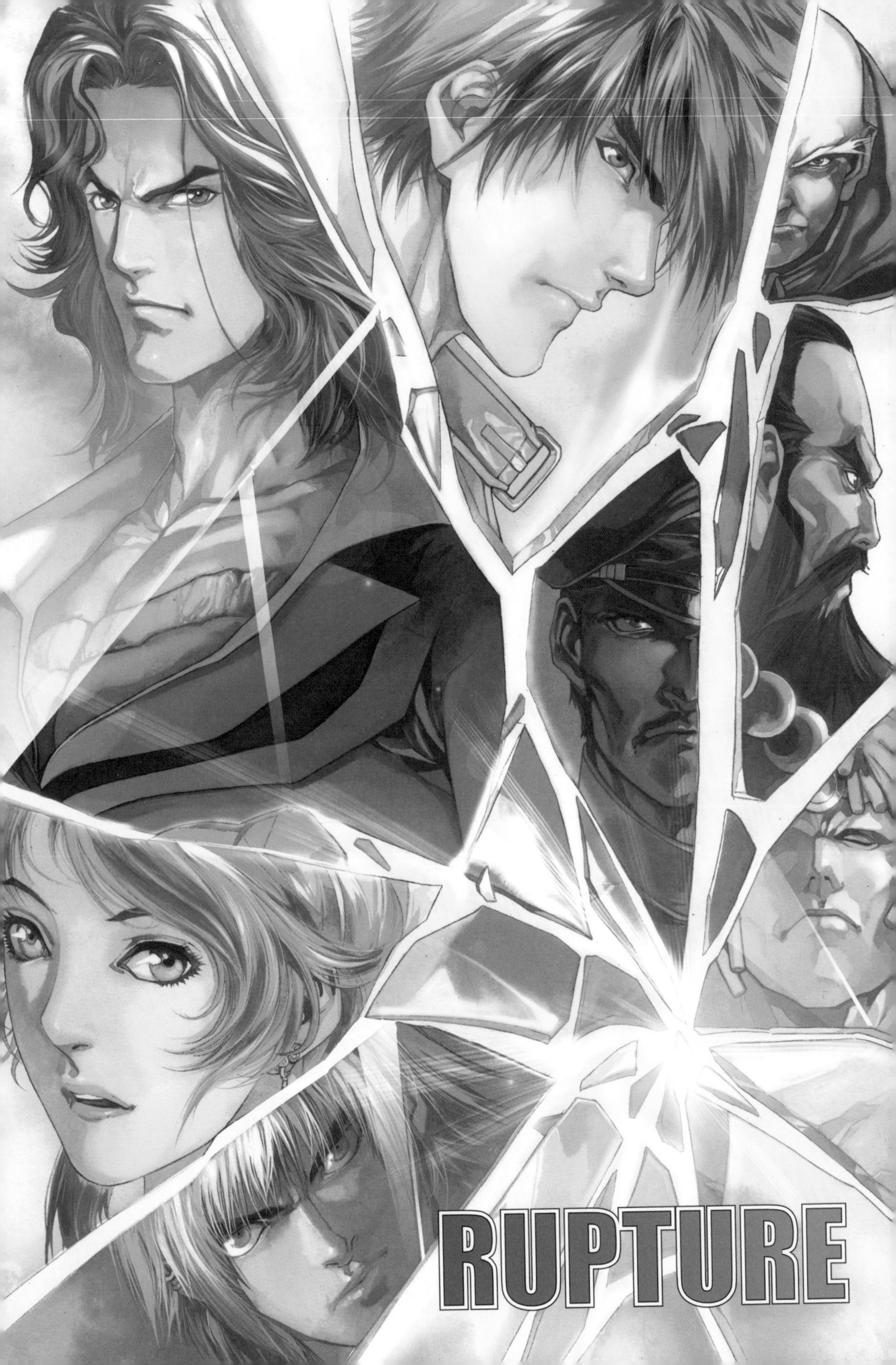
RUPTURE

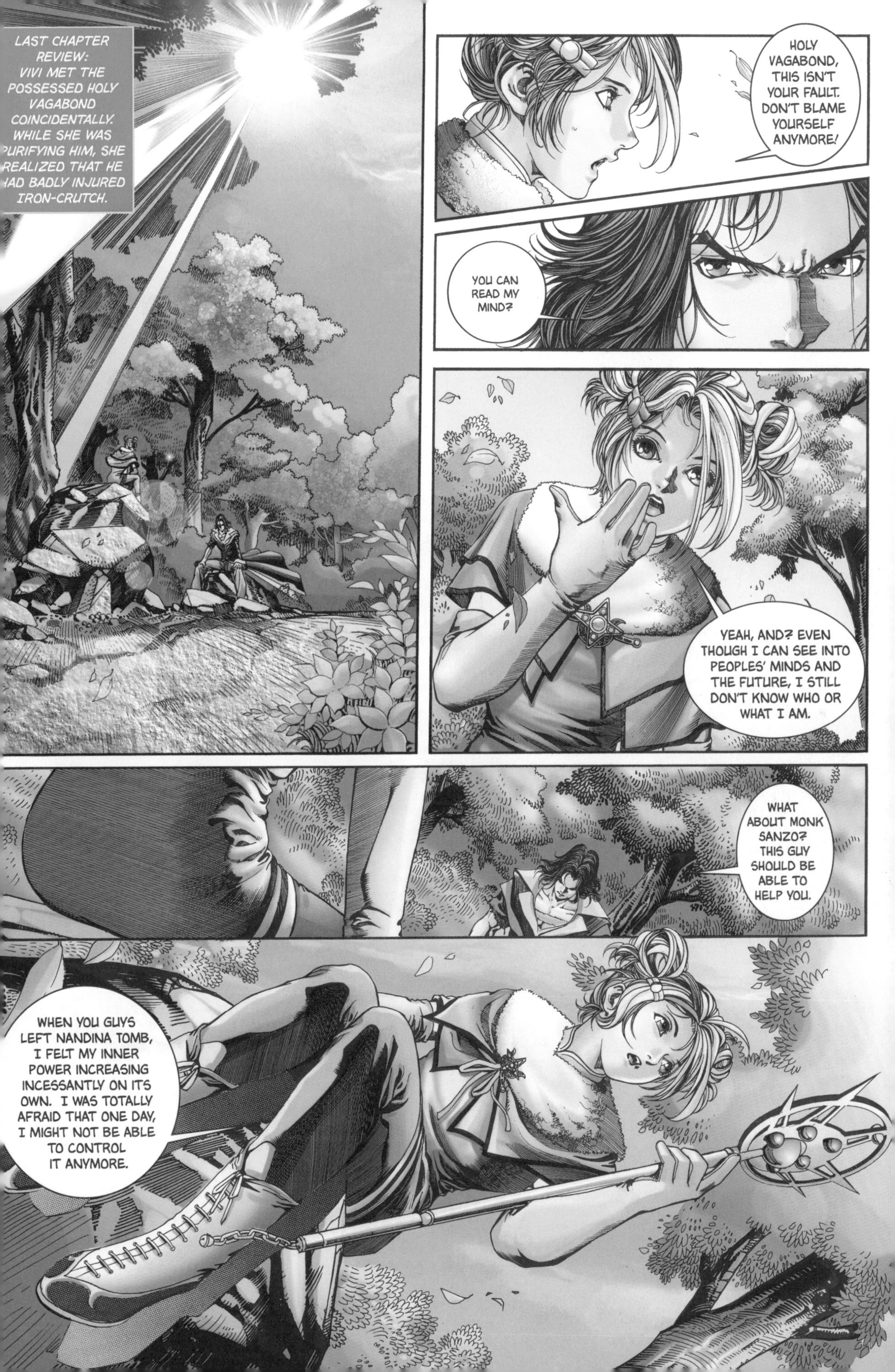
LAST CHAPTER REVIEW: VIVI MET THE POSSESSED HOLY VAGABOND COINCIDENTALLY. WHILE SHE WAS PURIFYING HIM, SHE REALIZED THAT HE HAD BADLY INJURED IRON-CRUTCH.
HOLY VAGABOND, THIS ISN'T YOUR FAULT. DON'T BLAME YOURSELF ANYMORE!
YOU CAN READ MY MIND?
YEAH, AND? EVEN THOUGH I CAN SEE INTO PEOPLES' MINDS AND THE FUTURE, I STILL DON'T KNOW WHO OR WHAT I AM.
WHAT ABOUT MONK SANZO? THIS GUY SHOULD BE ABLE TO HELP YOU.
WHEN YOU GUYS LEFT NANDINA TOMB, I FELT MY INNER POWER INCREASING INCESSANTLY ON ITS OWN. I WAS TOTALLY AFRAID THAT ONE DAY, I MIGHT NOT BE ABLE TO CONTROL IT ANYMORE.

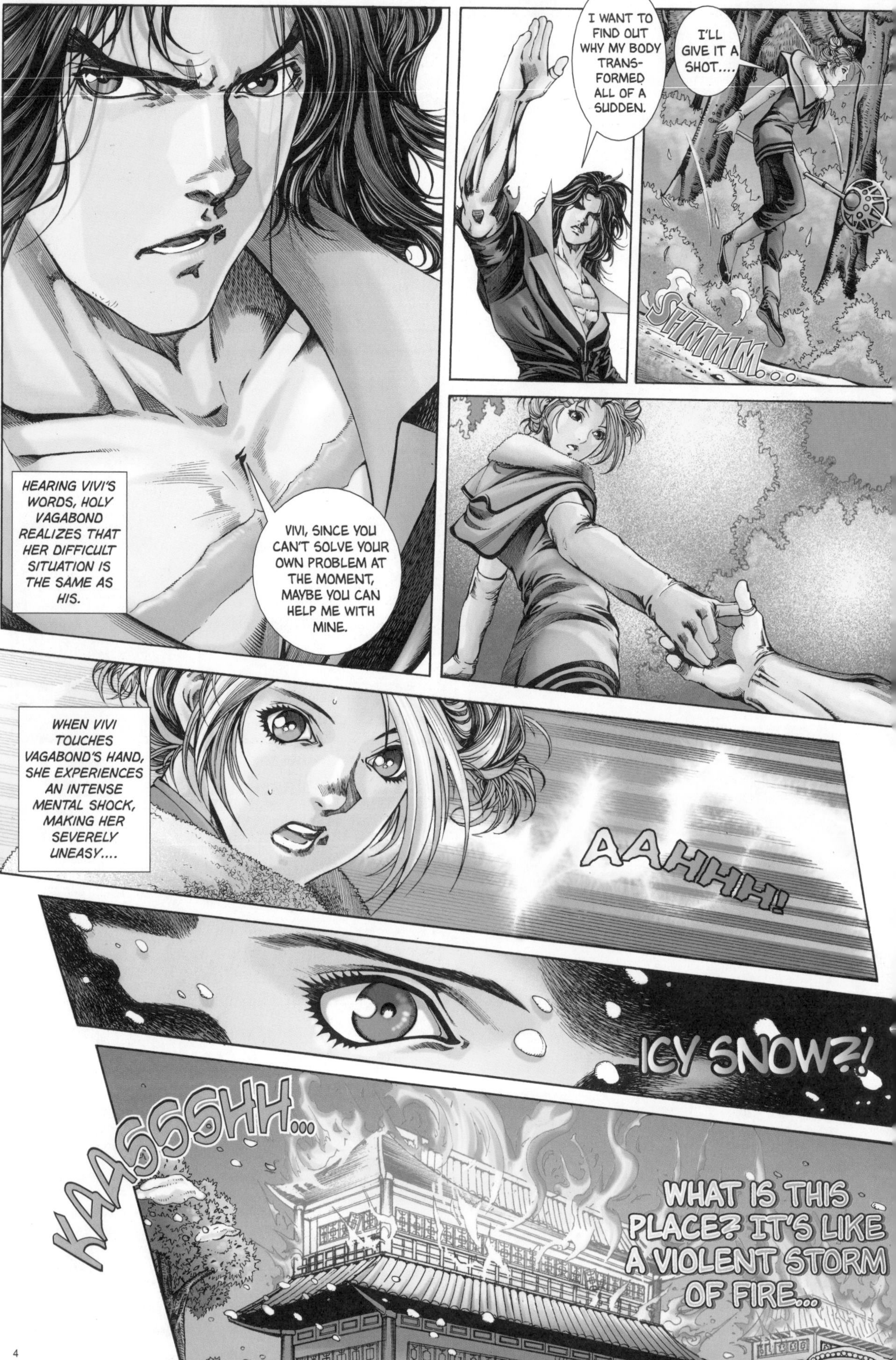
I WANT TO FIND OUT WHY MY BODY TRANS-FORMED ALL OF A SUDDEN.
I'LL GIVE IT A SHOT....
SHMMM...
HEARING VIVI'S WORDS, HOLY VAGABOND REALIZES THAT HER DIFFICULT SITUATION IS THE SAME AS HIS.
VIVI, SINCE YOU CAN'T SOLVE YOUR OWN PROBLEM AT THE MOMENT, MAYBE YOU CAN HELP ME WITH MINE.
WHEN VIVI TOUCHES VAGABOND'S HAND, SHE EXPERIENCES AN INTENSE MENTAL SHOCK, MAKING HER SEVERELY UNEASY....
AAHHHH!
ICY SNOW?!
KAASSSHH...
WHAT IS THIS PLACE? IT'S LIKE A VIOLENT STORM OF FIRE...

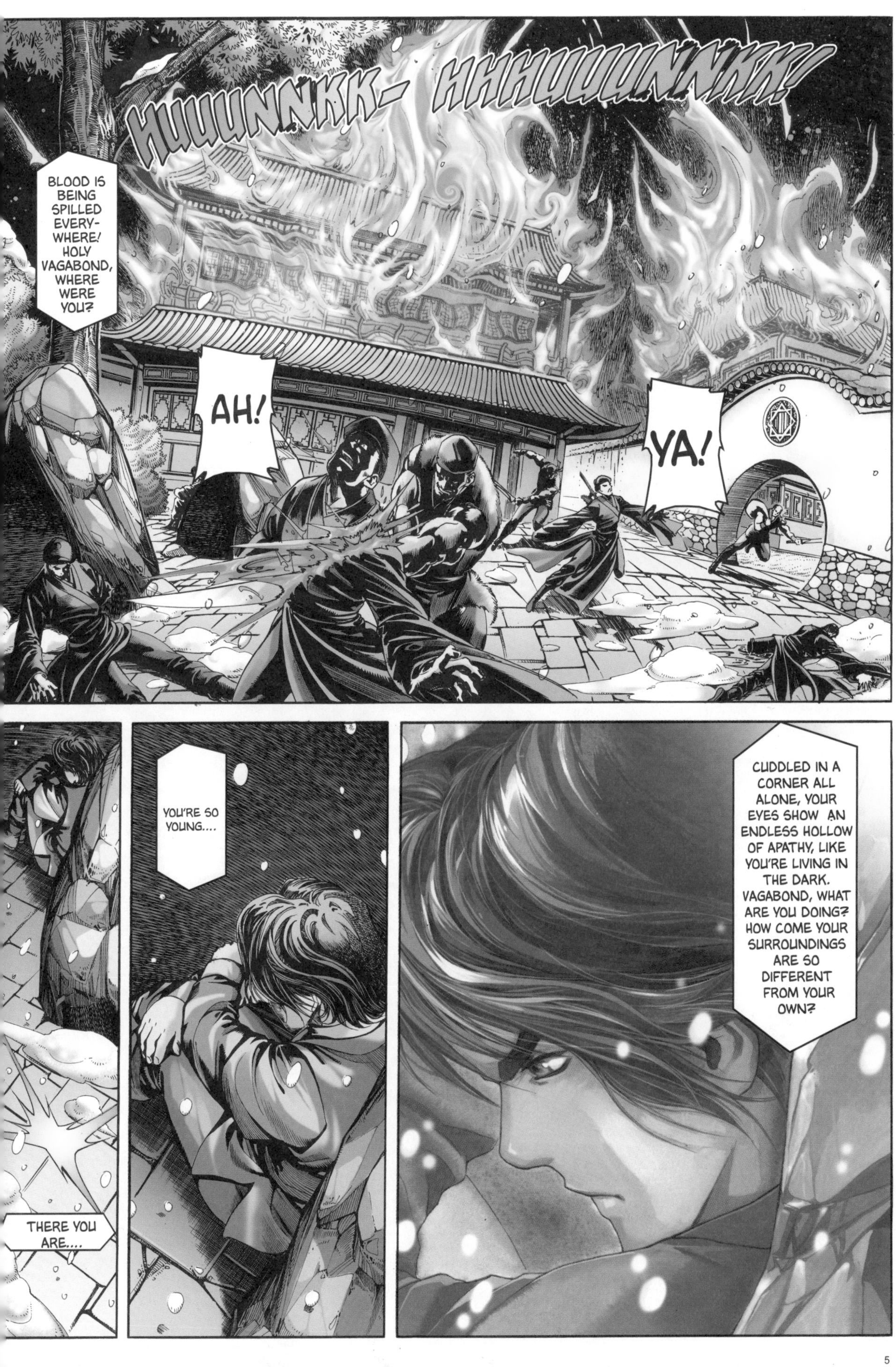
HUUUNNKK- HHHUUUUNNKK!
BLOOD IS BEING SPILLED EVERY-WHERE! HOLY VAGABOND, WHERE WERE YOU?
AH!
YA!
THERE YOU ARE....
YOU'RE SO YOUNG....
CUDDLED IN A CORNER ALL ALONE, YOUR EYES SHOW AN ENDLESS HOLLOW OF APATHY, LIKE YOU'RE LIVING IN THE DARK. VAGABOND, WHAT ARE YOU DOING? HOW COME YOUR SURROUNDINGS ARE SO DIFFERENT FROM YOUR OWN?

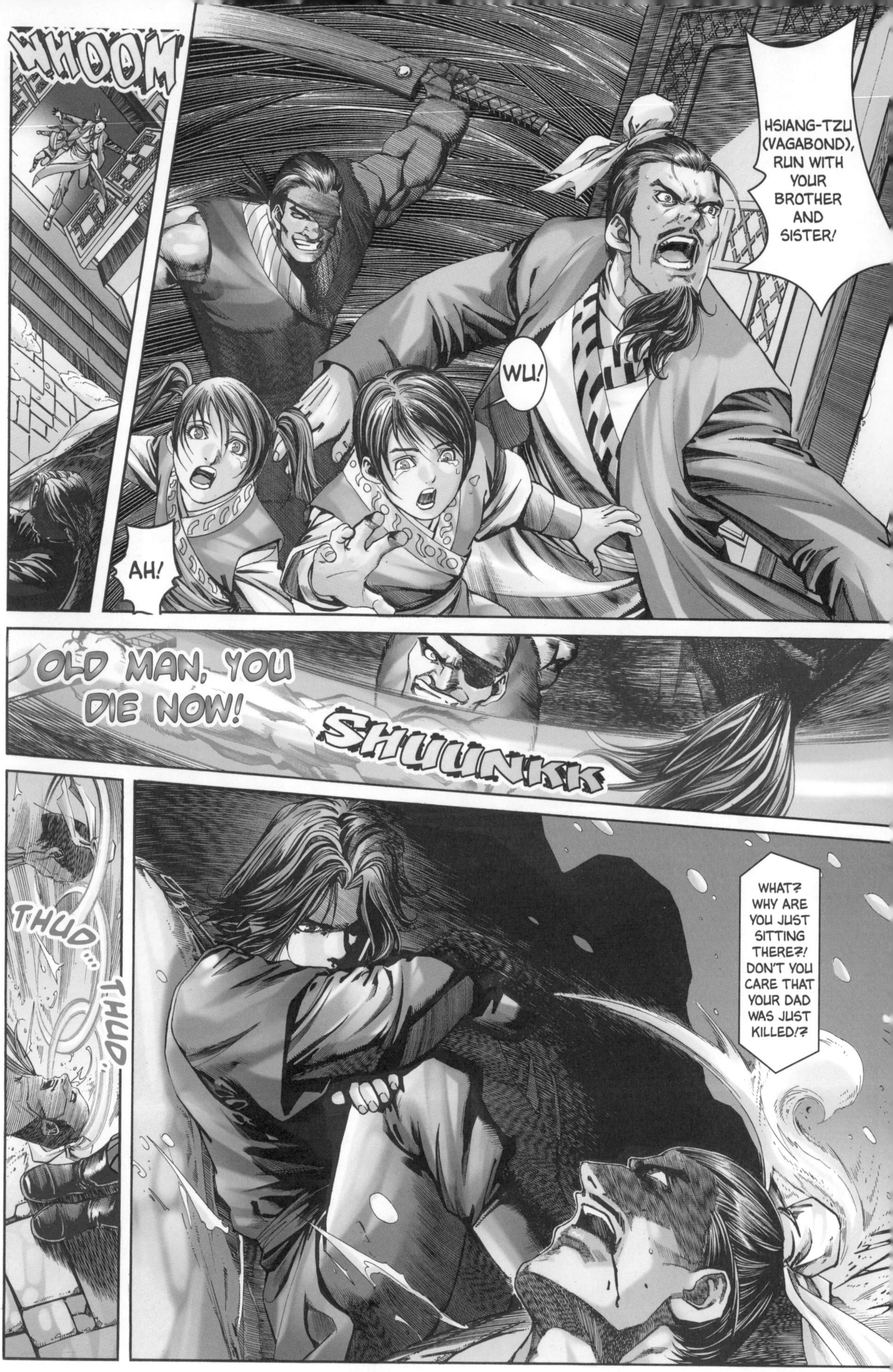
WHOOM
HSIANG-TZU (VAGABOND), RUN WITH YOUR BROTHER AND SISTER!
WU!
AH!
OLD MAN, YOU DIE NOW!
SHUUNKK
WHAT? WHY ARE YOU JUST SITTING THERE?! DON'T YOU CARE THAT YOUR DAD WAS JUST KILLED!?
THUD... THUD.

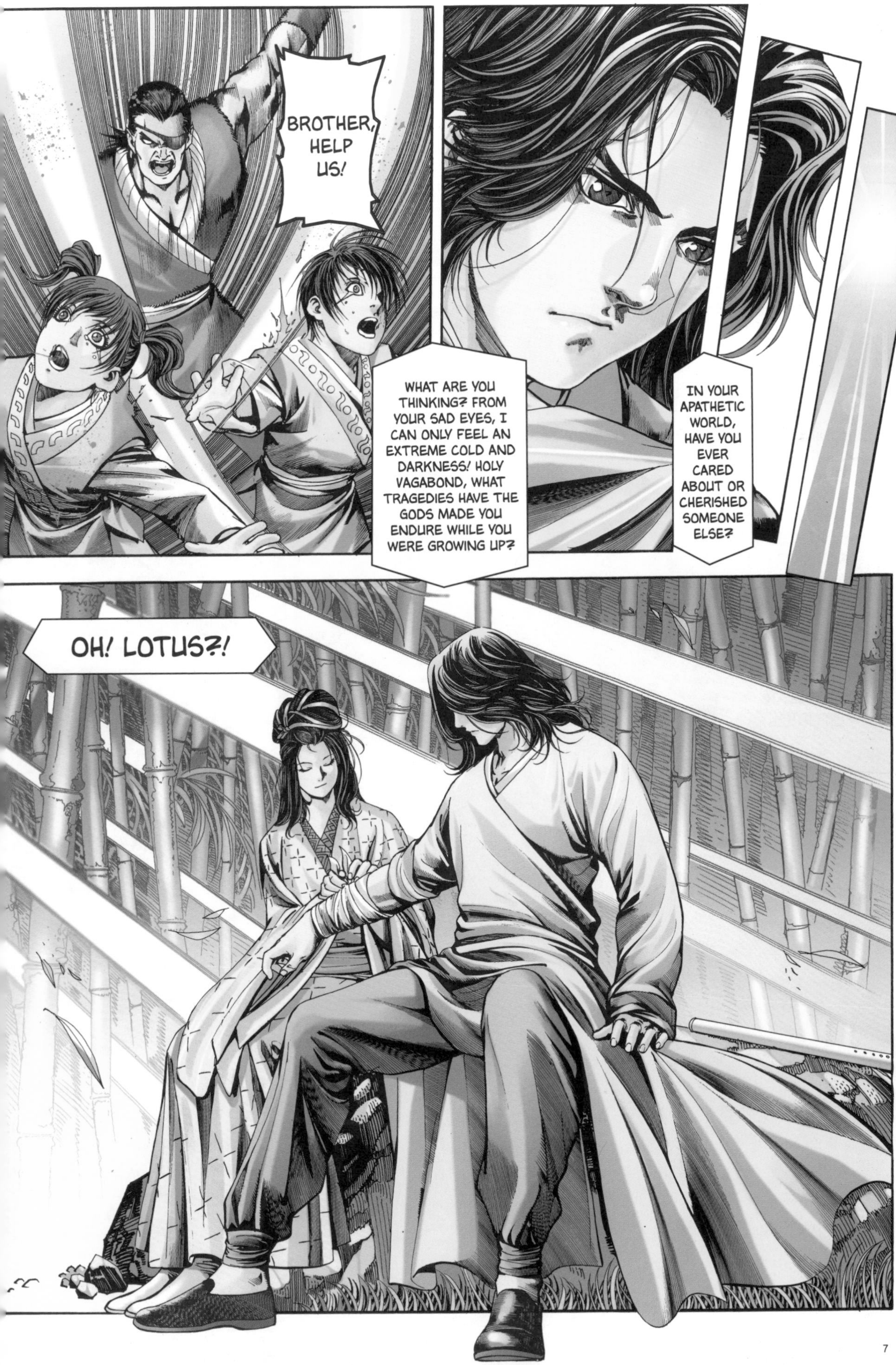
BROTHER, HELP US!
WHAT ARE YOU THINKING? FROM YOUR SAD EYES, I CAN ONLY FEEL AN EXTREME COLD AND DARKNESS! HOLY VAGABOND, WHAT TRAGEDIES HAVE THE GODS MADE YOU ENDURE WHILE YOU WERE GROWING UP?
IN YOUR APATHETIC WORLD, HAVE YOU EVER CARED ABOUT OR CHERISHED SOMEONE ELSE?
OH! LOTUS?!

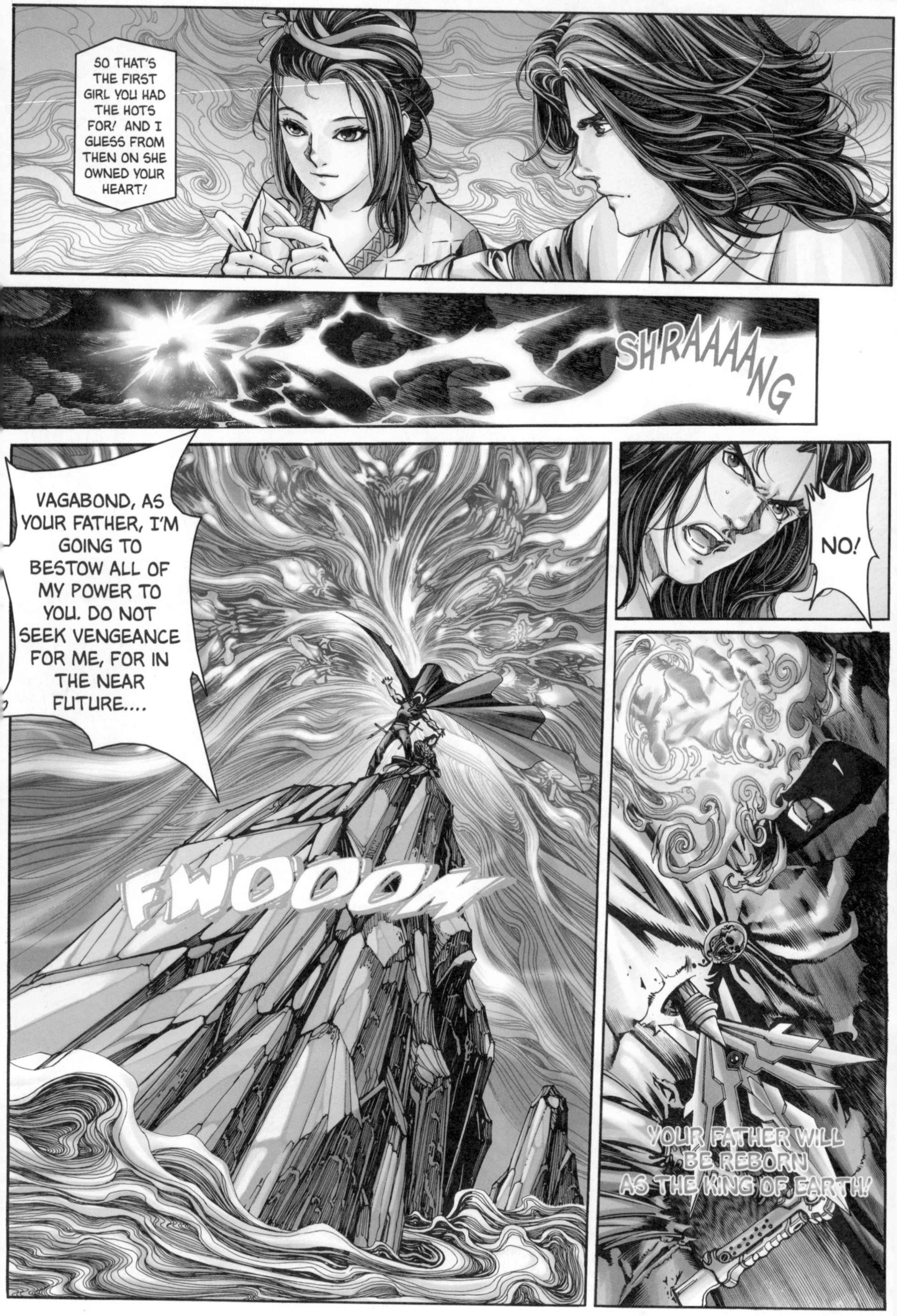
SO THAT'S THE FIRST GIRL YOU HAD THE HOTS FOR! AND I GUESS FROM THEN ON SHE OWNED YOUR HEART!
SHRAAAANG
VAGABOND, AS YOUR FATHER, I'M GOING TO BESTOW ALL OF MY POWER TO YOU. DO NOT SEEK VENGEANCE FOR ME, FOR IN THE NEAR FUTURE....
NO!
FWOOOM
YOUR FATHER WILL BE REBORN AS THE KING OF EARTH!

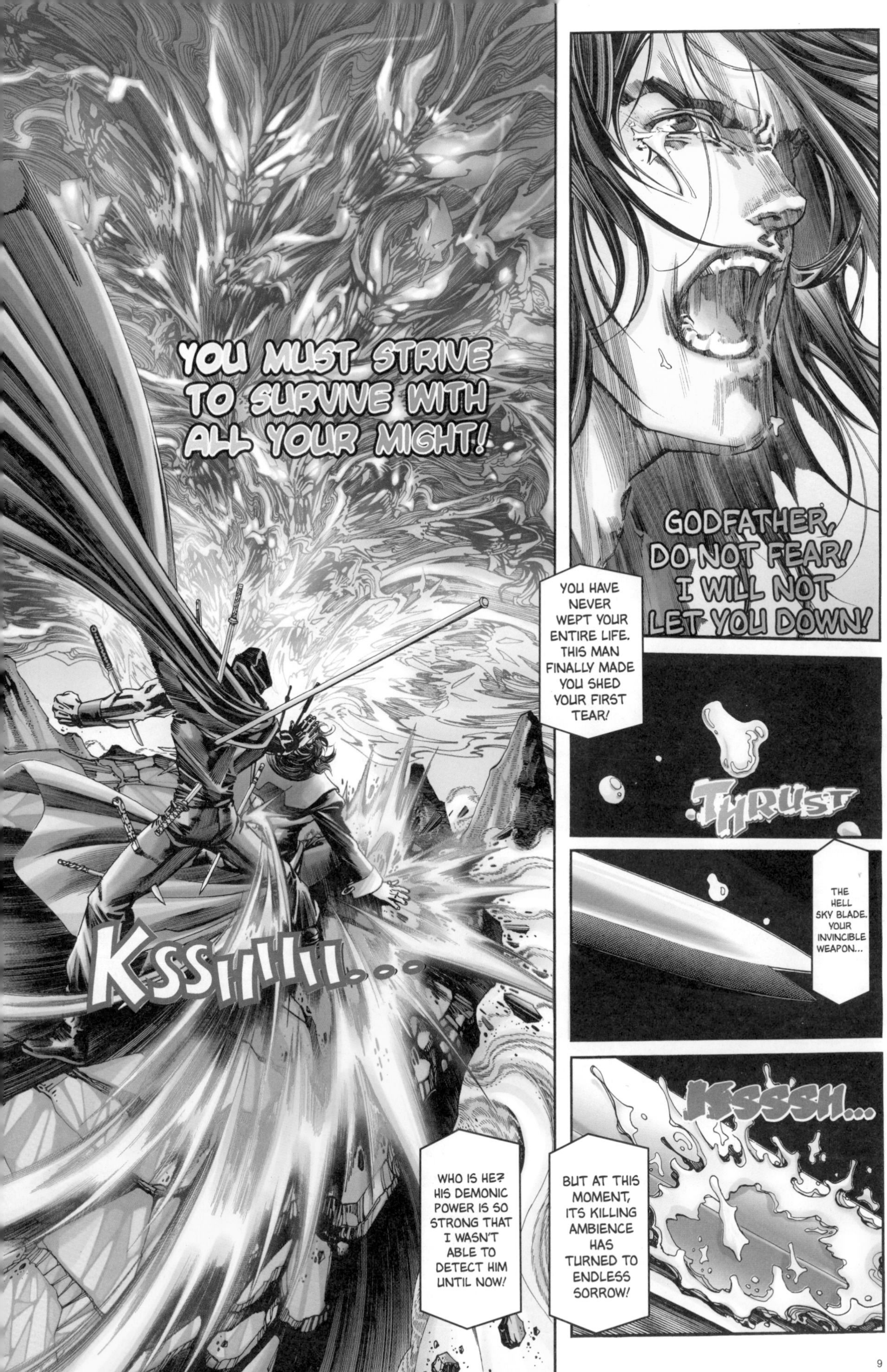

YOU MUST STRIVE TO SURVIVE WITH ALL YOUR MIGHT!
KSSHHHHH...
WHO IS HE? HIS DEMONIC POWER IS SO STRONG THAT I WASN'T ABLE TO DETECT HIM UNTIL NOW!
GODFATHER, DO NOT FEAR! I WILL NOT LET YOU DOWN!
YOU HAVE NEVER WEPT YOUR ENTIRE LIFE. THIS MAN FINALLY MADE YOU SHED YOUR FIRST TEAR!
THRUST
THE HELL SKY BLADE. YOUR INVINCIBLE WEAPON...
KSSSH...
BUT AT THIS MOMENT, ITS KILLING AMBIENCE HAS TURNED TO ENDLESS SORROW!

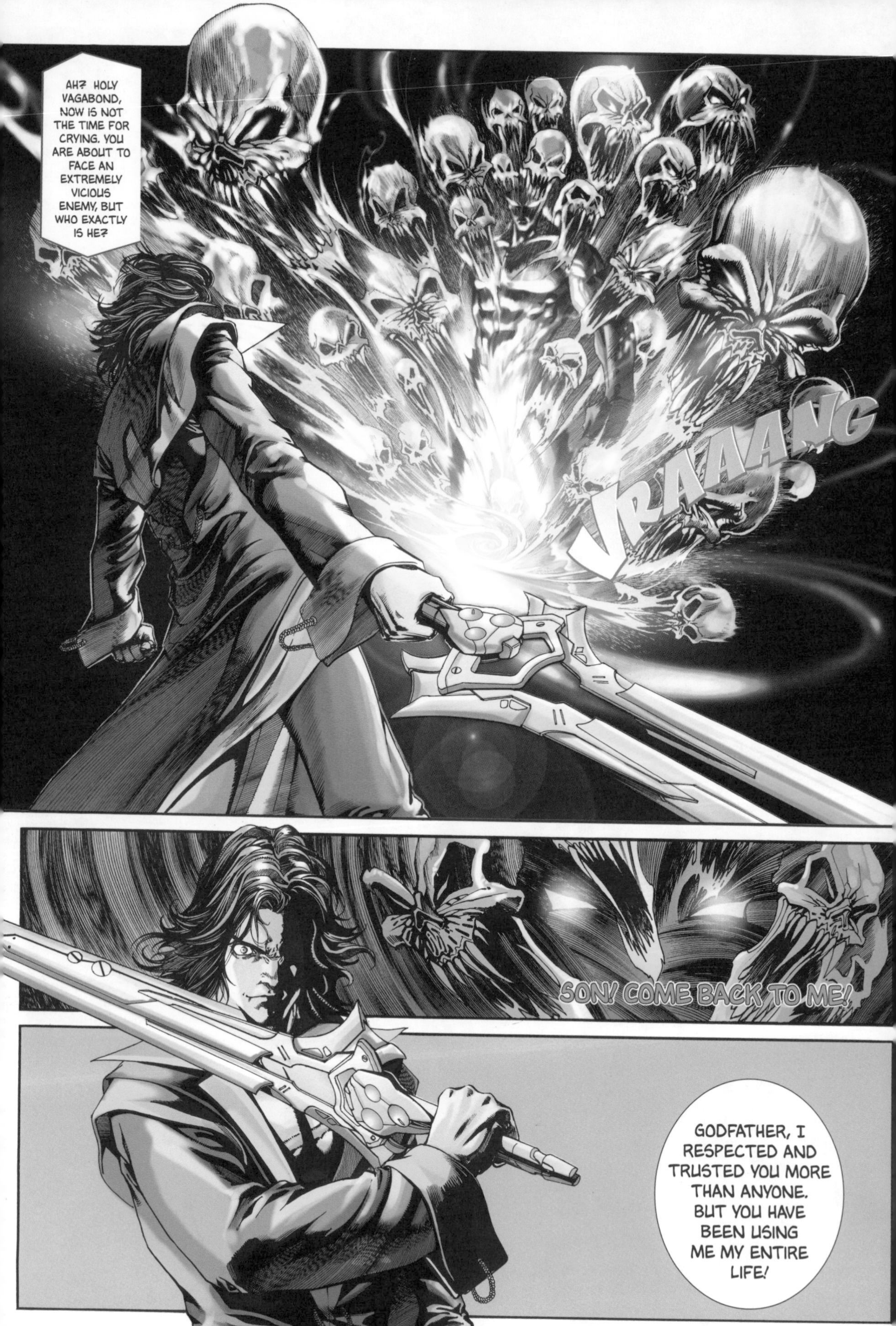
AH? HOLY VAGABOND, NOW IS NOT THE TIME FOR CRYING. YOU ARE ABOUT TO FACE AN EXTREMELY VICIOUS ENEMY, BUT WHO EXACTLY IS HE?
VRAAANG
SON! COME BACK TO ME!
GODFATHER, I RESPECTED AND TRUSTED YOU MORE THAN ANYONE. BUT YOU HAVE BEEN USING ME MY ENTIRE LIFE!

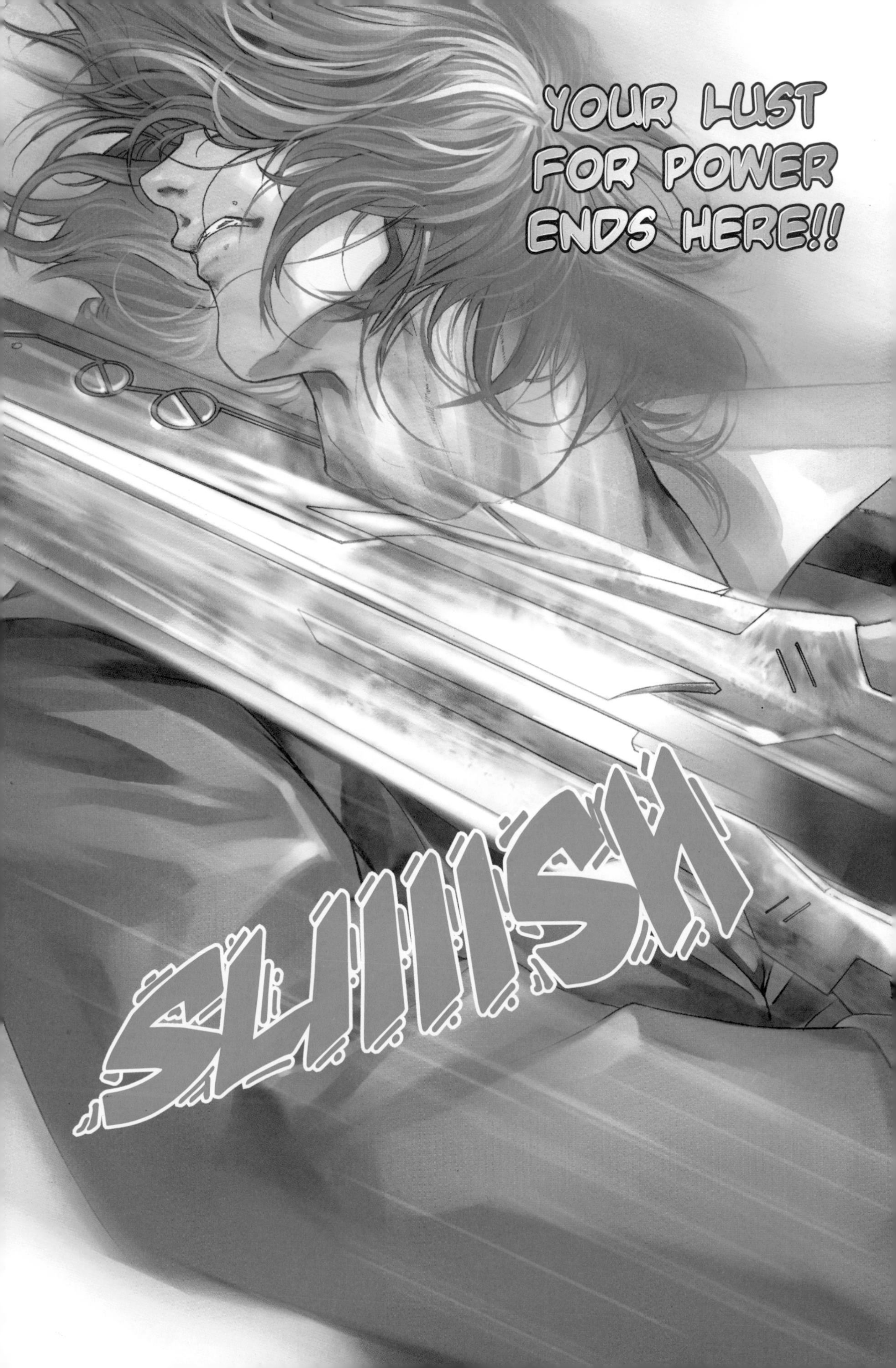
YOUR LUST FOR POWER ENDS HERE!!
SLIIIISH

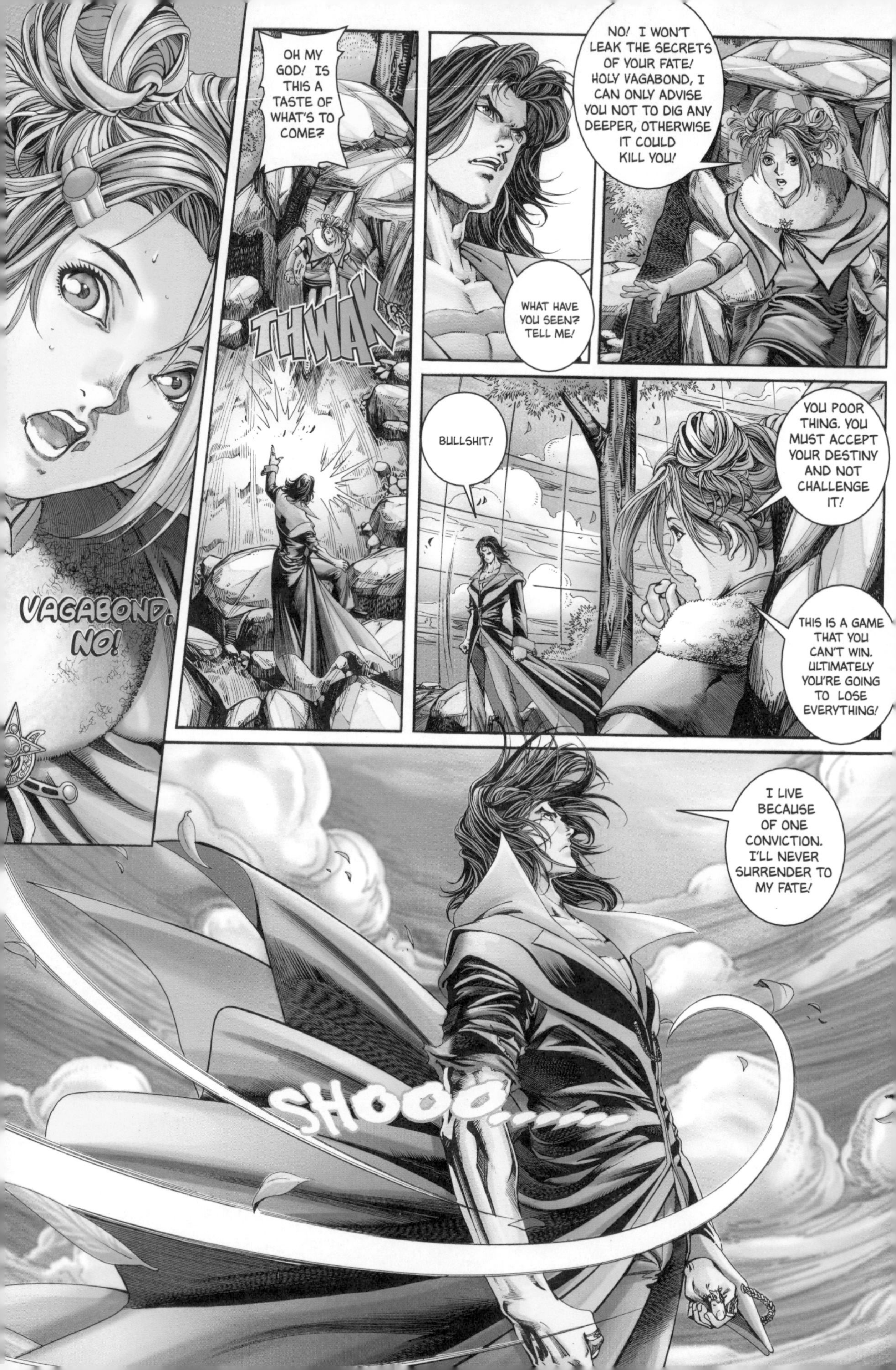
VAGABOND, NO!
OH MY GOD! IS THIS A TASTE OF WHAT'S TO COME?
THWAK
WHAT HAVE YOU SEEN? TELL ME!
NO! I WON'T LEAK THE SECRETS OF YOUR FATE! HOLY VAGABOND, I CAN ONLY ADVISE YOU NOT TO DIG ANY DEEPER, OTHERWISE IT COULD KILL YOU!
BULLSHIT!
YOU POOR THING. YOU MUST ACCEPT YOUR DESTINY AND NOT CHALLENGE IT!
THIS IS A GAME THAT YOU CAN'T WIN. ULTIMATELY YOU'RE GOING TO LOSE EVERYTHING!
I LIVE BECAUSE OF ONE CONVICTION. I'LL NEVER SURRENDER TO MY FATE!
SHOOO......

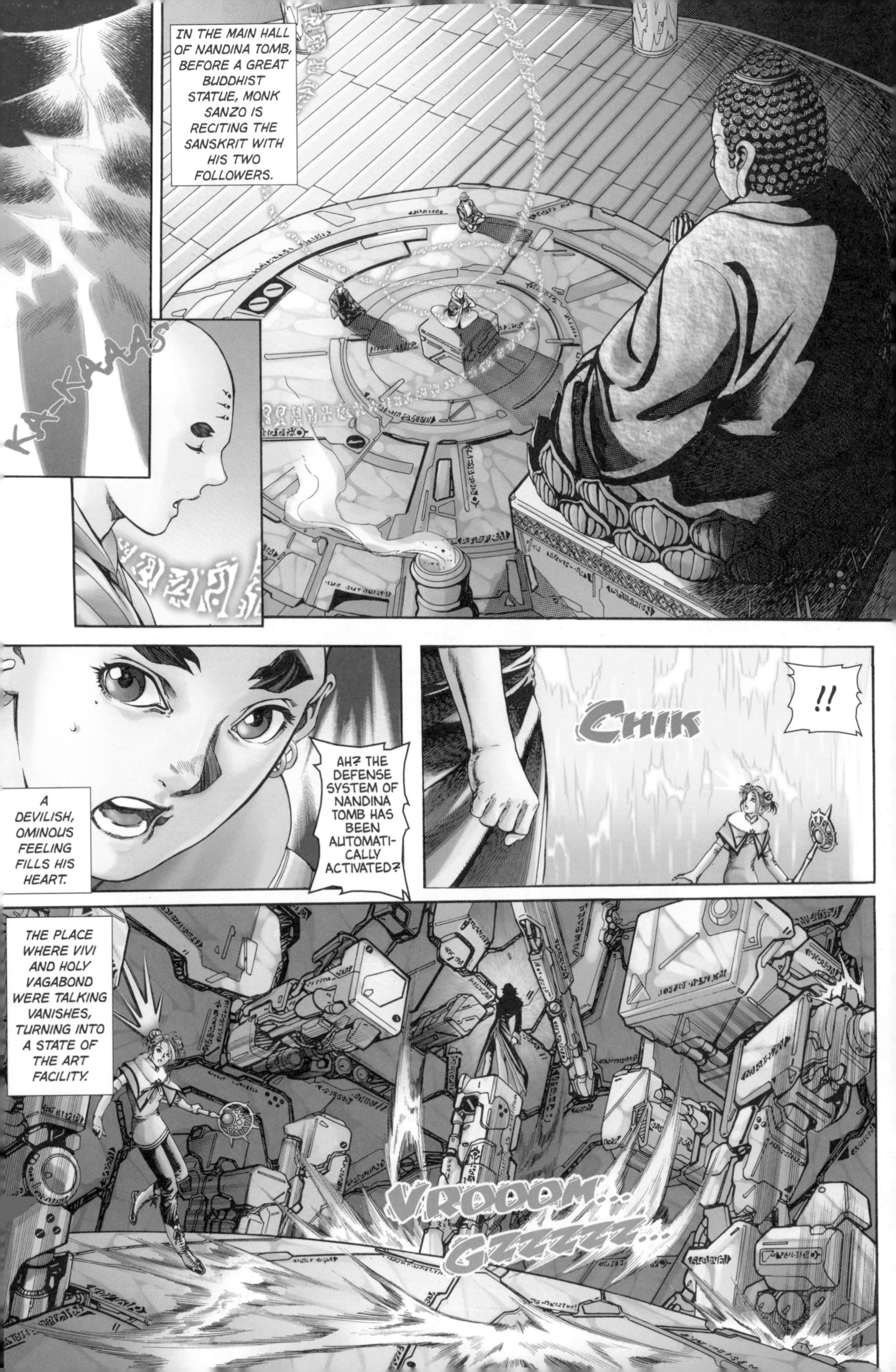
IN THE MAIN HALL OF NANDINA TOMB, BEFORE A GREAT BUDDHIST STATUE, MONK SANZO IS RECITING THE SANSKRIT WITH HIS TWO FOLLOWERS.
KA-KAAAS
A DEVILISH, OMINOUS FEELING FILLS HIS HEART.
AH? THE DEFENSE SYSTEM OF NANDINA TOMB HAS BEEN AUTOMATICALLY ACTIVATED?
CHIK
!!
THE PLACE WHERE VIVI AND HOLY VAGABOND WERE TALKING VANISHES, TURNING INTO A STATE OF THE ART FACILITY.
VROOOM...
GZZZZZ...

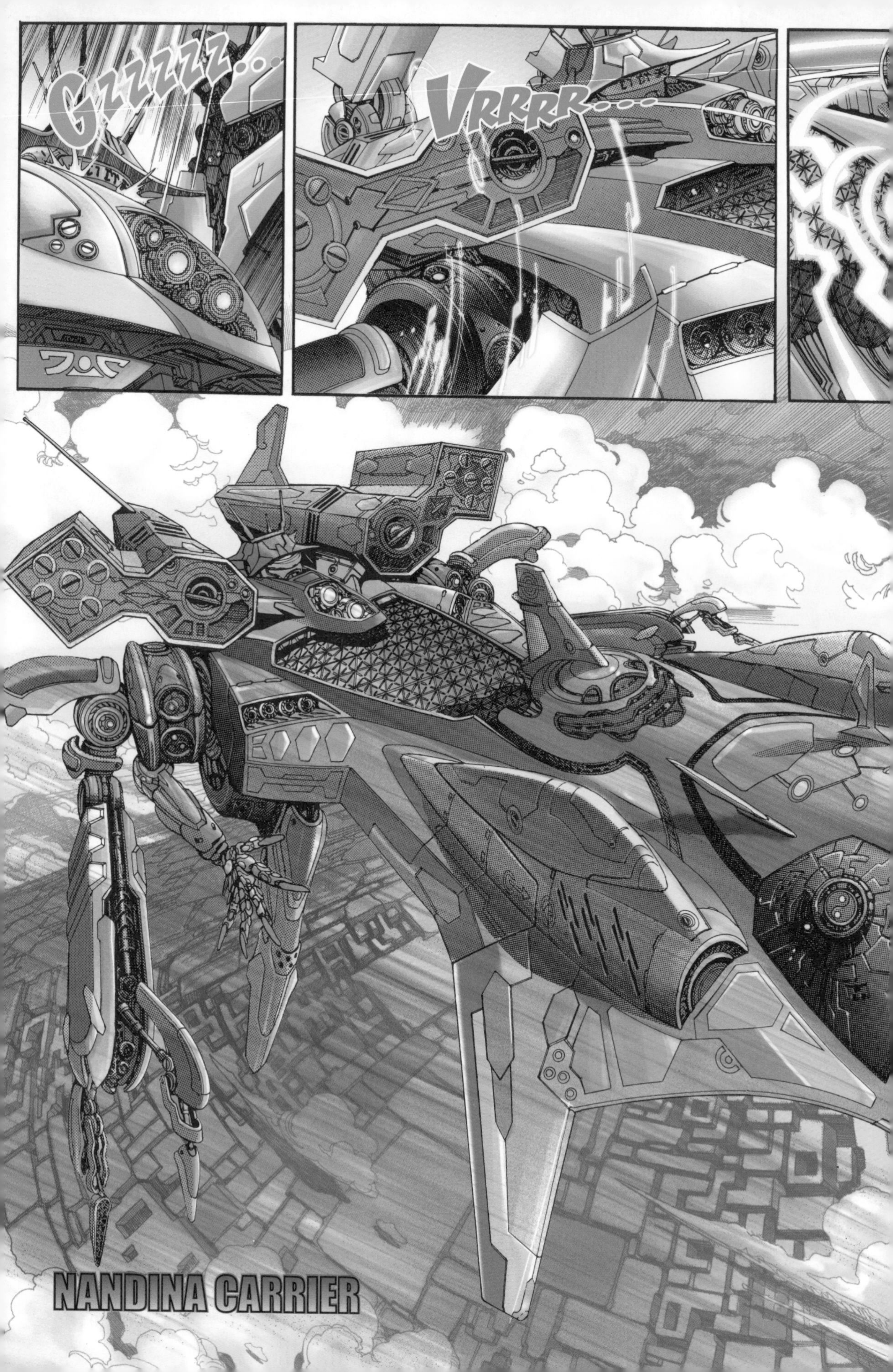
Gzzzzz...
Vrrrr....
NANDINA CARRIER

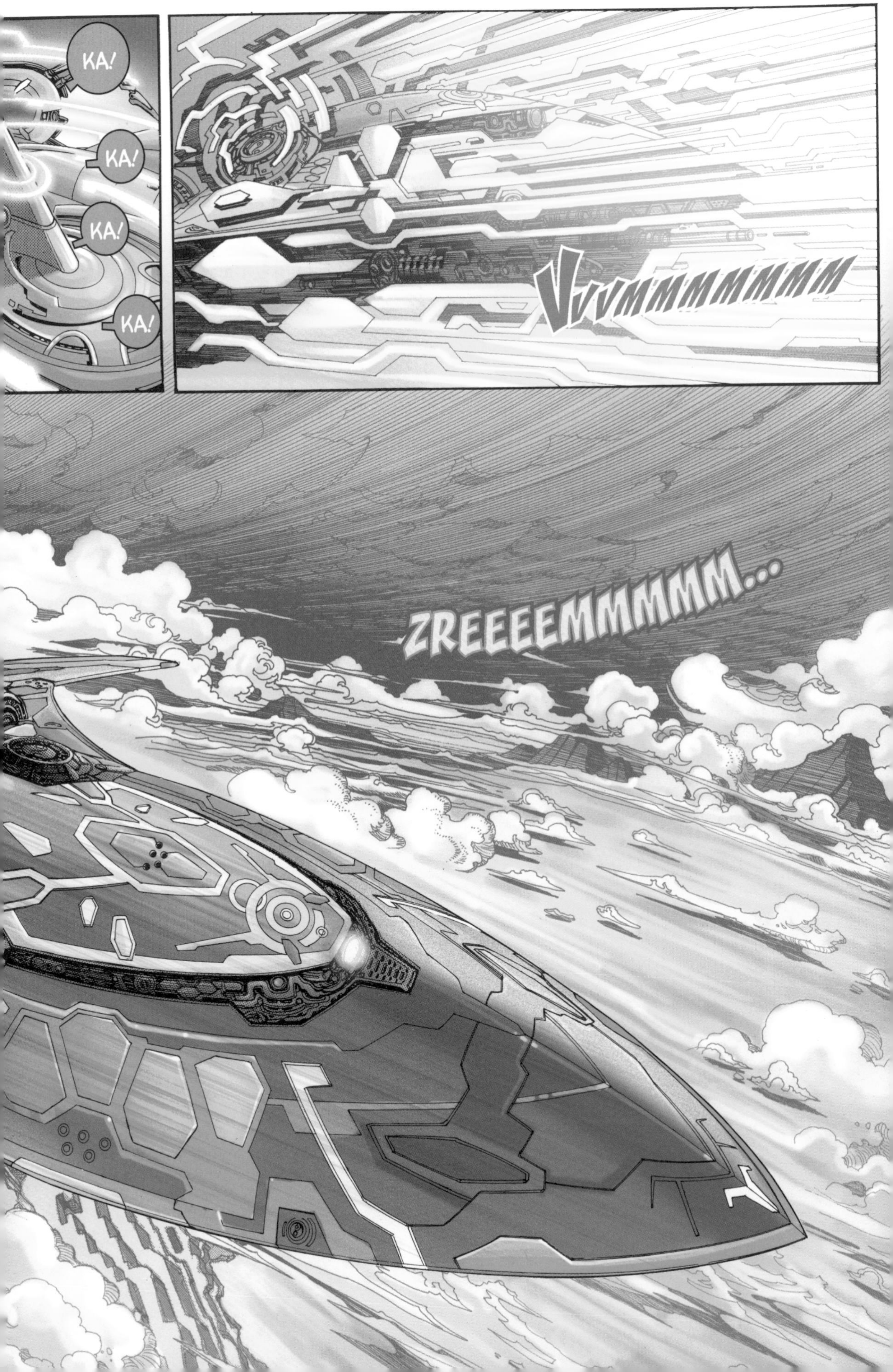
KA!
KA!
KA!
KA!
VVVMMMMMMMM
ZREEEEMMMMMM...

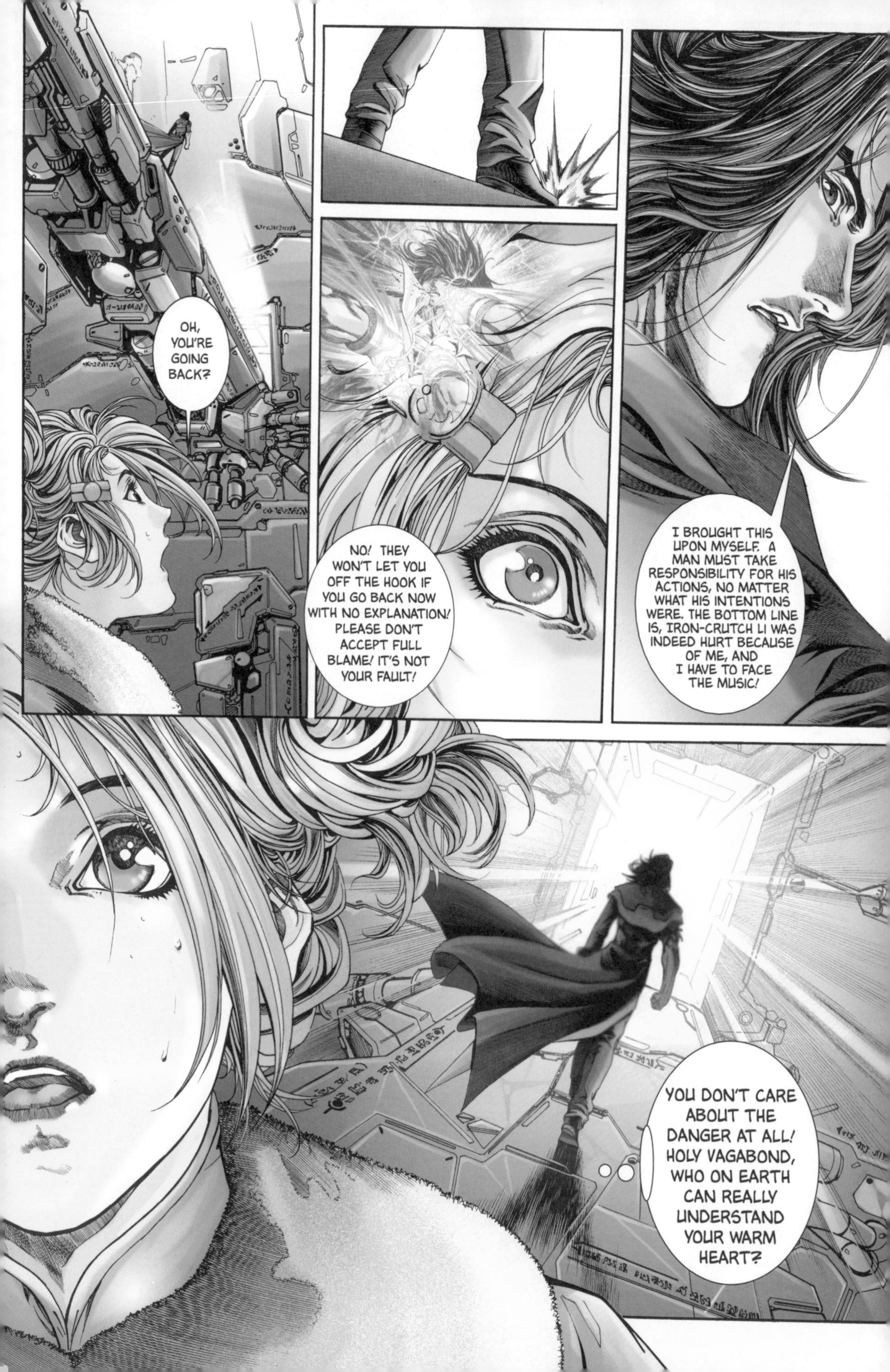
OH, YOU'RE GOING BACK?
NO! THEY WON'T LET YOU OFF THE HOOK IF YOU GO BACK NOW WITH NO EXPLANATION! PLEASE DON'T ACCEPT FULL BLAME! IT'S NOT YOUR FAULT!
I BROUGHT THIS UPON MYSELF. A MAN MUST TAKE RESPONSIBILITY FOR HIS ACTIONS, NO MATTER WHAT HIS INTENTIONS WERE. THE BOTTOM LINE IS, IRON-CRUTCH LI WAS INDEED HURT BECAUSE OF ME, AND I HAVE TO FACE THE MUSIC!
YOU DON'T CARE ABOUT THE DANGER AT ALL! HOLY VAGABOND, WHO ON EARTH CAN REALLY UNDERSTAND YOUR WARM HEART?

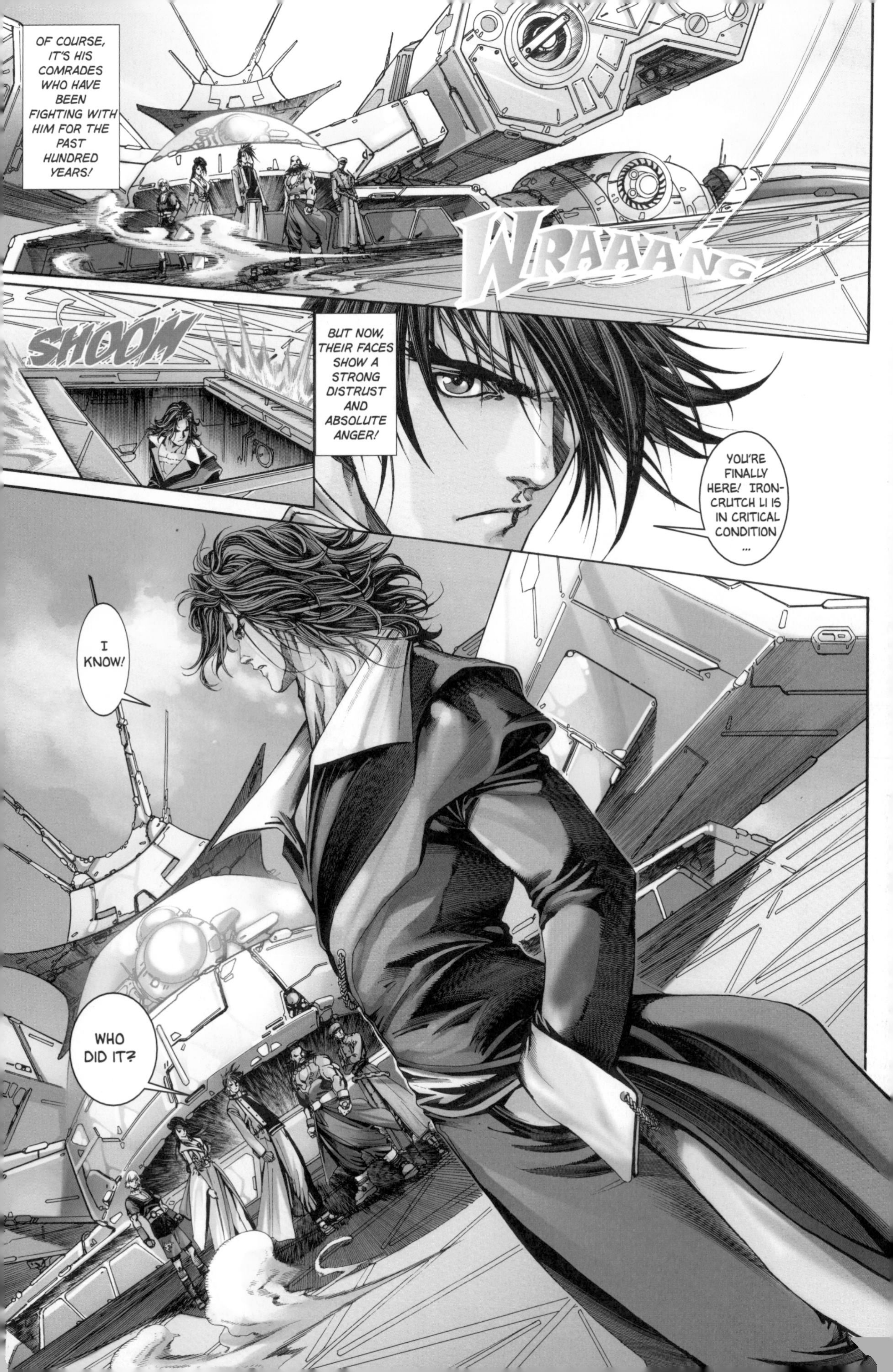
OF COURSE, IT'S HIS COMRADES WHO HAVE BEEN FIGHTING WITH HIM FOR THE PAST HUNDRED YEARS!
WRAAANG
SHOOM
BUT NOW, THEIR FACES SHOW A STRONG DISTRUST AND ABSOLUTE ANGER!
YOU'RE FINALLY HERE! IRON-CRUTCH LI IS IN CRITICAL CONDITION ...
I KNOW!
WHO DID IT?

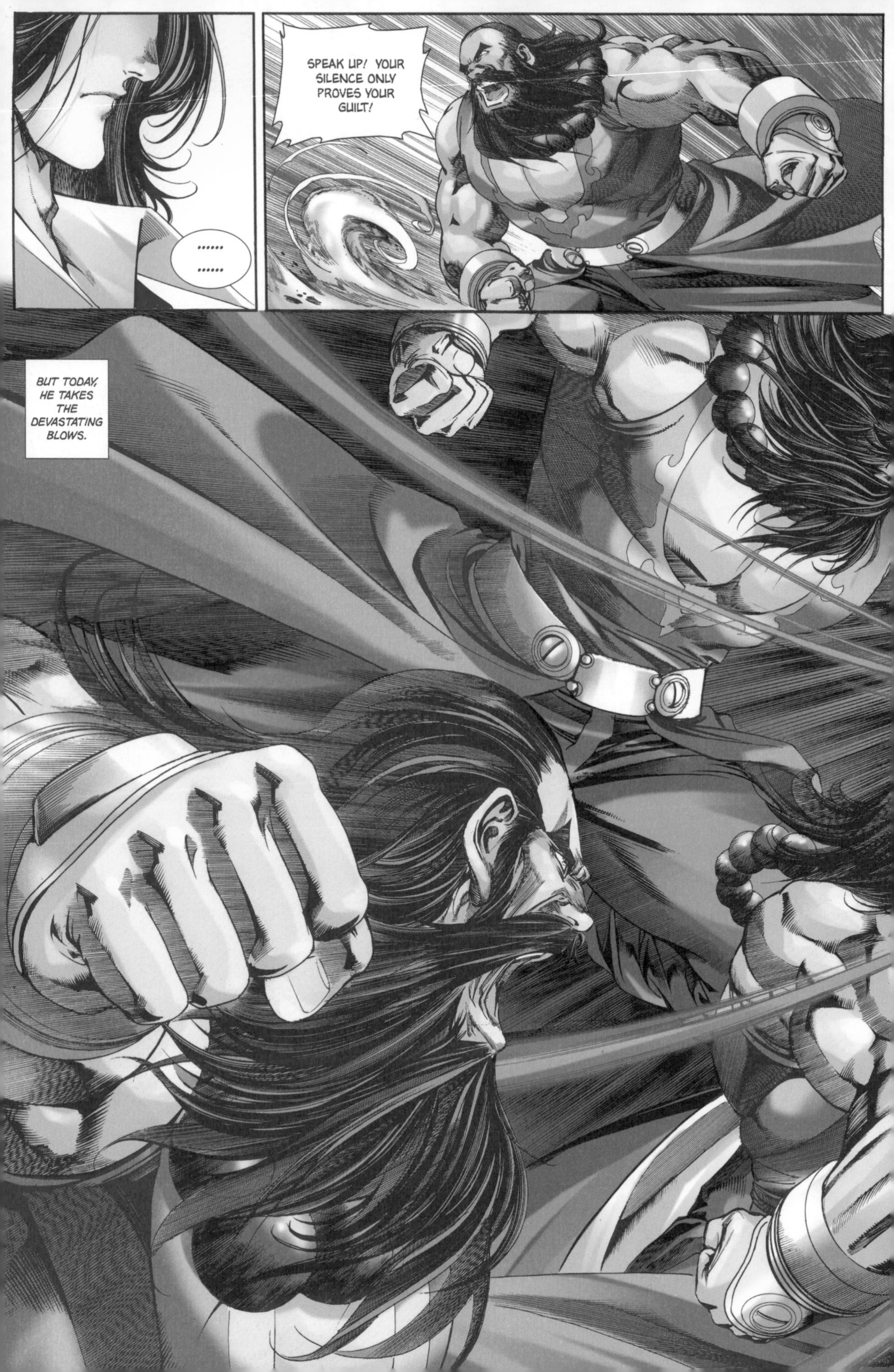
......
......
SPEAK UP! YOUR SILENCE ONLY PROVES YOUR GUILT!
BUT TODAY, HE TAKES THE DEVASTATING BLOWS.

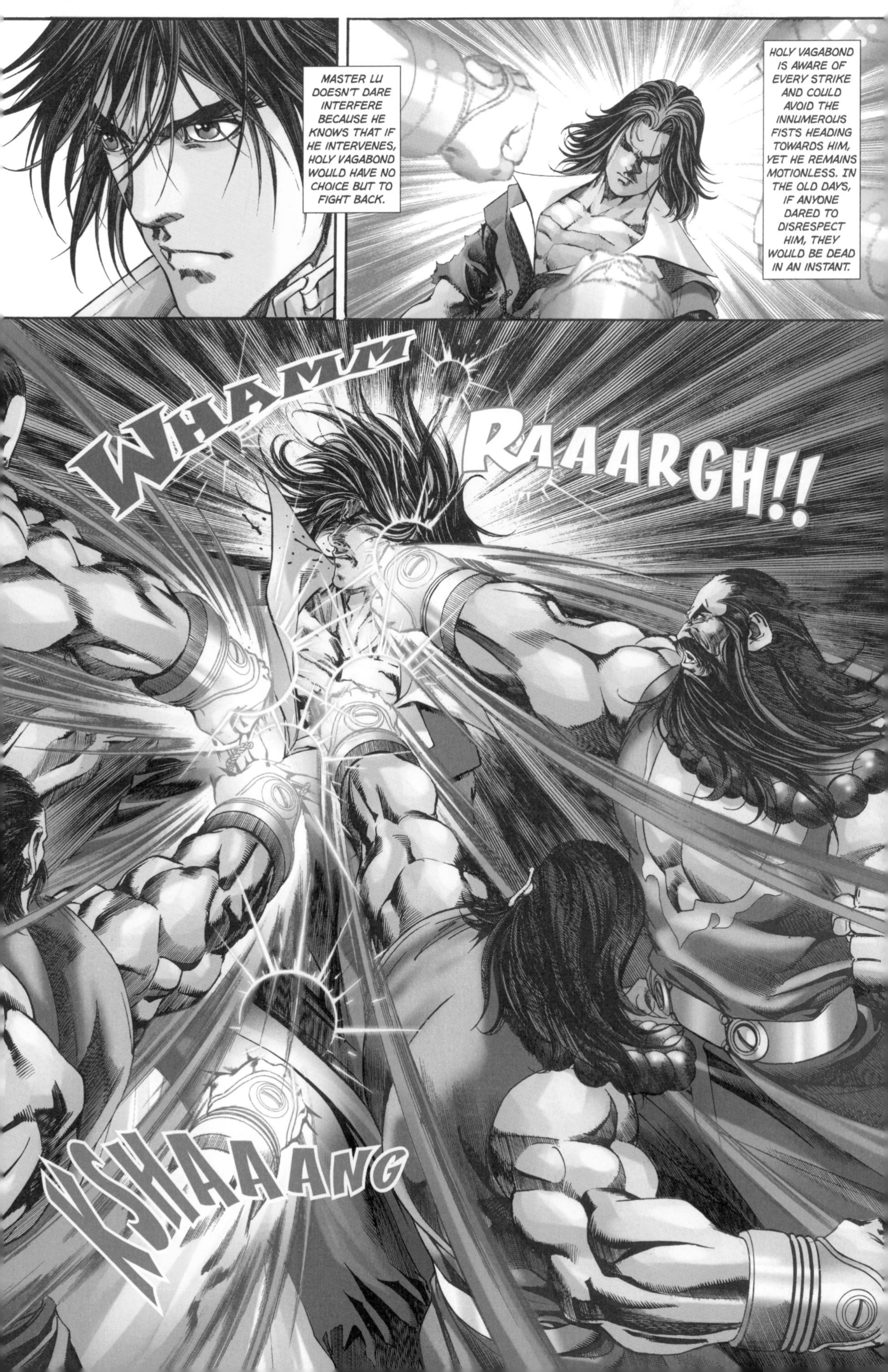
MASTER LU DOESN'T DARE INTERFERE BECAUSE HE KNOWS THAT IF HE INTERVENES, HOLY VAGABOND WOULD HAVE NO CHOICE BUT TO FIGHT BACK.
HOLY VAGABOND IS AWARE OF EVERY STRIKE AND COULD AVOID THE INNUMEROUS FISTS HEADING TOWARDS HIM, YET HE REMAINS MOTIONLESS. IN THE OLD DAYS, IF ANYONE DARED TO DISRESPECT HIM, THEY WOULD BE DEAD IN AN INSTANT.
WHAMM
RAAARGH!!
XSHAAAANG

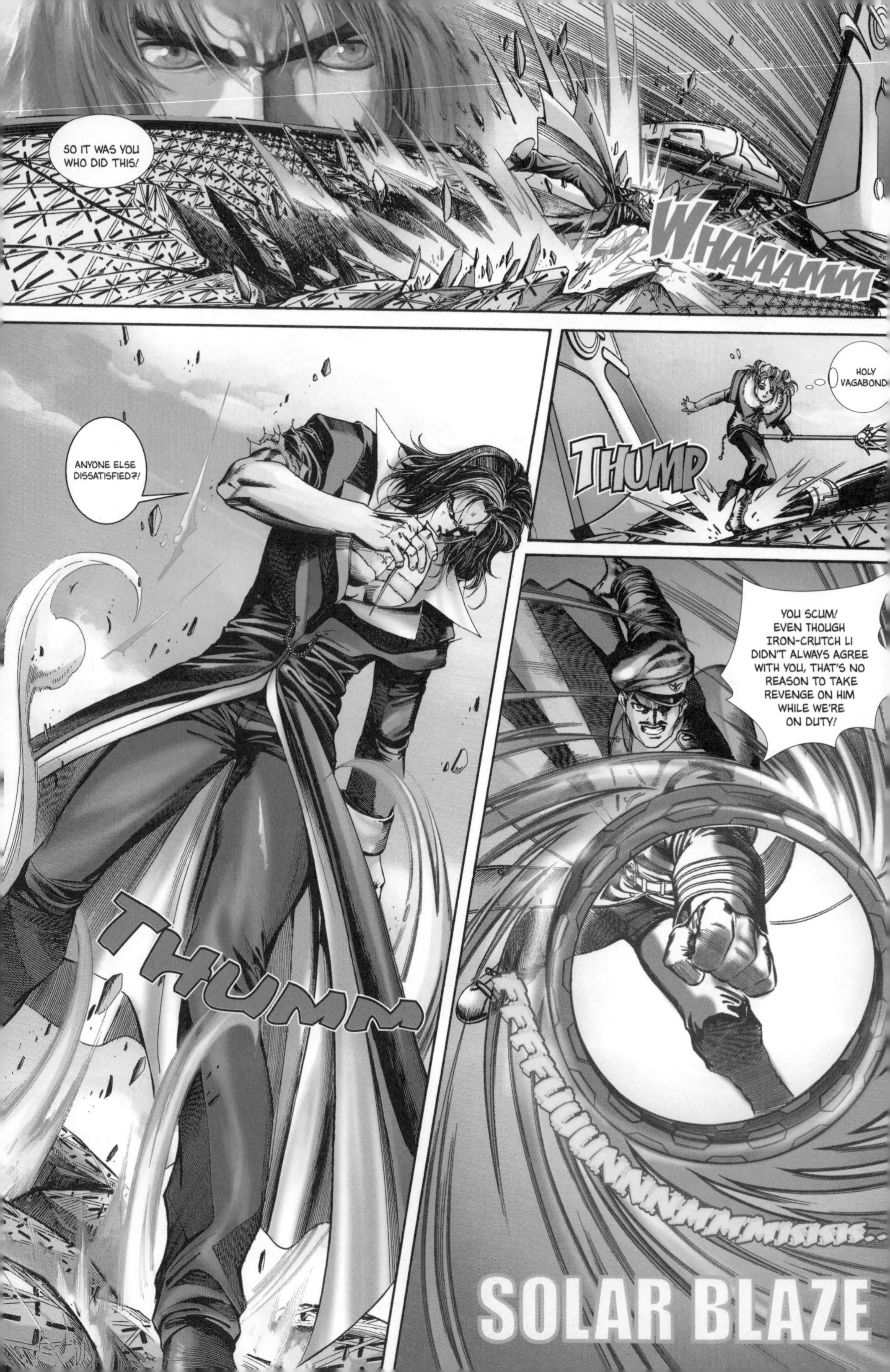
SO IT WAS YOU WHO DID THIS!
WHAAAAMM
ANYONE ELSE DISSATISFIED?!
HOLY VAGABOND!
THUMP
YOU SCUM! EVEN THOUGH IRON-CRUTCH LI DIDN'T ALWAYS AGREE WITH YOU, THAT'S NO REASON TO TAKE REVENGE ON HIM WHILE WE'RE ON DUTY!
THUMM
FFFUUUNNNNNMMMSSSS...
SOLAR BLAZE

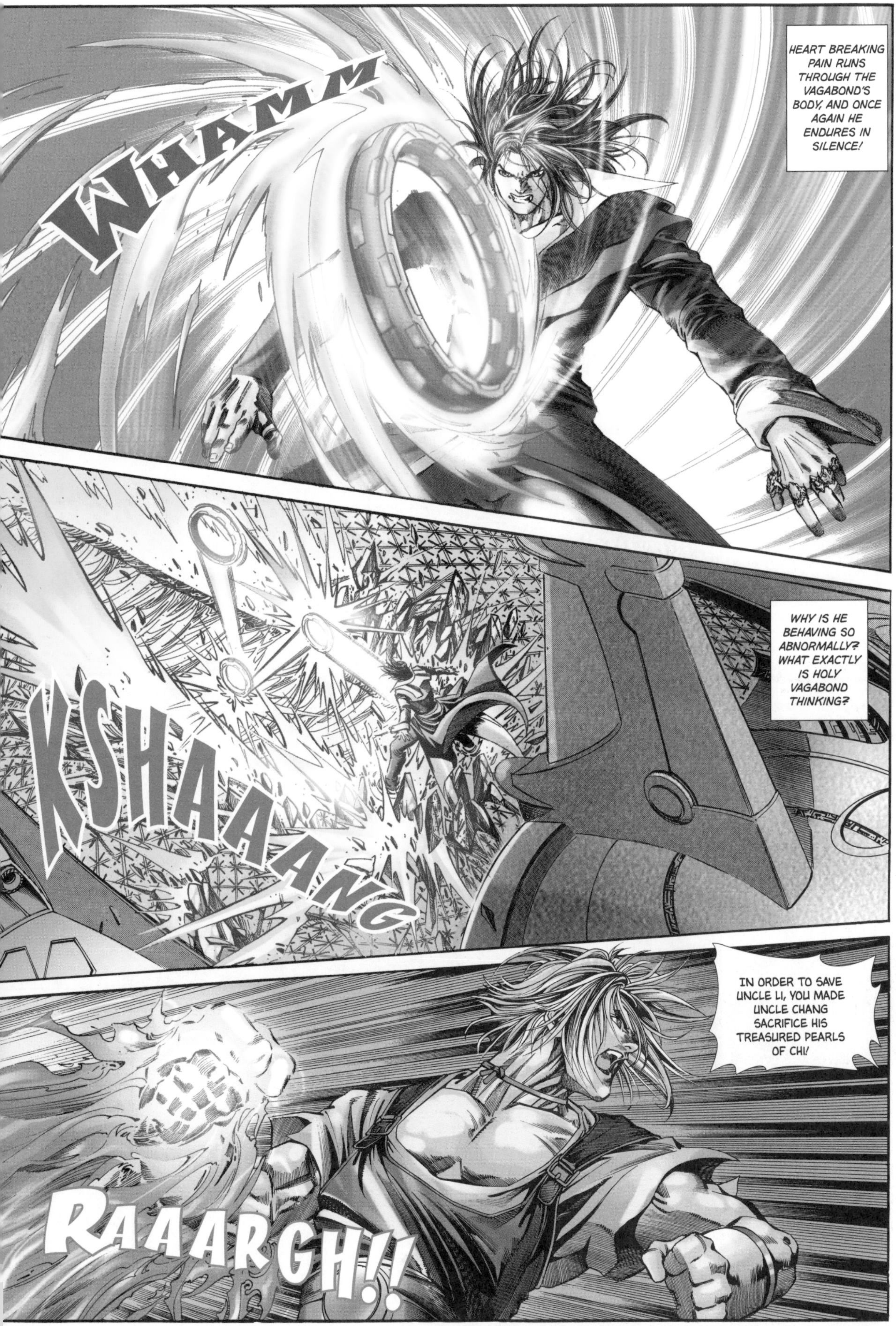
HEART BREAKING PAIN RUNS THROUGH THE VAGABOND'S BODY, AND ONCE AGAIN HE ENDURES IN SILENCE!
WHAMM
WHY IS HE BEHAVING SO ABNORMALLY? WHAT EXACTLY IS HOLY VAGABOND THINKING?
KSHAAAANG
IN ORDER TO SAVE UNCLE LI, YOU MADE UNCLE CHANG SACRIFICE HIS TREASURED PEARLS OF CHI!
RAAARGH!!

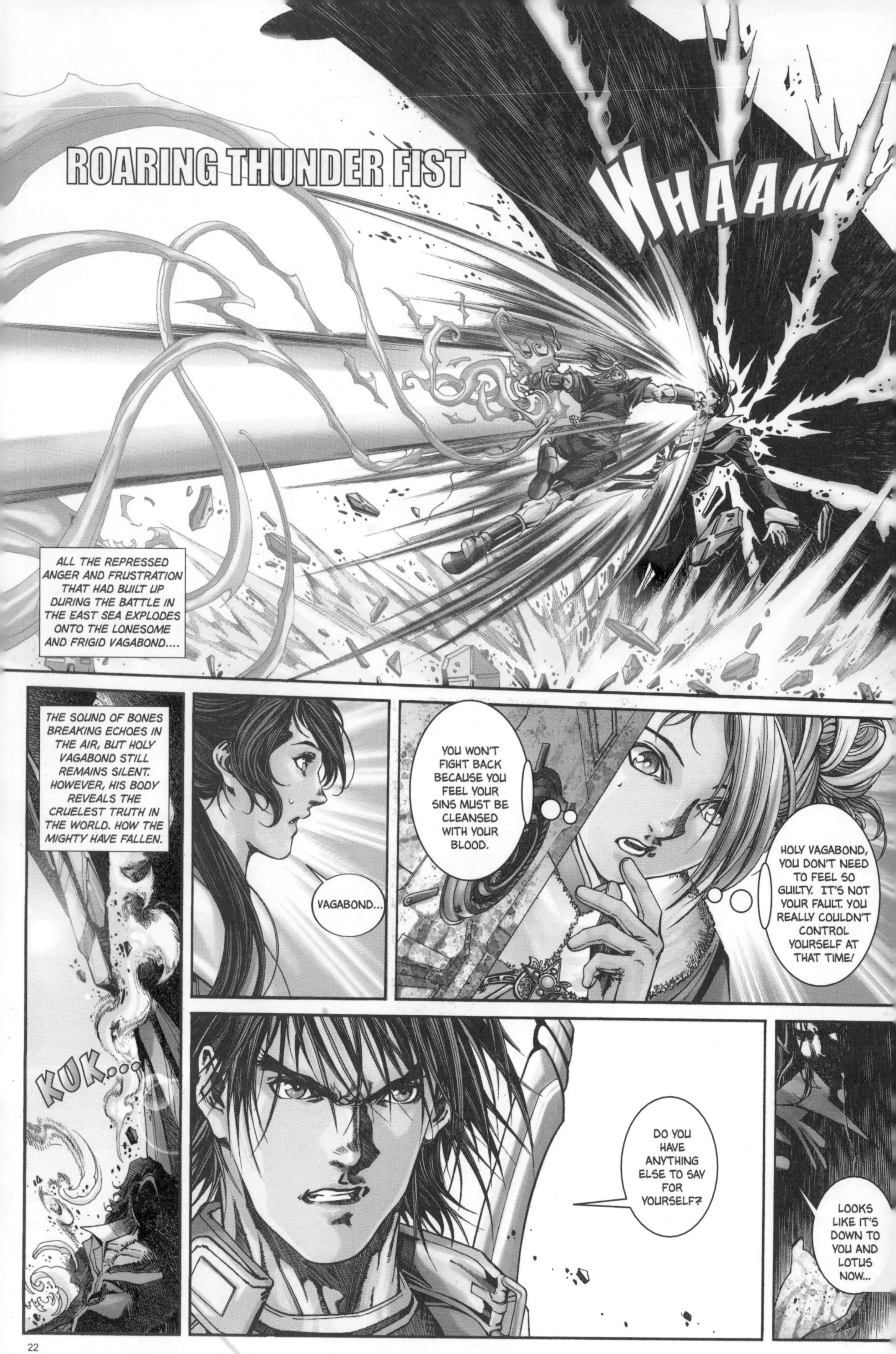
ROARING THUNDER FIST
WHAAM
ALL THE REPRESSED ANGER AND FRUSTRATION THAT HAD BUILT UP DURING THE BATTLE IN THE EAST SEA EXPLODES ONTO THE LONESOME AND FRIGID VAGABOND....
THE SOUND OF BONES BREAKING ECHOES IN THE AIR, BUT HOLY VAGABOND STILL REMAINS SILENT. HOWEVER, HIS BODY REVEALS THE CRUELEST TRUTH IN THE WORLD. HOW THE MIGHTY HAVE FALLEN.
VAGABOND...
YOU WON'T FIGHT BACK BECAUSE YOU FEEL YOUR SINS MUST BE CLEANSED WITH YOUR BLOOD.
HOLY VAGABOND, YOU DON'T NEED TO FEEL SO GUILTY. IT'S NOT YOUR FAULT. YOU REALLY COULDN'T CONTROL YOURSELF AT THAT TIME!
KUK...
DO YOU HAVE ANYTHING ELSE TO SAY FOR YOURSELF?
LOOKS LIKE IT'S DOWN TO YOU AND LOTUS NOW...

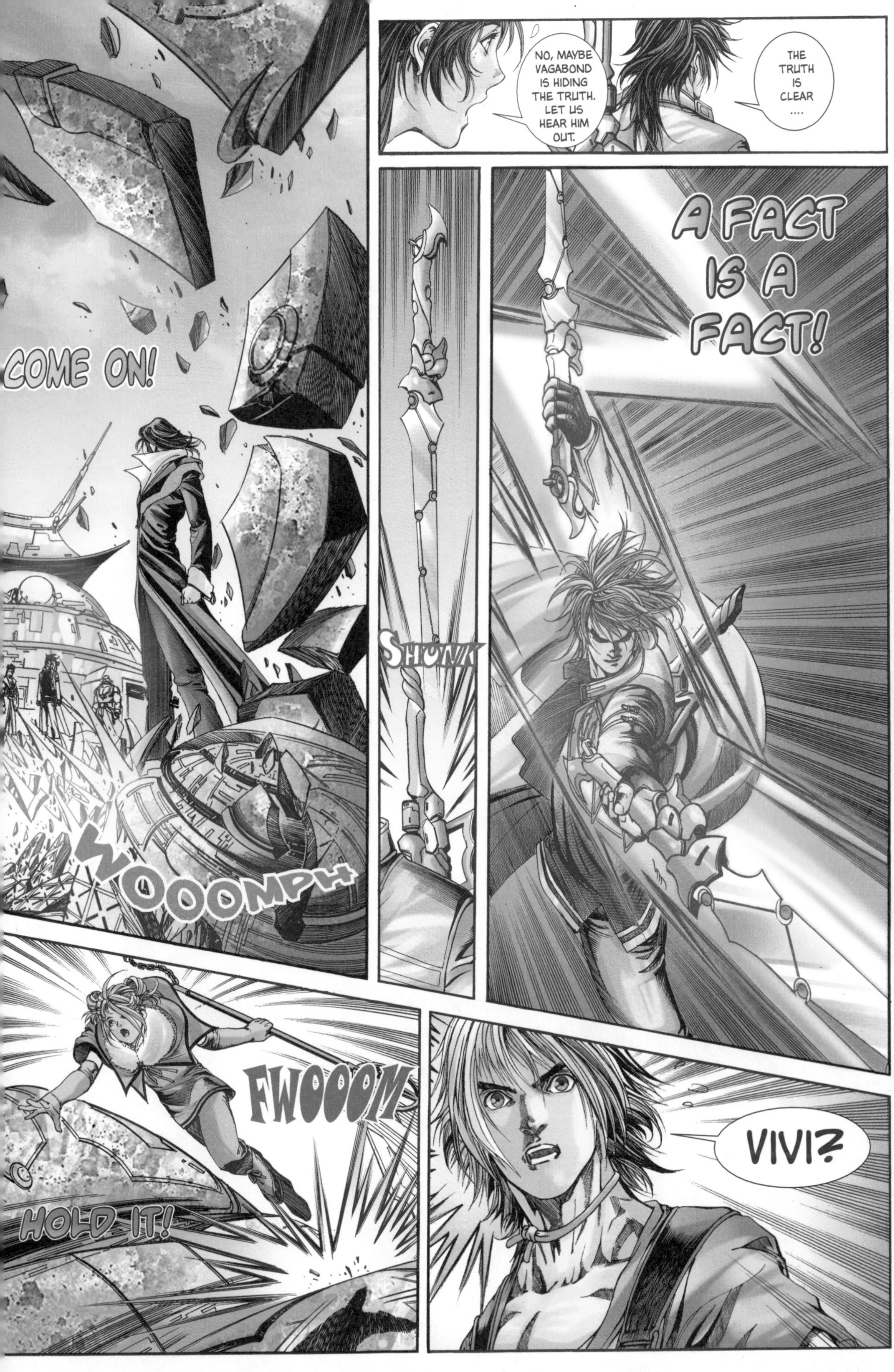

COME ON!
WOOOMPH
NO, MAYBE VAGABOND IS HIDING THE TRUTH. LET US HEAR HIM OUT.
THE TRUTH IS CLEAR ....
SHUNK
A FACT IS A FACT!
FWOOOM
HOLD IT!
VIVI?

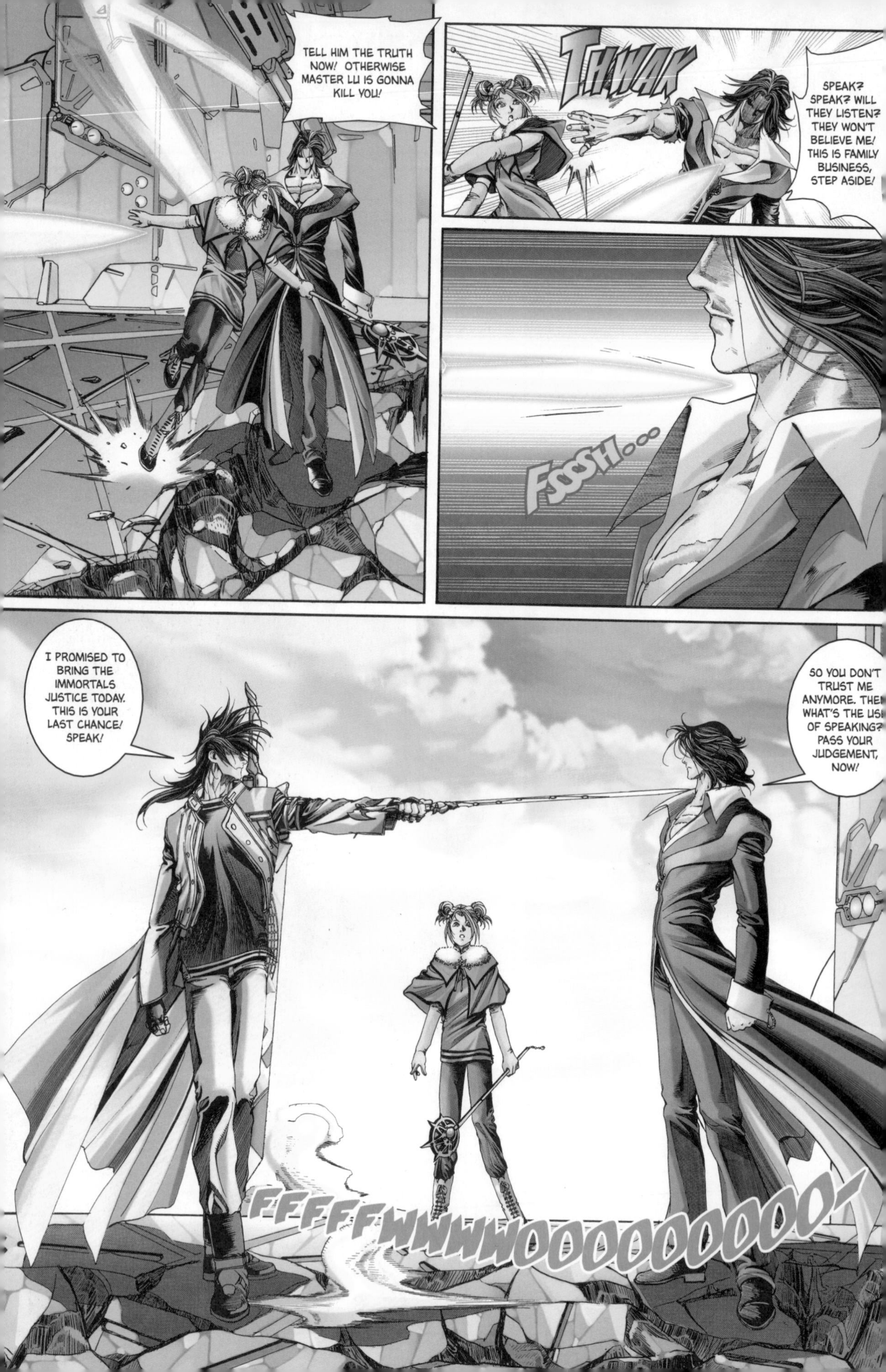
TELL HIM THE TRUTH NOW! OTHERWISE MASTER LU IS GONNA KILL YOU!
THWAK
SPEAK? SPEAK? WILL THEY LISTEN? THEY WON'T BELIEVE ME! THIS IS FAMILY BUSINESS, STEP ASIDE!
FSSSH...
I PROMISED TO BRING THE IMMORTALS JUSTICE TODAY. THIS IS YOUR LAST CHANCE! SPEAK!
SO YOU DON'T TRUST ME ANYMORE. THE WHAT'S THE US OF SPEAKING? PASS YOUR JUDGEMENT, NOW!
FFFFFWWWWOOOOOOOOOO-

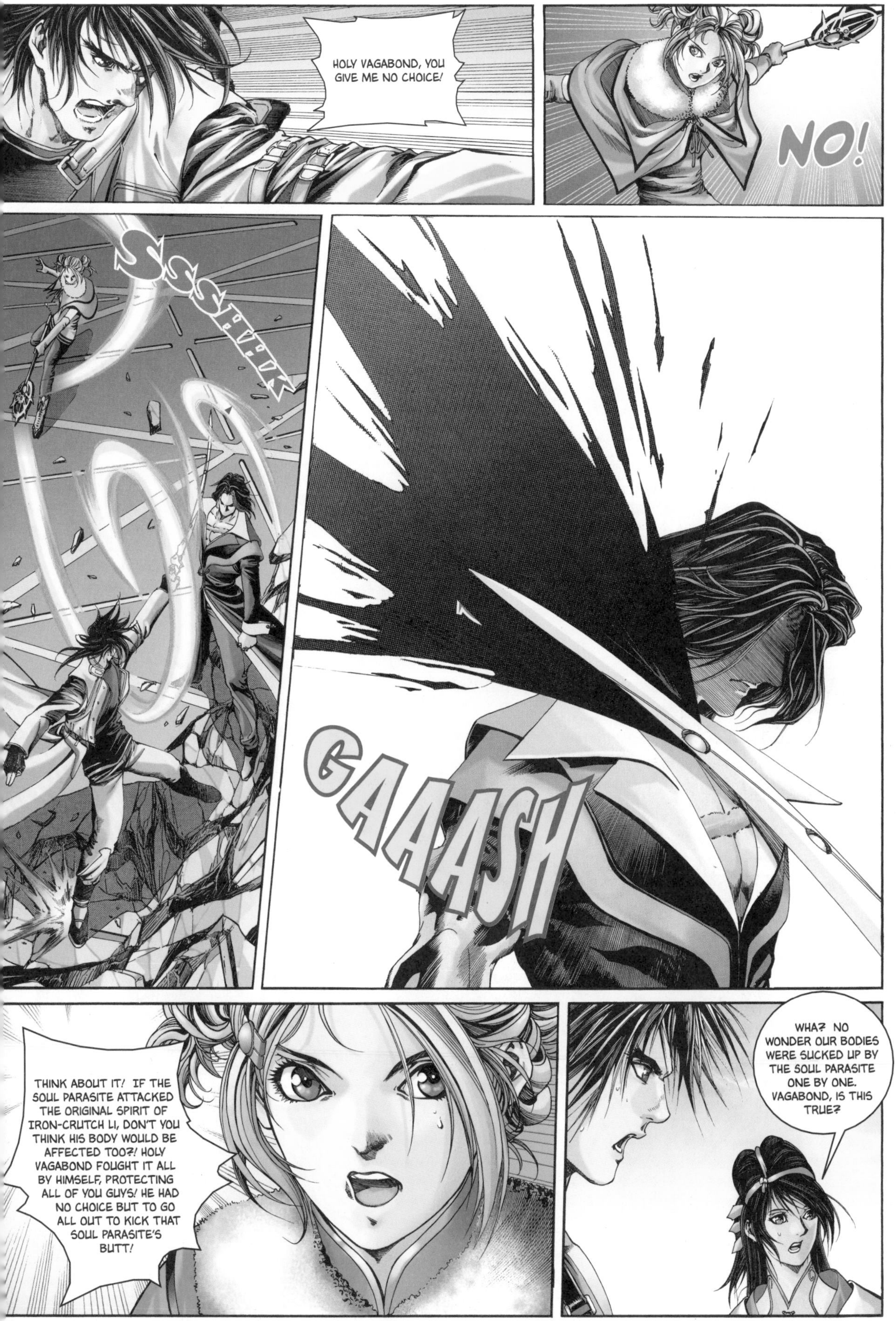
HOLY VAGABOND, YOU GIVE ME NO CHOICE!
NO!
SSSHHHK
GAAASH
THINK ABOUT IT! IF THE SOUL PARASITE ATTACKED THE ORIGINAL SPIRIT OF IRON-CRUTCH LI, DON'T YOU THINK HIS BODY WOULD BE AFFECTED TOO?! HOLY VAGABOND FOUGHT IT ALL BY HIMSELF, PROTECTING ALL OF YOU GUYS! HE HAD NO CHOICE BUT TO GO ALL OUT TO KICK THAT SOUL PARASITE'S BUTT!
WHA? NO WONDER OUR BODIES WERE SUCKED UP BY THE SOUL PARASITE ONE BY ONE. VAGABOND, IS THIS TRUE?

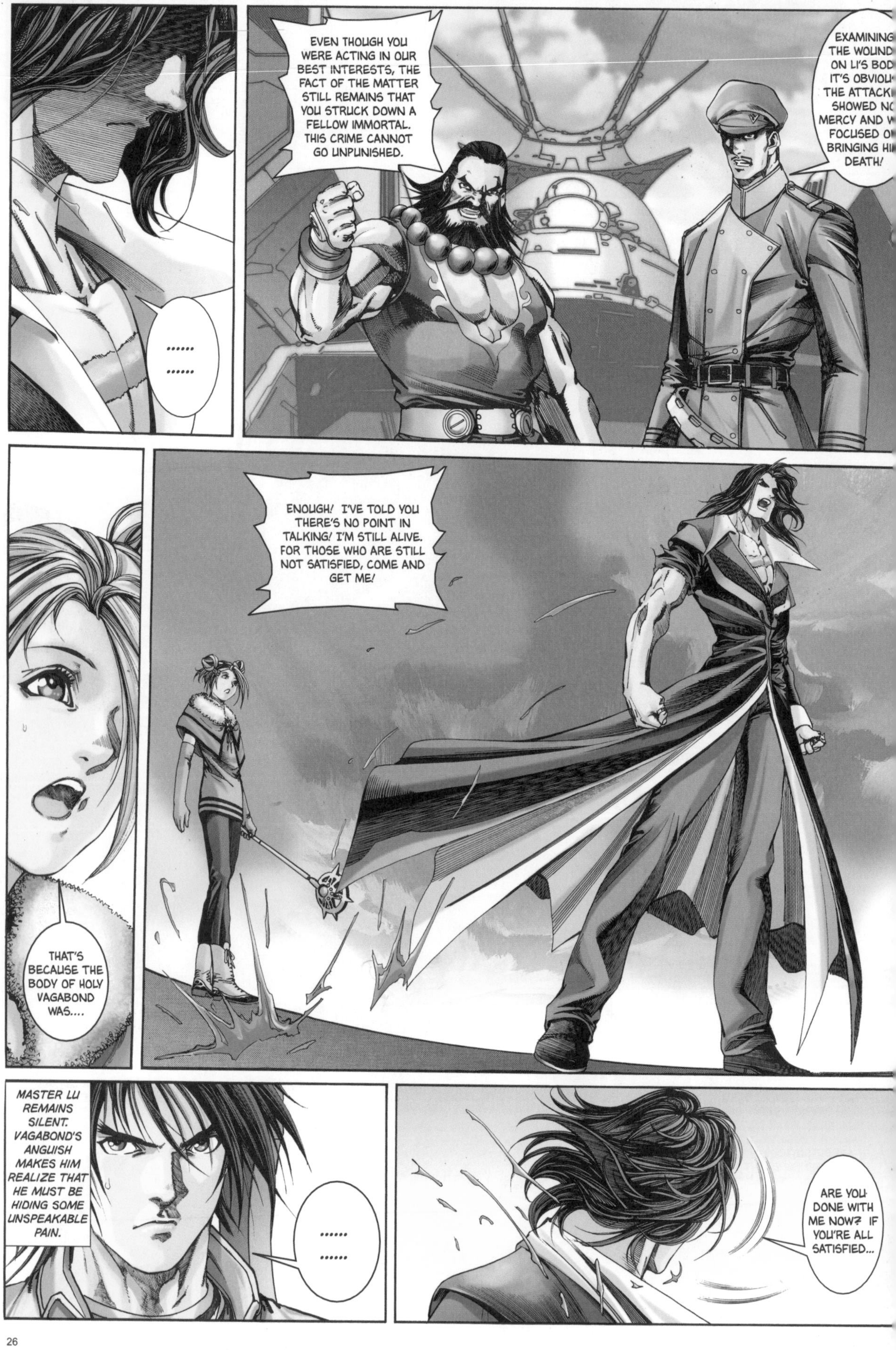

....
EVEN THOUGH YOU WERE ACTING IN OUR BEST INTERESTS, THE FACT OF THE MATTER STILL REMAINS THAT YOU STRUCK DOWN A FELLOW IMMORTAL. THIS CRIME CANNOT GO UNPUNISHED.
EXAMINING THE WOUND ON LI'S BOD IT'S OBVIOU THE ATTACK SHOWED NO MERCY AND W FOCUSED O BRINGING HI DEATH!
ENOUGH! I'VE TOLD YOU THERE'S NO POINT IN TALKING! I'M STILL ALIVE. FOR THOSE WHO ARE STILL NOT SATISFIED, COME AND GET ME!
THAT'S BECAUSE THE BODY OF HOLY VAGABOND WAS....
MASTER LU REMAINS SILENT. VAGABOND'S ANGUISH MAKES HIM REALIZE THAT HE MUST BE HIDING SOME UNSPEAKABLE PAIN.
....
ARE YOU DONE WITH ME NOW? IF YOU'RE ALL SATISFIED...

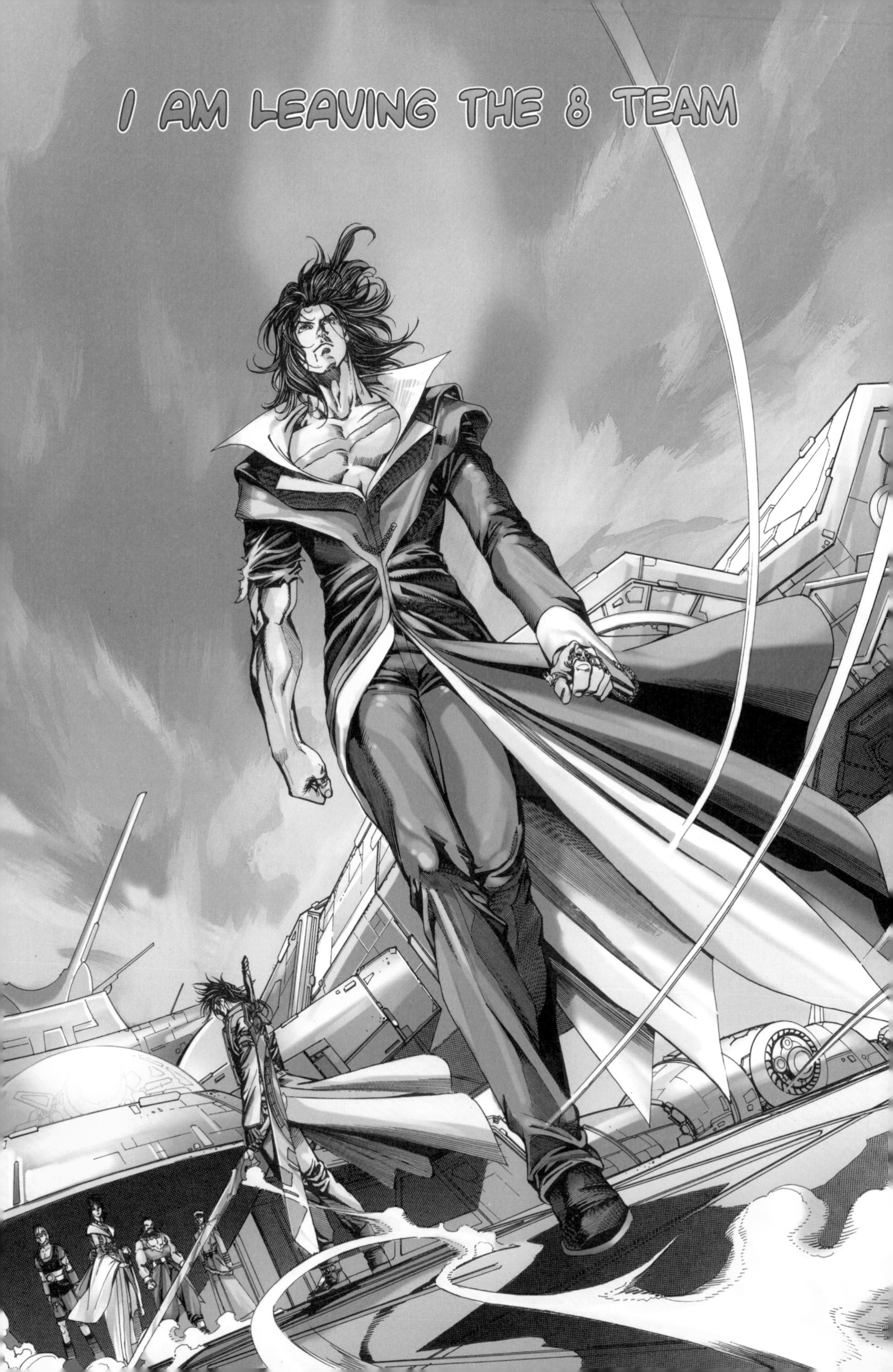
I AM LEAVING THE 8 TEAM

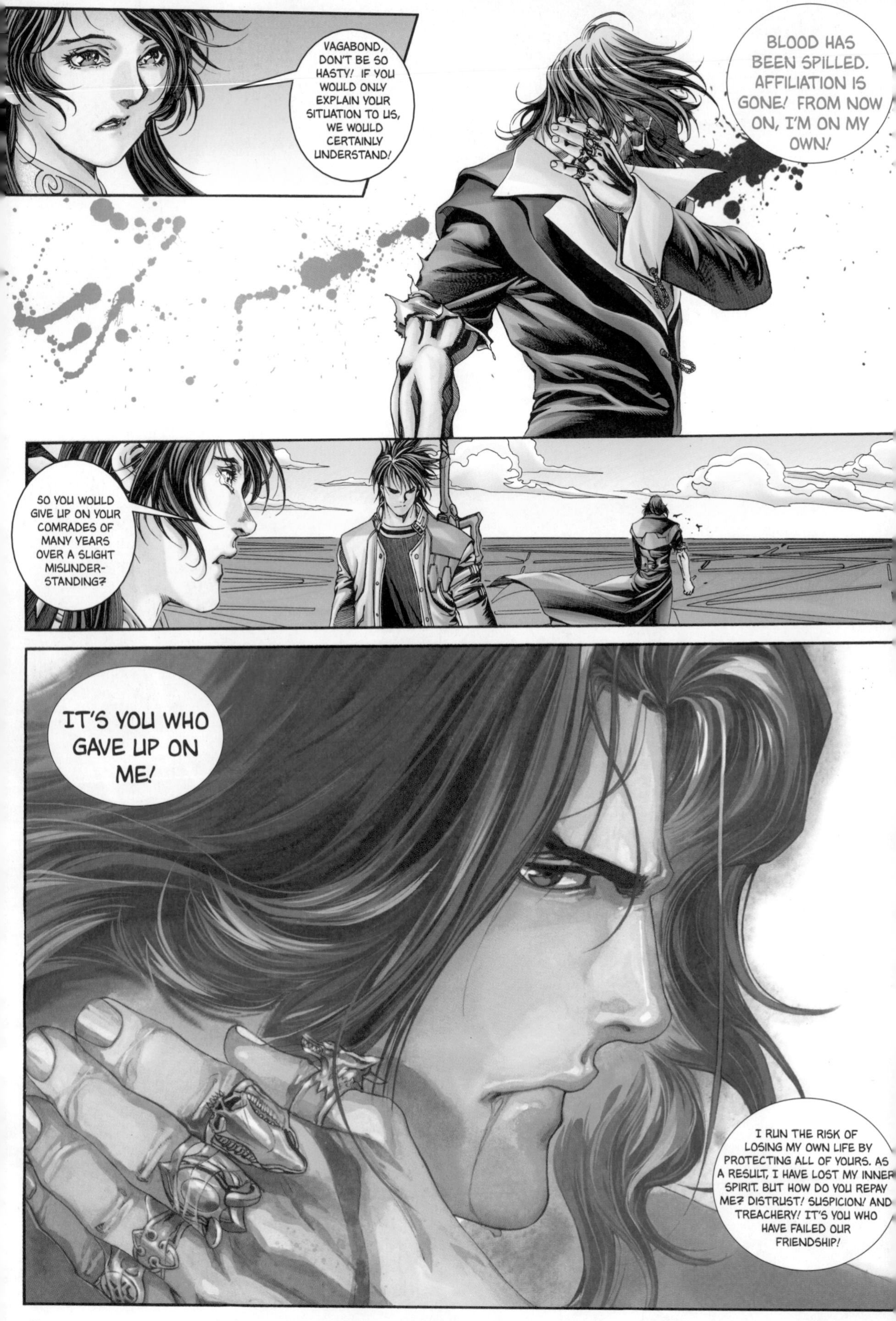
VAGABOND, DON'T BE SO HASTY! IF YOU WOULD ONLY EXPLAIN YOUR SITUATION TO US, WE WOULD CERTAINLY UNDERSTAND!
BLOOD HAS BEEN SPILLED. AFFILIATION IS GONE! FROM NOW ON, I'M ON MY OWN!
SO YOU WOULD GIVE UP ON YOUR COMRADES OF MANY YEARS OVER A SLIGHT MISUNDER-STANDING?
IT'S YOU WHO GAVE UP ON ME!
I RUN THE RISK OF LOSING MY OWN LIFE BY PROTECTING ALL OF YOURS. AS A RESULT, I HAVE LOST MY INNER SPIRIT. BUT HOW DO YOU REPAY ME? DISTRUST! SUSPICION! AND TREACHERY! IT'S YOU WHO HAVE FAILED OUR FRIENDSHIP!

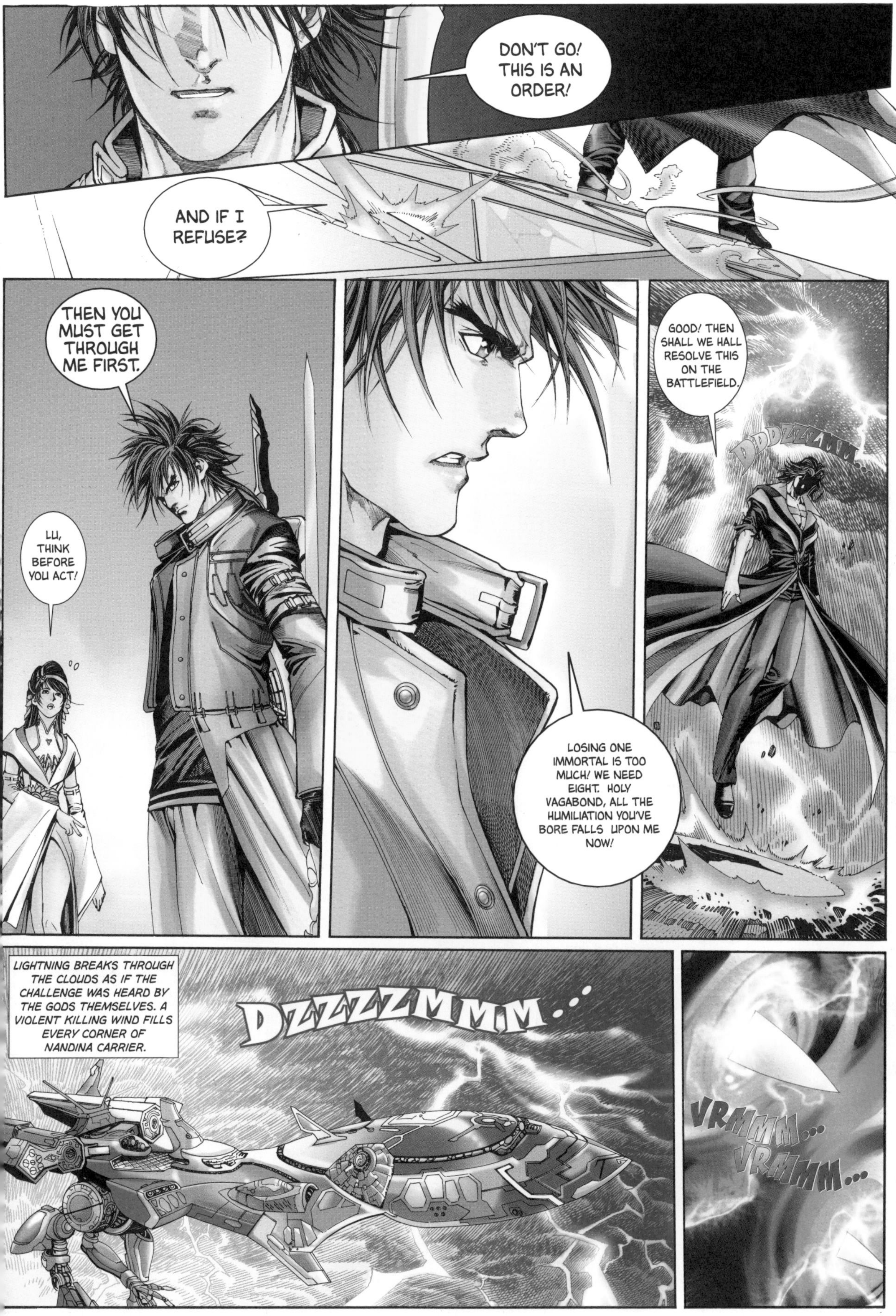
DON'T GO! THIS IS AN ORDER!
AND IF I REFUSE?
THEN YOU MUST GET THROUGH ME FIRST.
LU, THINK BEFORE YOU ACT!
LOSING ONE IMMORTAL IS TOO MUCH! WE NEED EIGHT. HOLY VAGABOND, ALL THE HUMILIATION YOU'VE BORE FALLS UPON ME NOW!
GOOD! THEN SHALL WE HALL RESOLVE THIS ON THE BATTLEFIELD.
DDDZZZZMM...
LIGHTNING BREAKS THROUGH THE CLOUDS AS IF THE CHALLENGE WAS HEARD BY THE GODS THEMSELVES. A VIOLENT KILLING WIND FILLS EVERY CORNER OF NANDINA CARRIER.
DZZZZMMM...
VRMMM...
VRMMM...

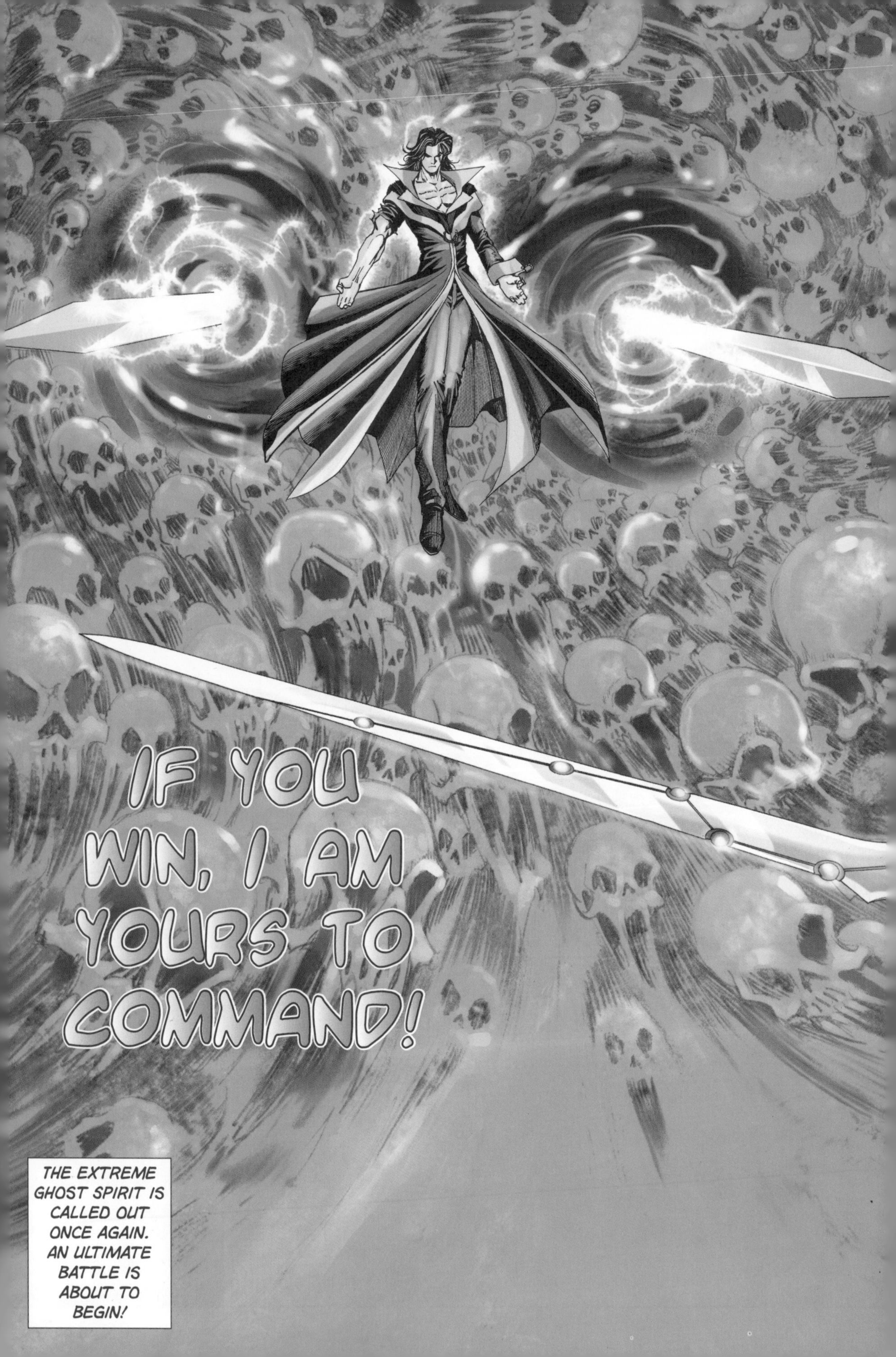

IF YOU WIN, I AM YOURS TO COMMAND!
THE EXTREME GHOST SPIRIT IS CALLED OUT ONCE AGAIN. AN ULTIMATE BATTLE IS ABOUT TO BEGIN!

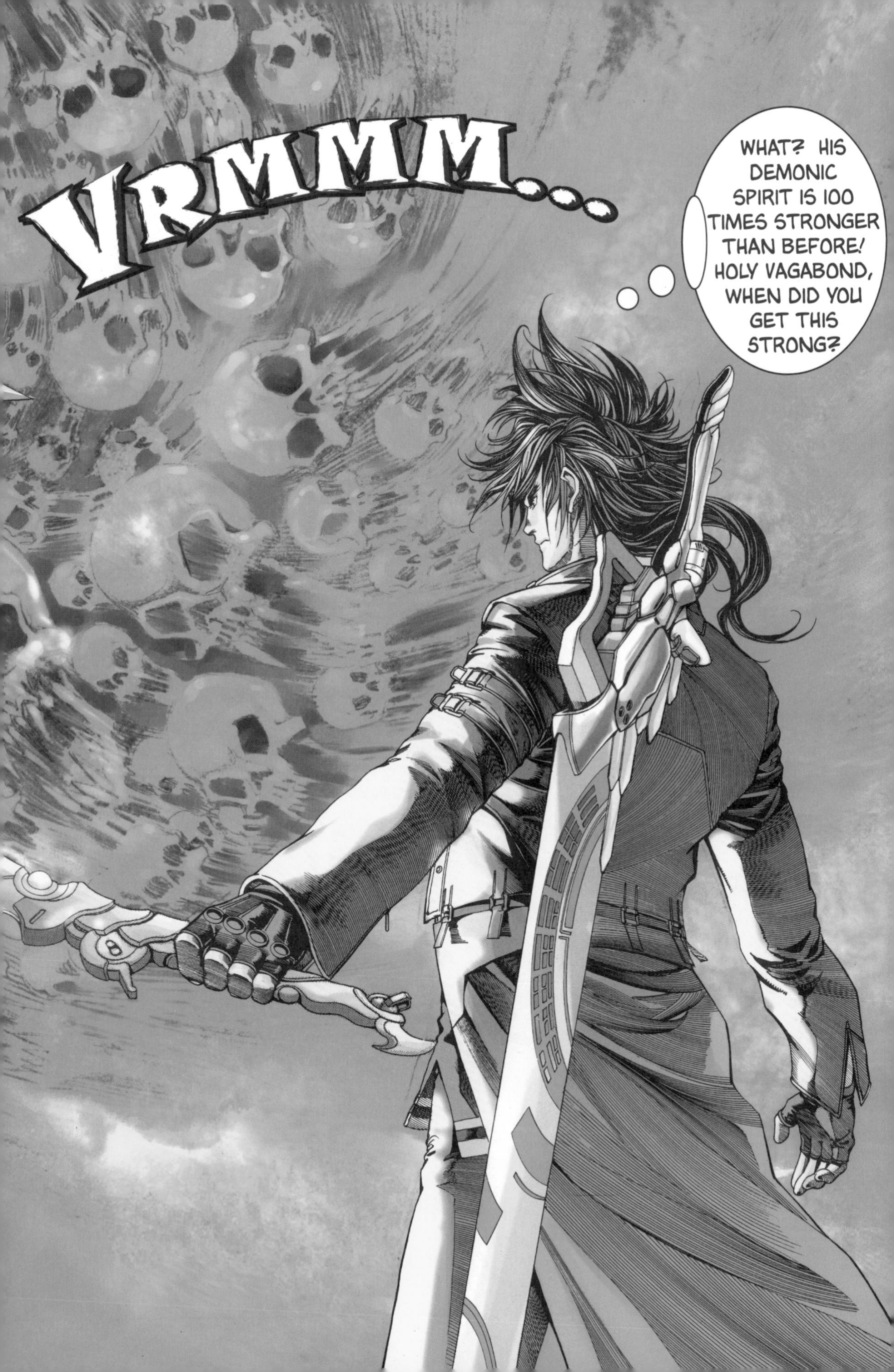
VRMMMM...
WHAT? HIS DEMONIC SPIRIT IS 100 TIMES STRONGER THAN BEFORE! HOLY VAGABOND, WHEN DID YOU GET THIS STRONG?

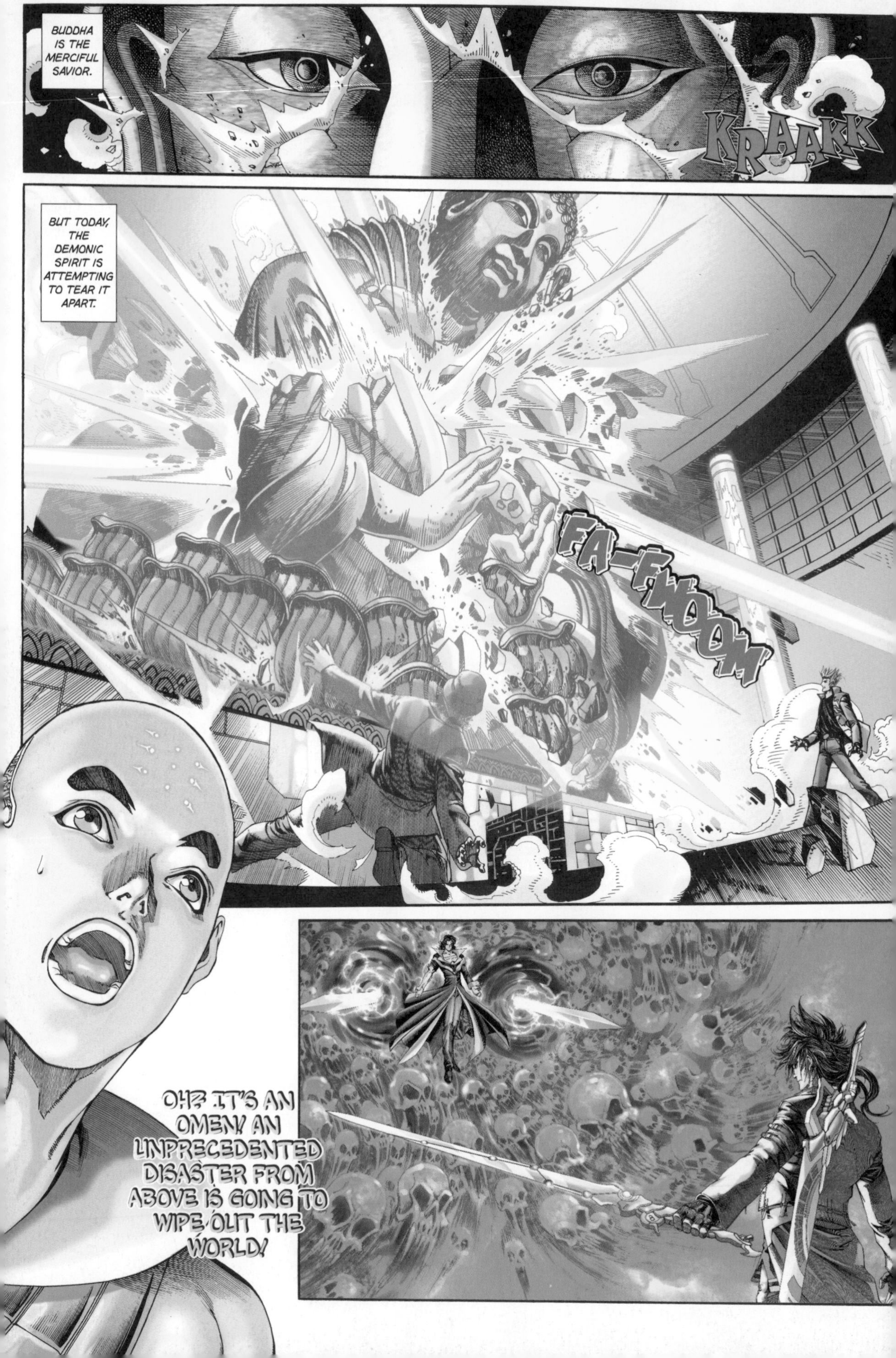

BUDDHA IS THE MERCIFUL SAVIOR.
KRAAKK
BUT TODAY, THE DEMONIC SPIRIT IS ATTEMPTING TO TEAR IT APART.
FA-FWOOM
OH? IT'S AN OMEN! AN UNPRECEDENTED DISASTER FROM ABOVE IS GOING TO WIPE OUT THE WORLD!

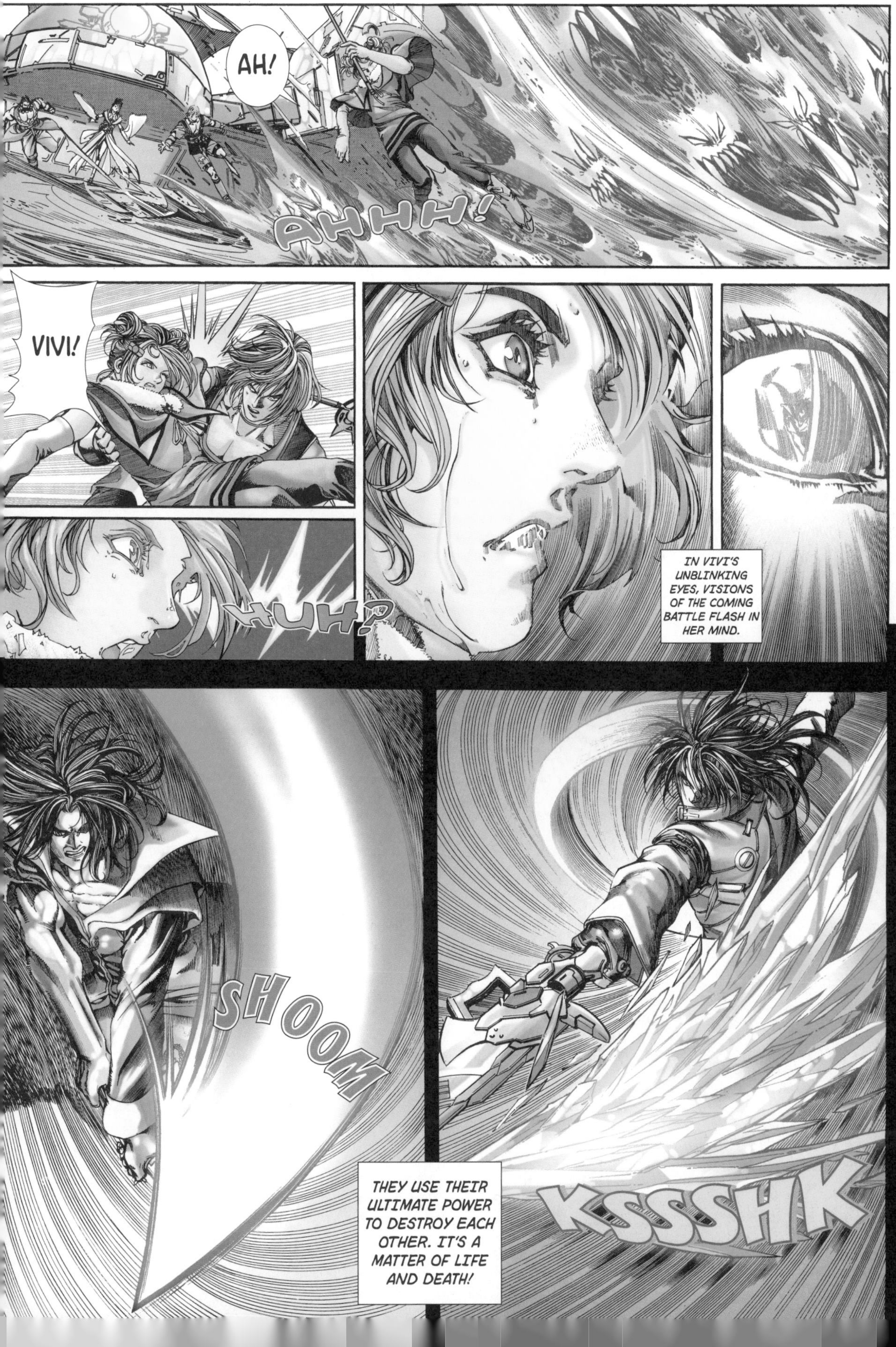
AH!
AHHH!
VIVI!
HUH?
IN VIVI'S UNBLINKING EYES, VISIONS OF THE COMING BATTLE FLASH IN HER MIND.
SHOOM
KSSSHK
THEY USE THEIR ULTIMATE POWER TO DESTROY EACH OTHER. IT'S A MATTER OF LIFE AND DEATH!

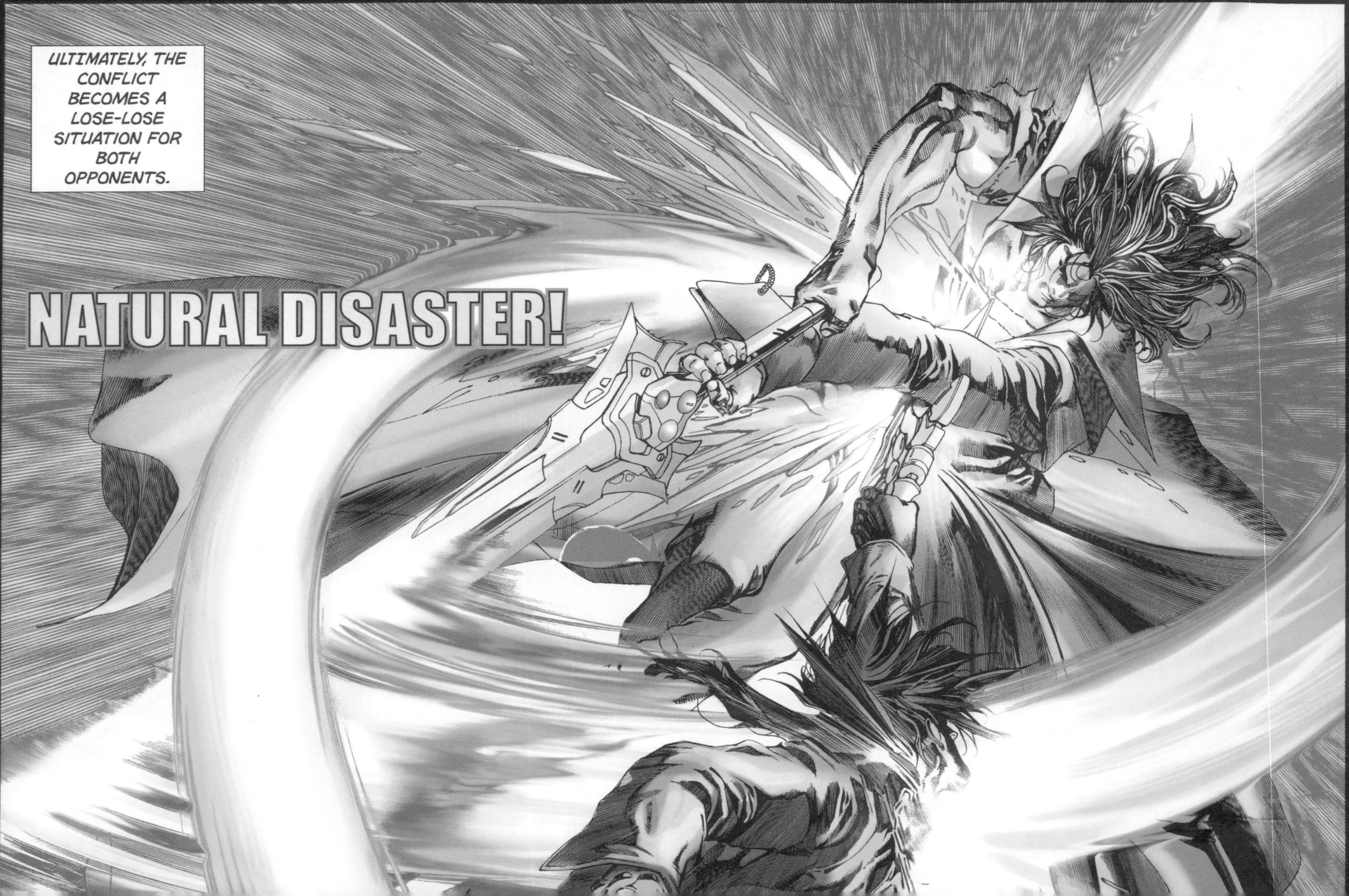
ULTIMATELY, THE CONFLICT BECOMES A LOSE-LOSE SITUATION FOR BOTH OPPONENTS.
NATURAL DISASTER!

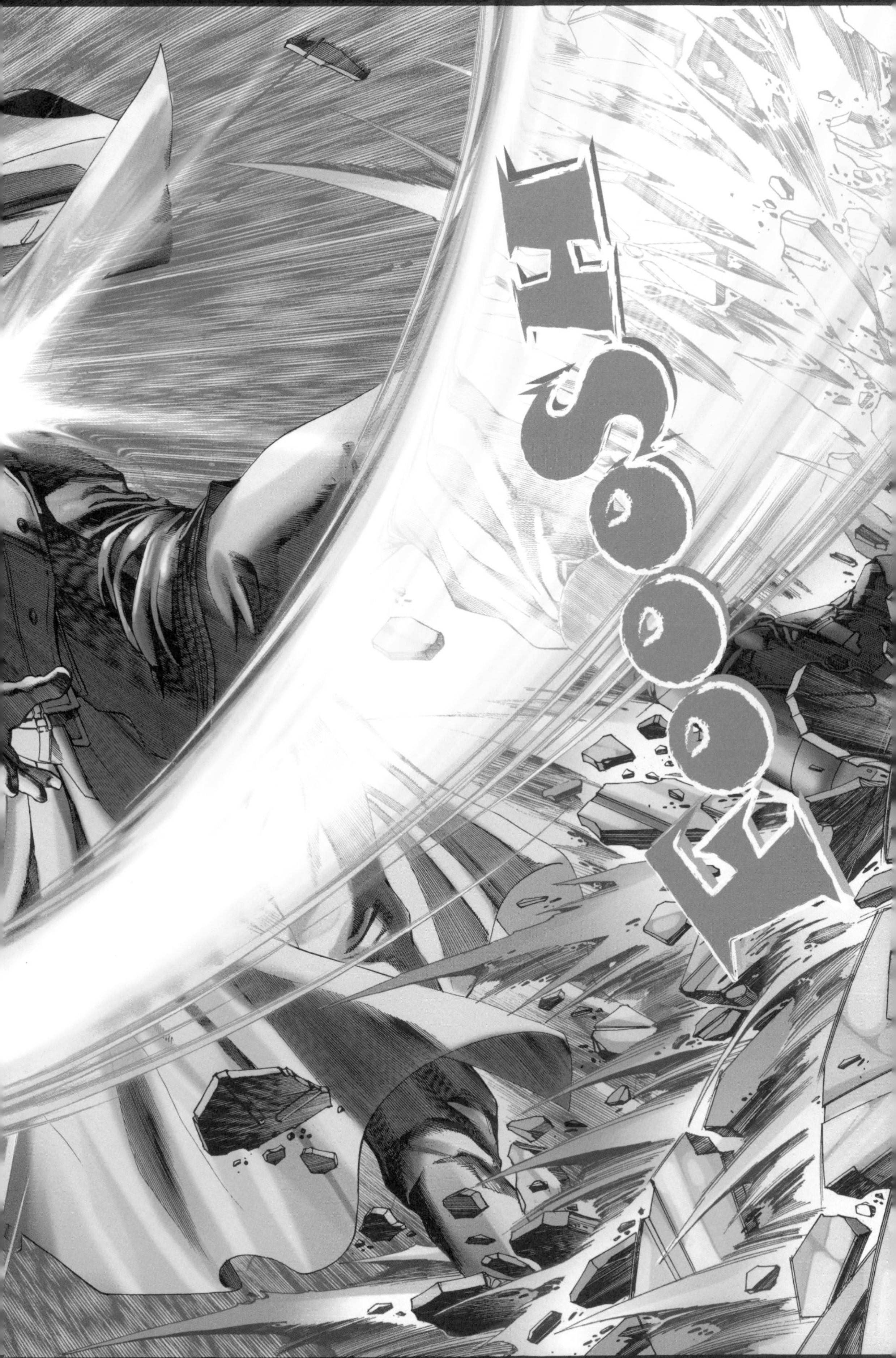

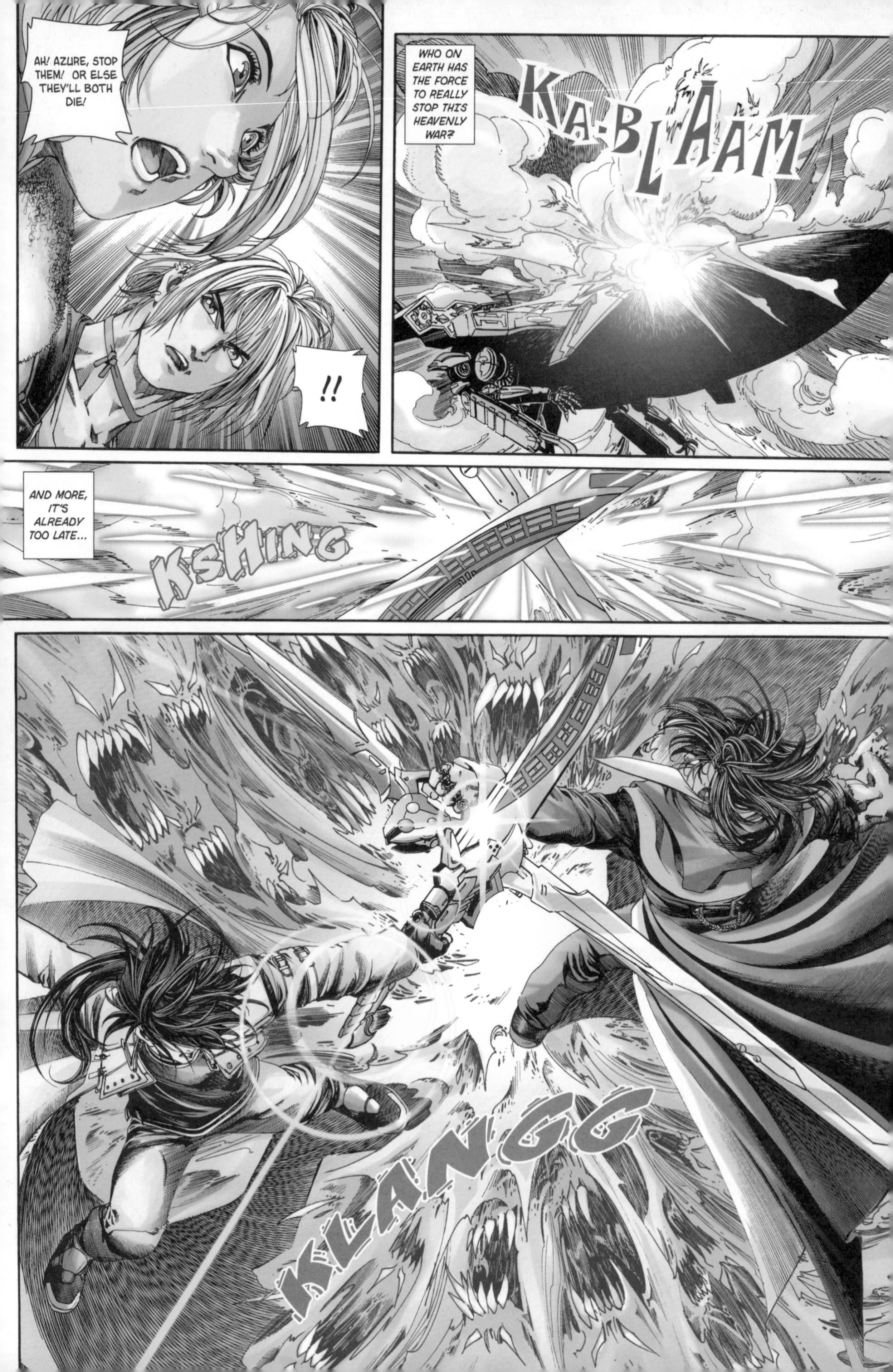
AH! AZURE, STOP THEM! OR ELSE THEY'LL BOTH DIE!
!!
WHO ON EARTH HAS THE FORCE TO REALLY STOP THIS HEAVENLY WAR?
KA-BLAAM
AND MORE, IT'S ALREADY TOO LATE...
KSHING
KLANGG

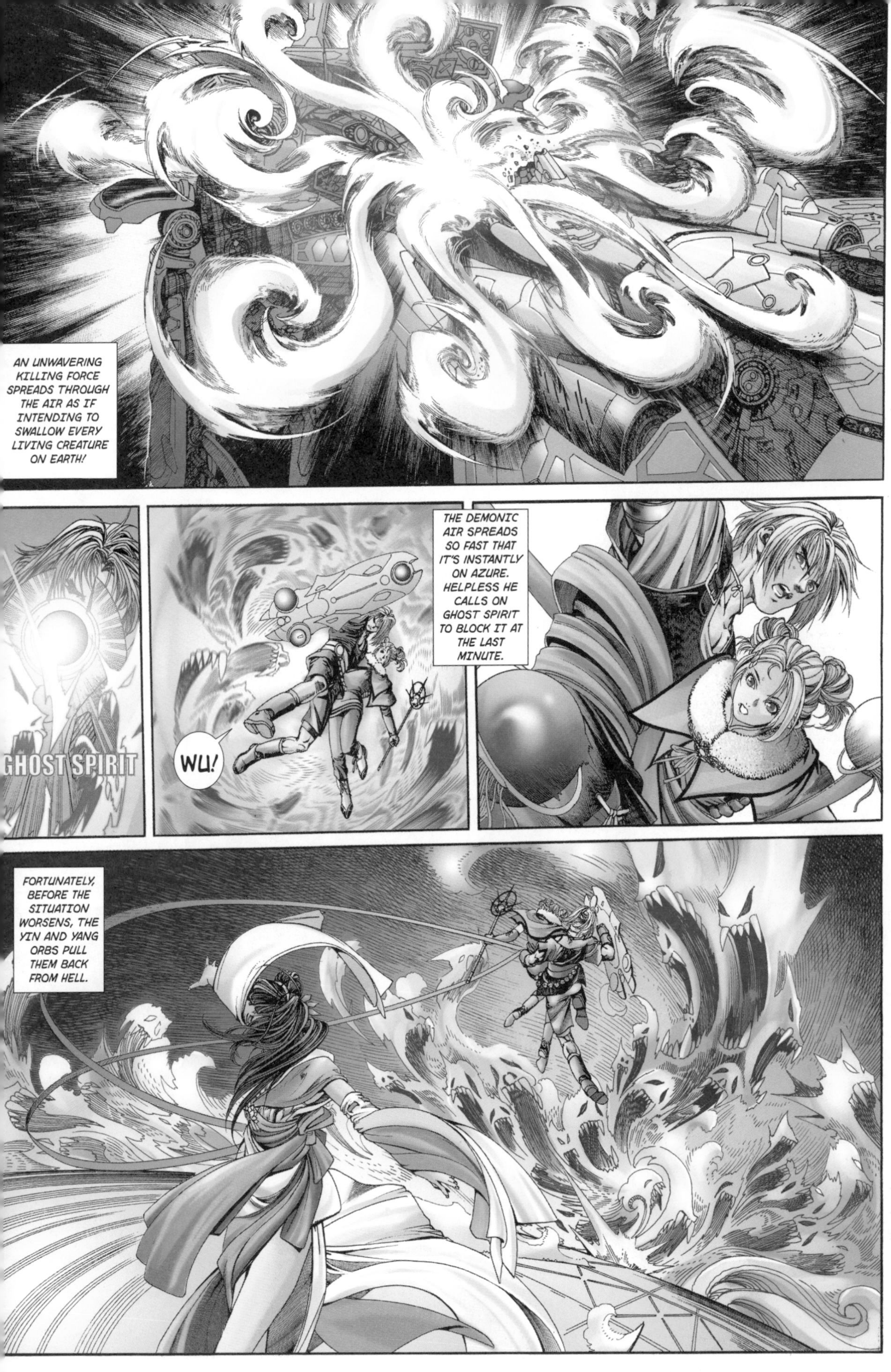
AN UNWAVERING KILLING FORCE SPREADS THROUGH THE AIR AS IF INTENDING TO SWALLOW EVERY LIVING CREATURE ON EARTH!
GHOST SPIRIT
WU!
THE DEMONIC AIR SPREADS SO FAST THAT IT'S INSTANTLY ON AZURE. HELPLESS HE CALLS ON GHOST SPIRIT TO BLOCK IT AT THE LAST MINUTE.
FORTUNATELY, BEFORE THE SITUATION WORSENS, THE YIN AND YANG ORBS PULL THEM BACK FROM HELL.

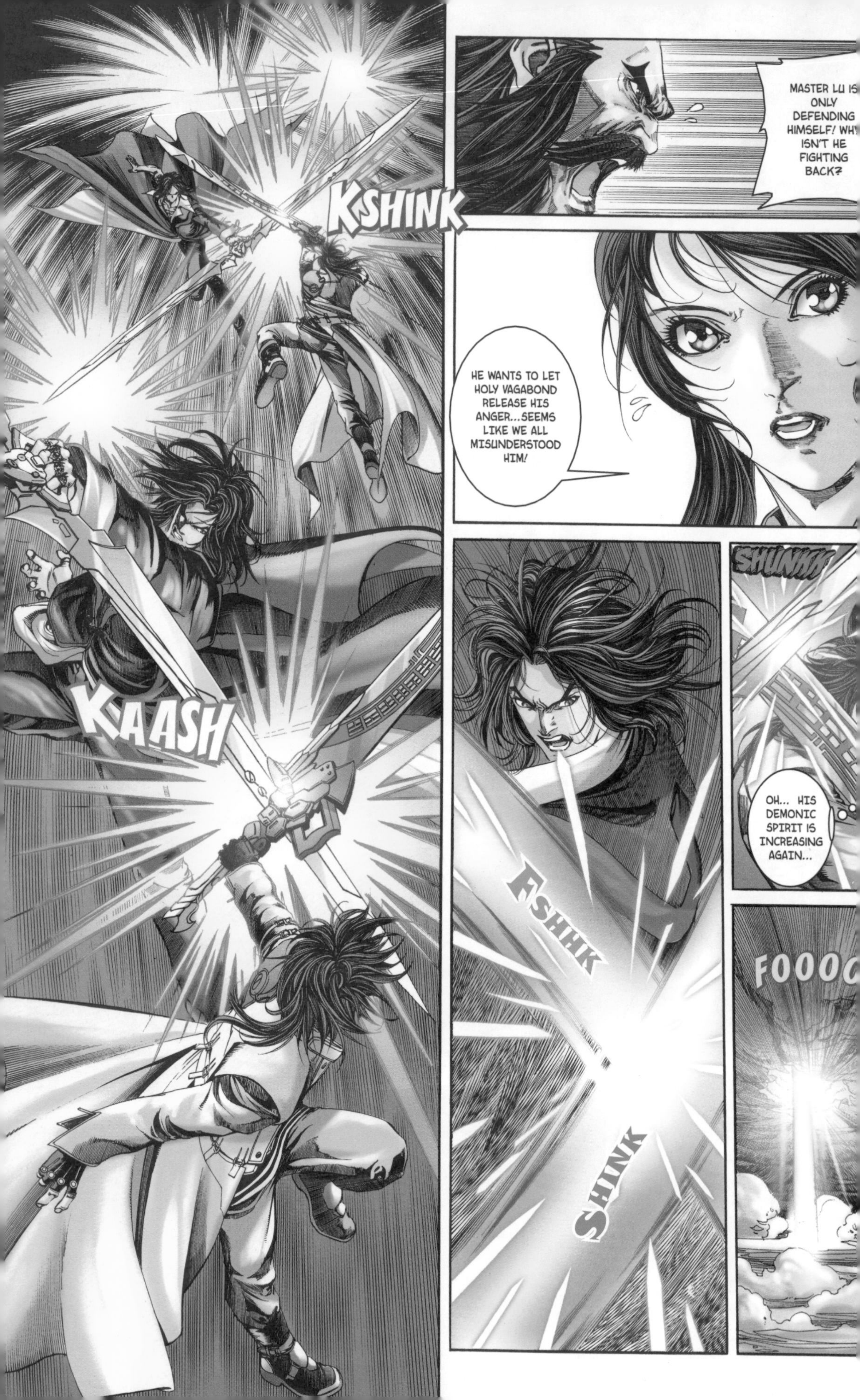
KSHINK
KAASH
MASTER LU IS ONLY DEFENDING HIMSELF! WHY ISN'T HE FIGHTING BACK?
HE WANTS TO LET HOLY VAGABOND RELEASE HIS ANGER...SEEMS LIKE WE ALL MISUNDERSTOOD HIM!
FSHHK
SHINK
SHUNKK
OH... HIS DEMONIC SPIRIT IS INCREASING AGAIN...
FOOOO

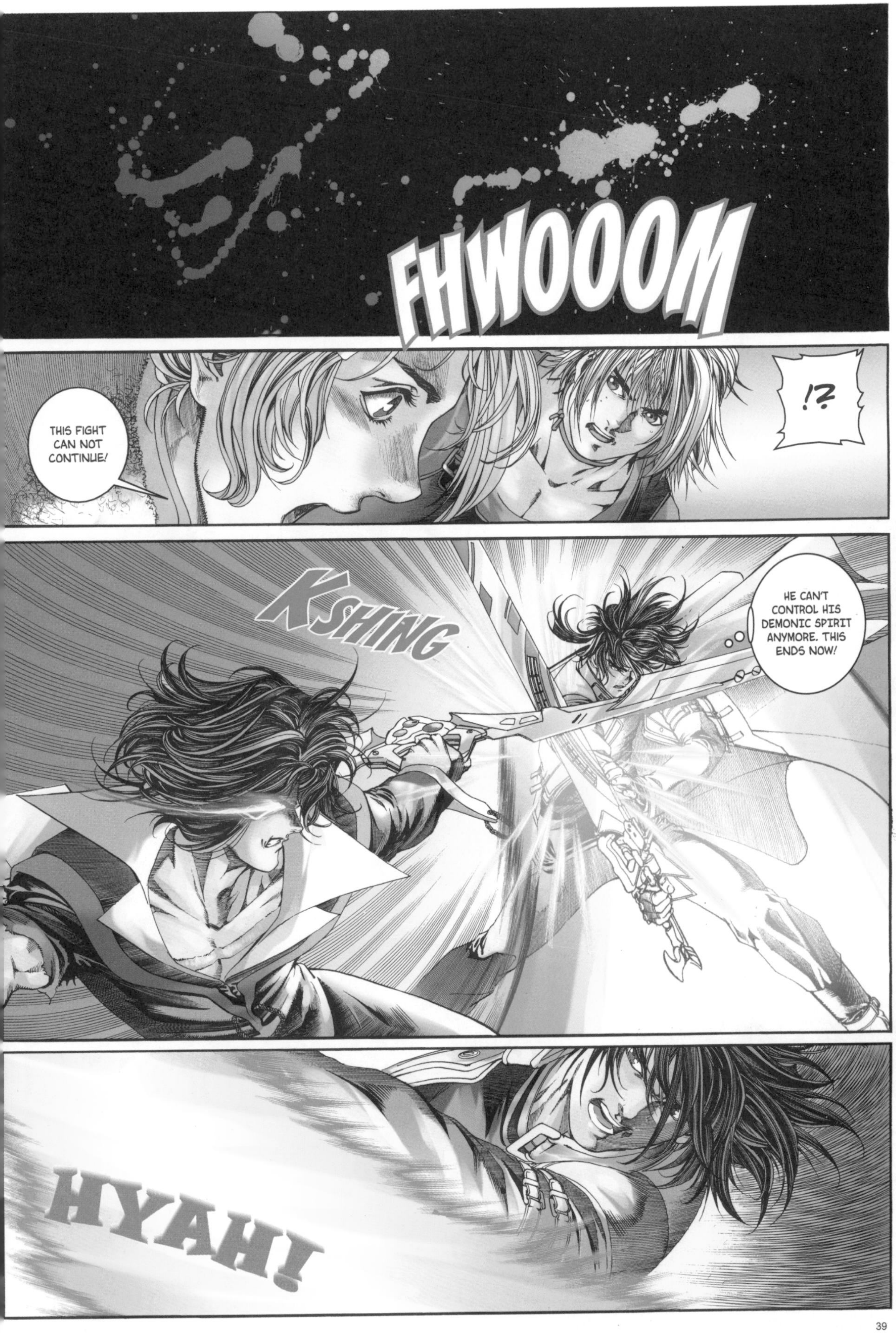

FHWOOOM
THIS FIGHT CAN NOT CONTINUE!
!?
K'SHING
HE CAN'T CONTROL HIS DEMONIC SPIRIT ANYMORE. THIS ENDS NOW!
HYAH!

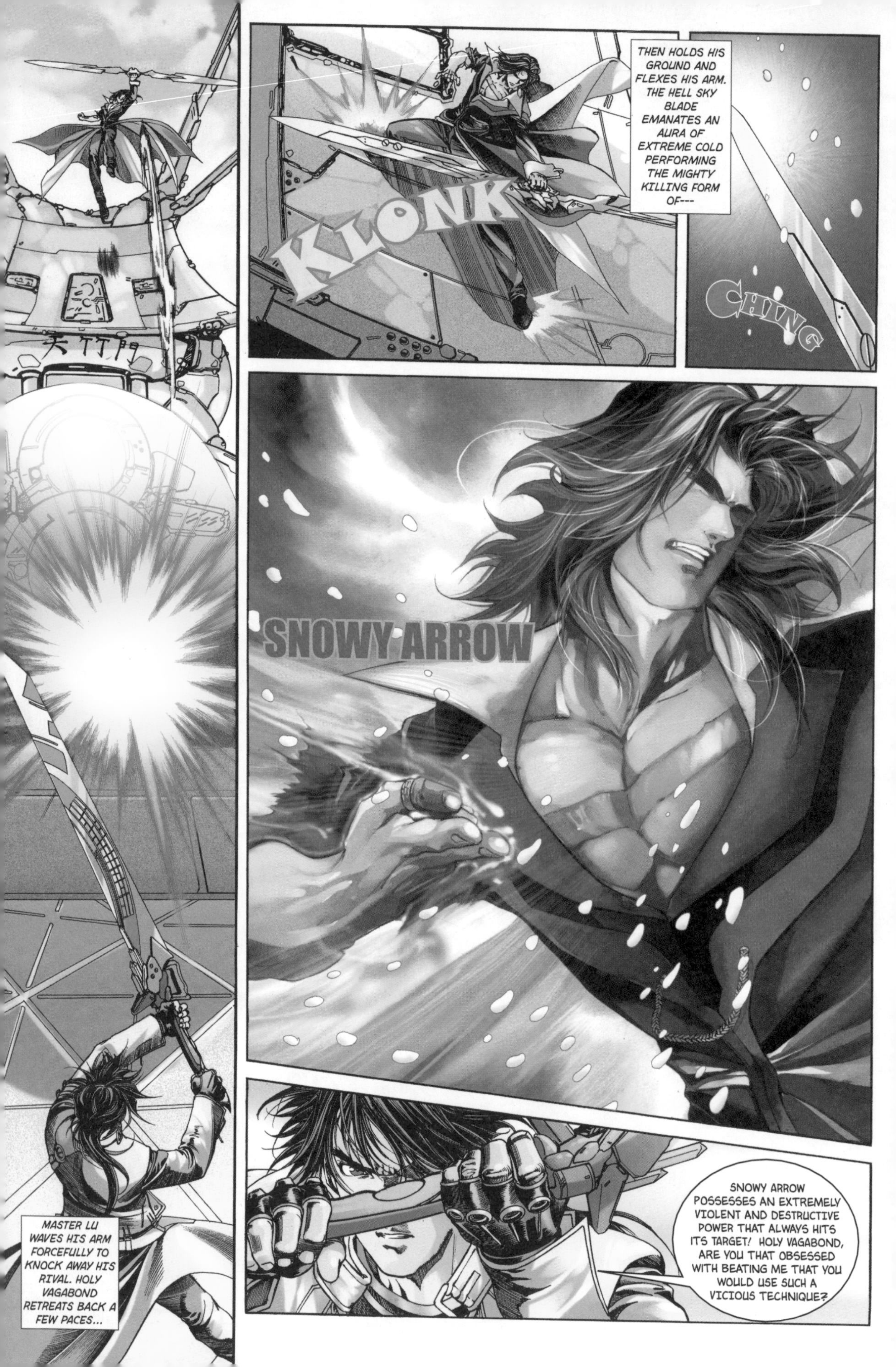
MASTER LU WAVES HIS ARM FORCEFULLY TO KNOCK AWAY HIS RIVAL. HOLY VAGABOND RETREATS BACK A FEW PACES...
KLONK
THEN HOLDS HIS GROUND AND FLEXES HIS ARM. THE HELL SKY BLADE EMANATES AN AURA OF EXTREME COLD PERFORMING THE MIGHTY KILLING FORM OF---
CHING
SNOWY ARROW
SNOWY ARROW POSSESSES AN EXTREMELY VIOLENT AND DESTRUCTIVE POWER THAT ALWAYS HITS ITS TARGET! HOLY VAGABOND, ARE YOU THAT OBSESSED WITH BEATING ME THAT YOU WOULD USE SUCH A VICIOUS TECHNIQUE?

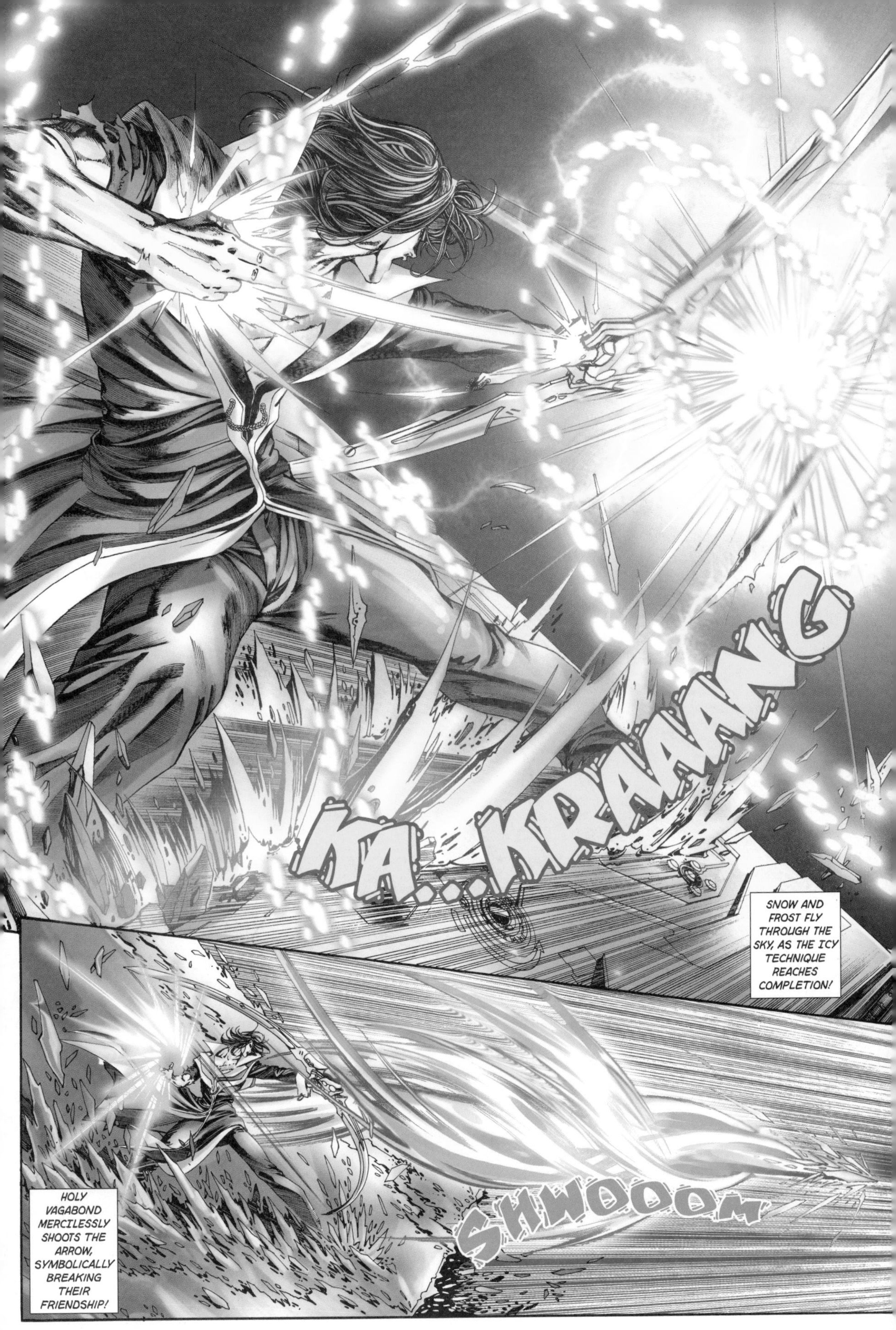
KA...KRAAANG
SNOW AND FROST FLY THROUGH THE SKY, AS THE ICY TECHNIQUE REACHES COMPLETION!
SHWOOOM
HOLY VAGABOND MERCILESSLY SHOOTS THE ARROW, SYMBOLICALLY BREAKING THEIR FRIENDSHIP!

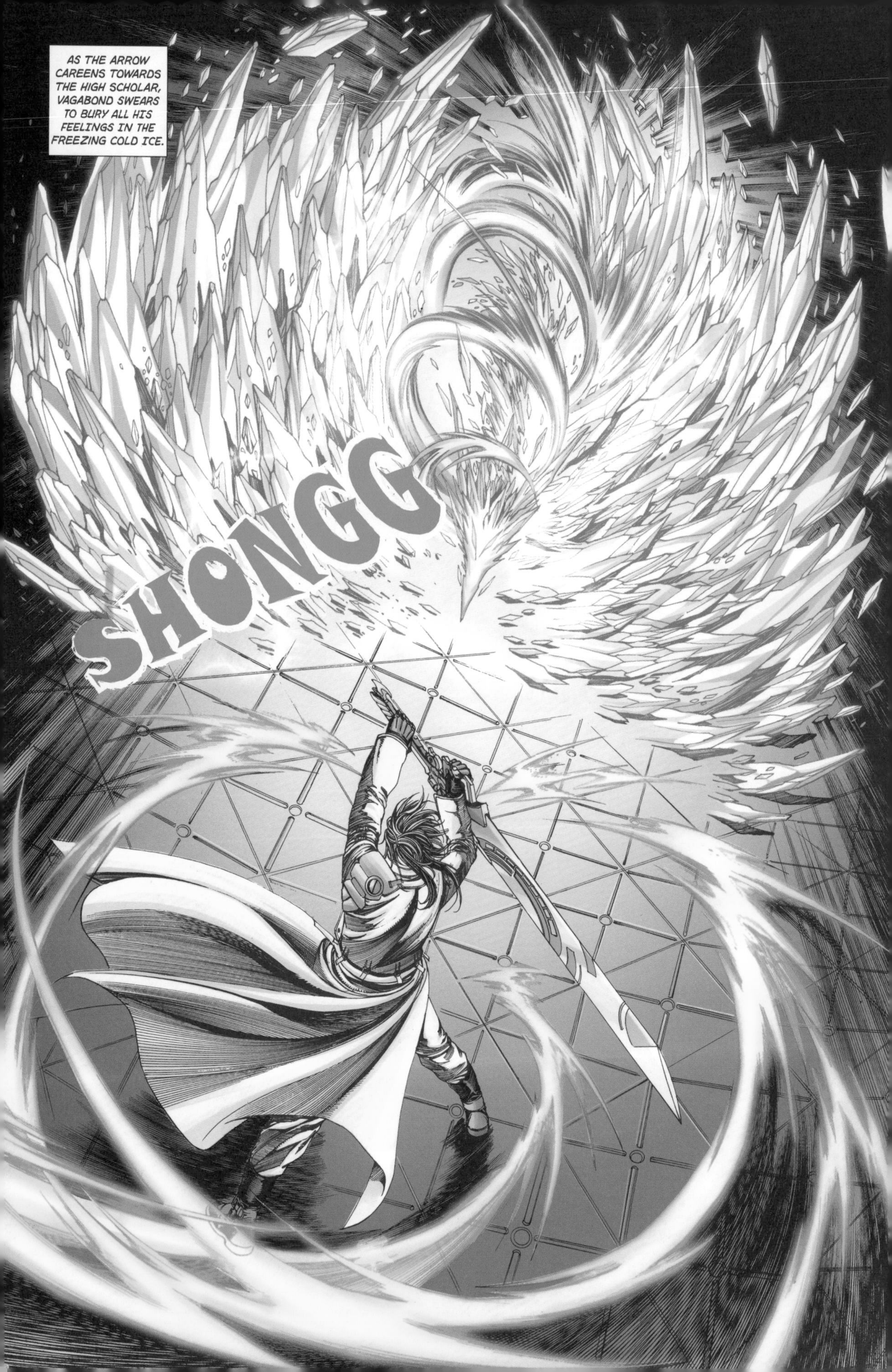
AS THE ARROW CAREENS TOWARDS THE HIGH SCHOLAR, VAGABOND SWEARS TO BURY ALL HIS FEELINGS IN THE FREEZING COLD ICE.
SHONGG

A Celestial Tale

Vivi is the reincarnation of the Goddess of the Celestial Realm. From the moment she met Azure, she has felt a close bond to him. During the 21st century Millennium celebration a great disaster was predicted. If not for the Goddess of the Celestial Realm, all would have been lost. But this victory was not without a price, for once the earth was saved she did not have the power to sustain her godly abilities and plummeted to earth. Her essence found a woman and she gave birth to Vivi. Now with the help of Azure and the other 8 immortals she continues to find new powers and search for her new purpose in life.

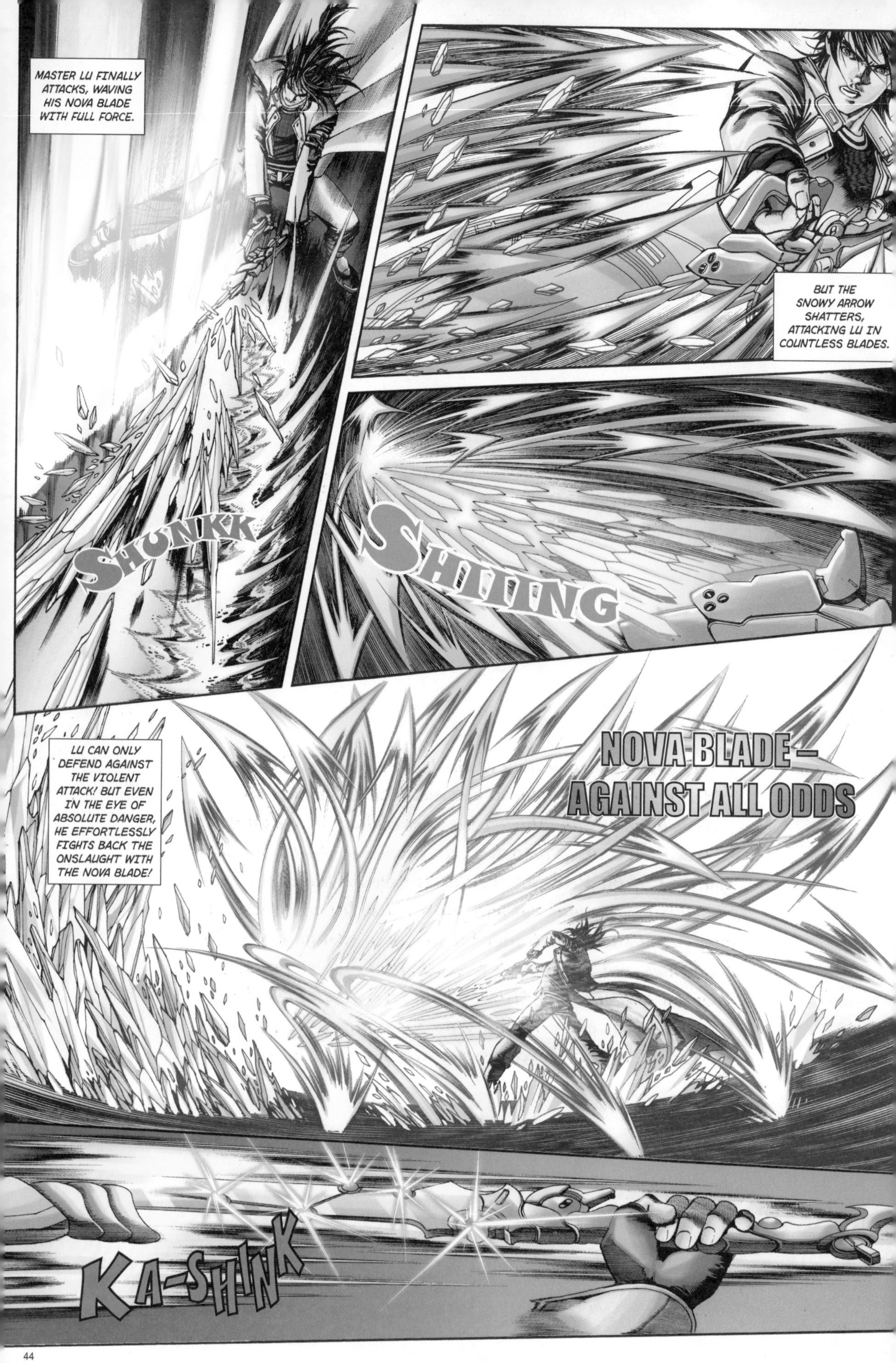

MASTER LU FINALLY ATTACKS, WAVING HIS NOVA BLADE WITH FULL FORCE.
BUT THE SNOWY ARROW SHATTERS, ATTACKING LU IN COUNTLESS BLADES.
SHUNKK
SHIIING
LU CAN ONLY DEFEND AGAINST THE VIOLENT ATTACK! BUT EVEN IN THE EYE OF ABSOLUTE DANGER, HE EFFORTLESSLY FIGHTS BACK THE ONSLAUGHT WITH THE NOVA BLADE!
NOVA BLADE – AGAINST ALL ODDS
KA-SHINK

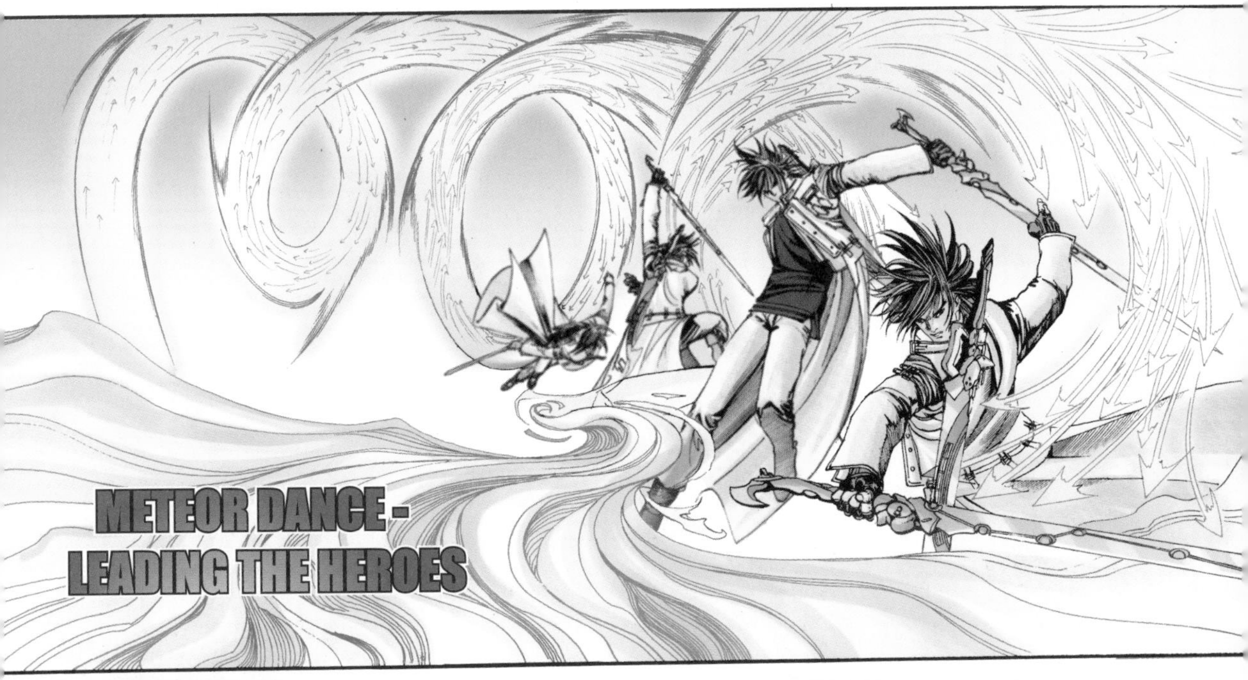
METEOR DANCE -
LEADING THE HEROES

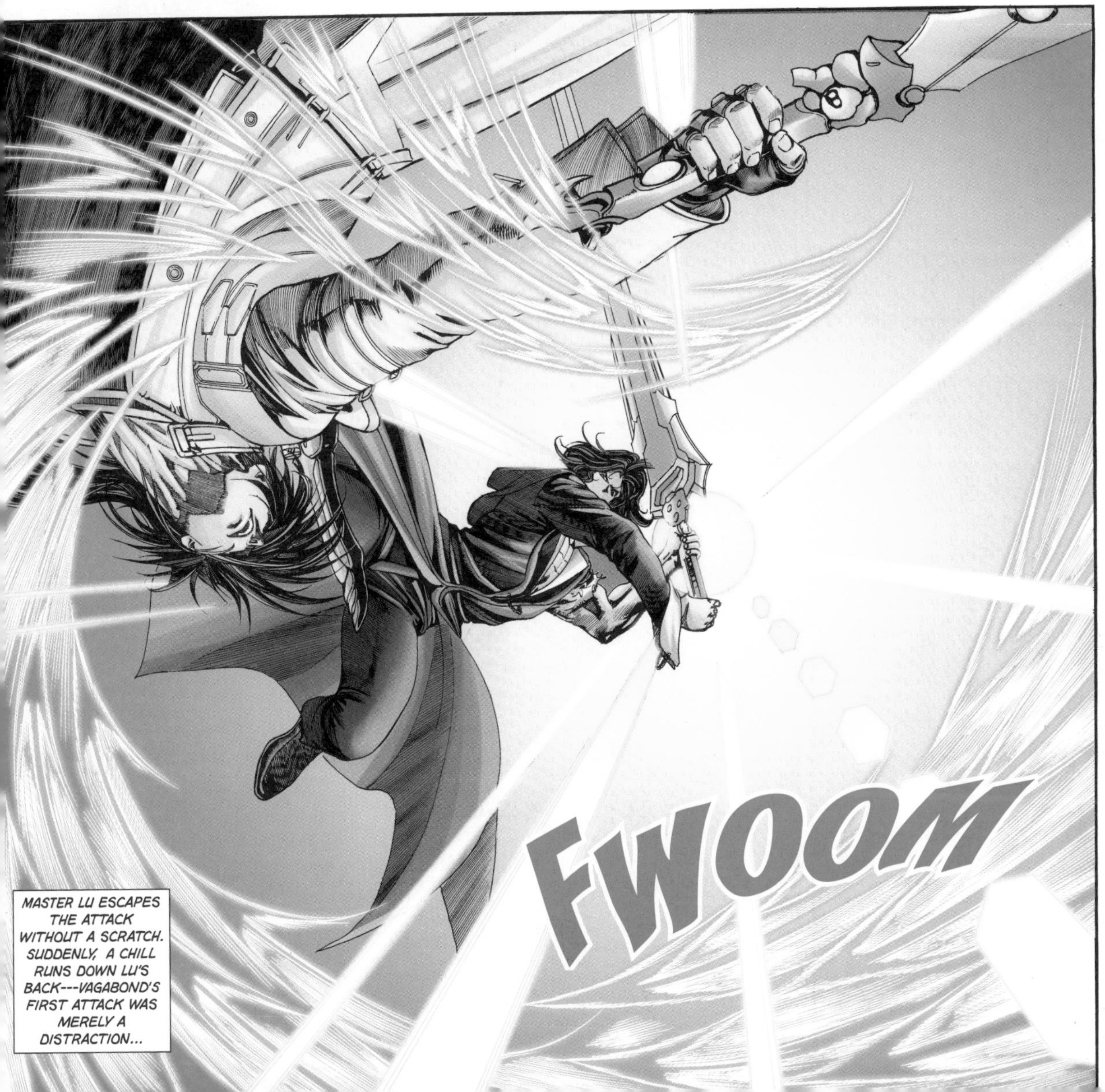
FWOOM
MASTER LU ESCAPES THE ATTACK WITHOUT A SCRATCH. SUDDENLY, A CHILL RUNS DOWN LU'S BACK---VAGABOND'S FIRST ATTACK WAS MERELY A DISTRACTION...

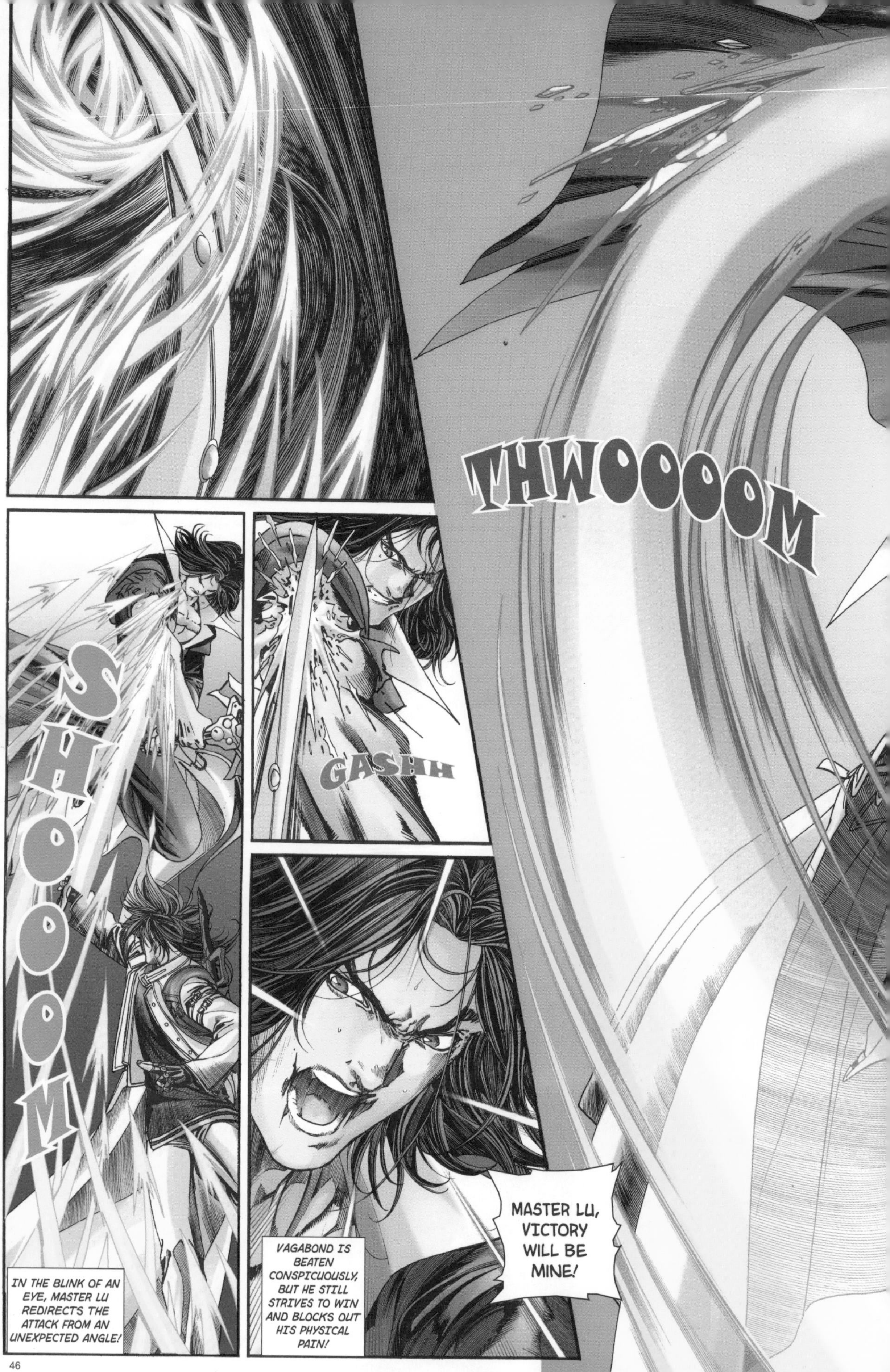
THWOOOOM
SHOOOOOM
GASHH
IN THE BLINK OF AN EYE, MASTER LU REDIRECTS THE ATTACK FROM AN UNEXPECTED ANGLE!
VAGABOND IS BEATEN CONSPICUOUSLY, BUT HE STILL STRIVES TO WIN AND BLOCKS OUT HIS PHYSICAL PAIN!
MASTER LU, VICTORY WILL BE MINE!

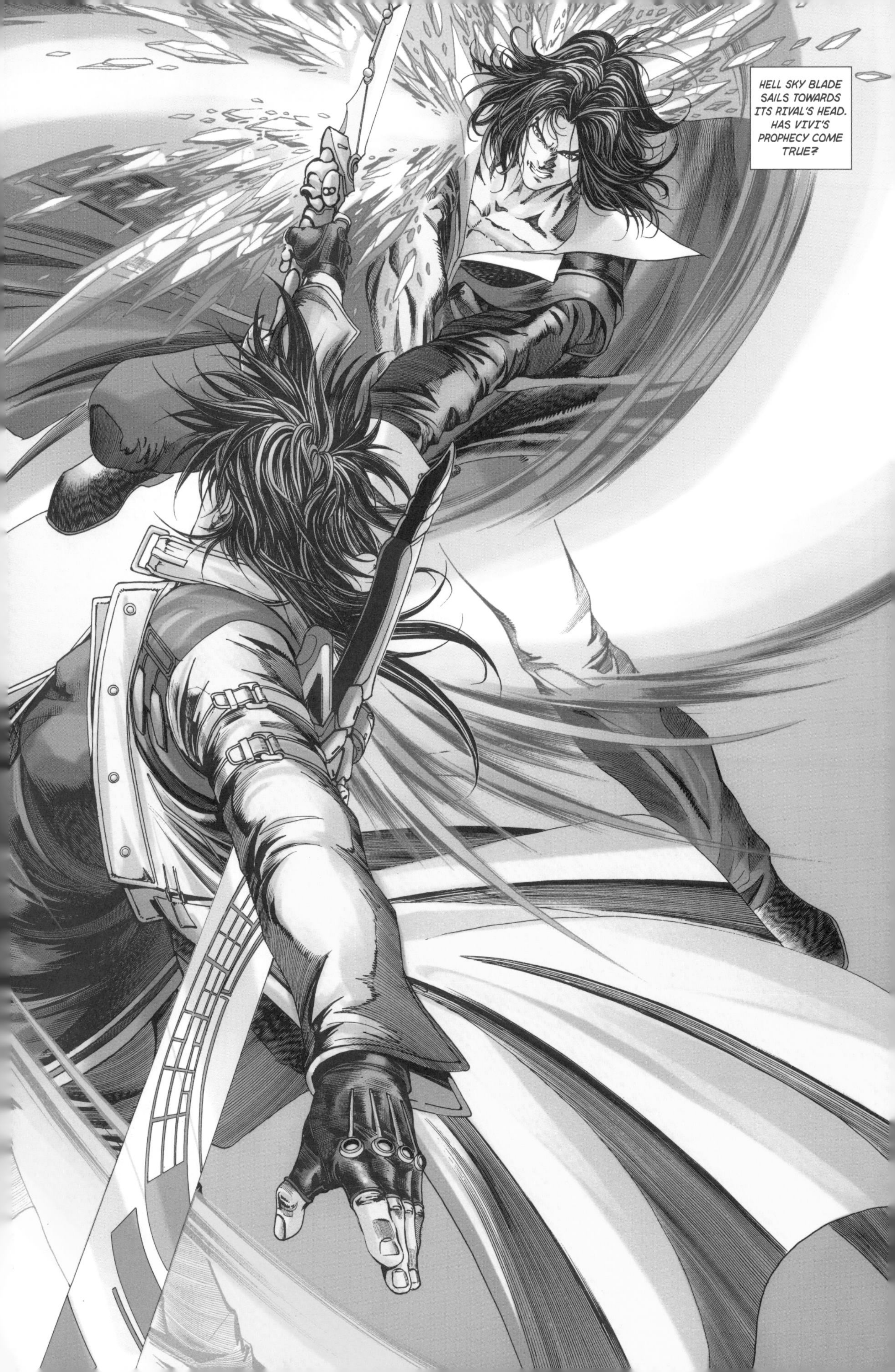
HELL SKY BLADE SAILS TOWARDS ITS RIVAL'S HEAD. HAS VIVI'S PROPHECY COME TRUE?

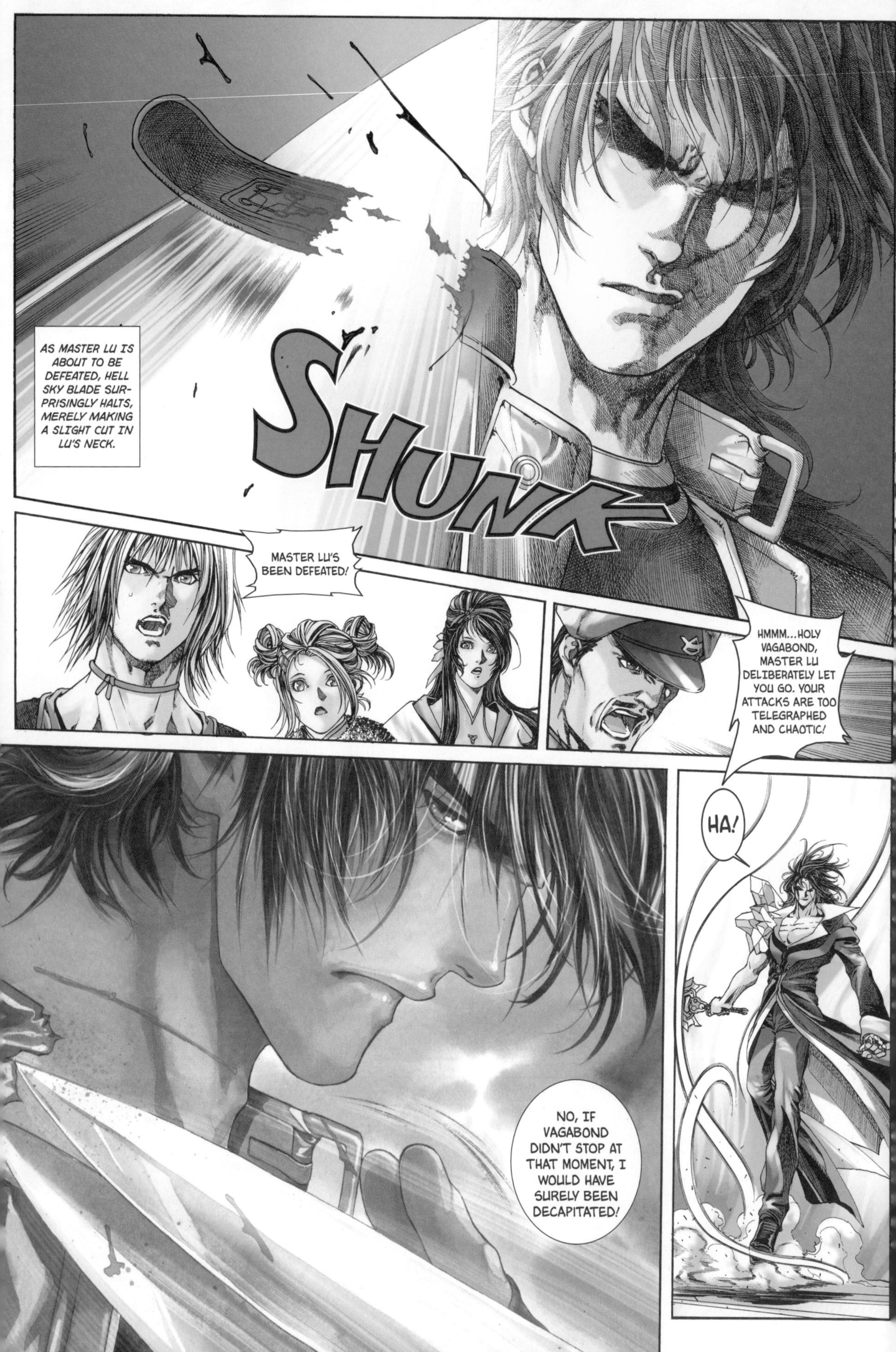
AS MASTER LU IS ABOUT TO BE DEFEATED, HELL SKY BLADE SURPRISINGLY HALTS, MERELY MAKING A SLIGHT CUT IN LU'S NECK.
SHUNK
MASTER LU'S BEEN DEFEATED!
HMMM...HOLY VAGABOND, MASTER LU DELIBERATELY LET YOU GO. YOUR ATTACKS ARE TOO TELEGRAPHED AND CHAOTIC!
HA!
NO, IF VAGABOND DIDN'T STOP AT THAT MOMENT, I WOULD HAVE SURELY BEEN DECAPITATED!

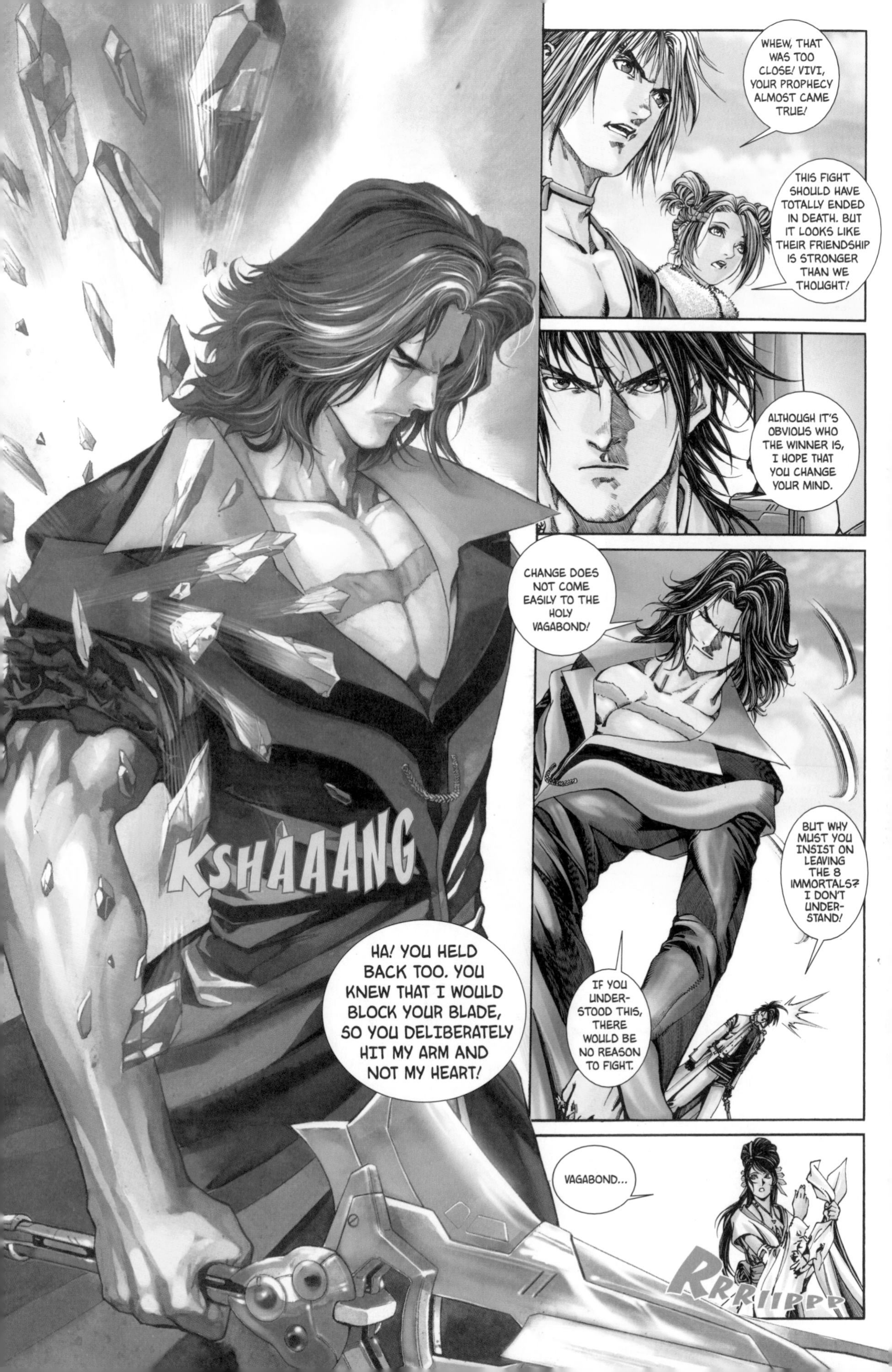
WHEW, THAT WAS TOO CLOSE! VIVI, YOUR PROPHECY ALMOST CAME TRUE!
THIS FIGHT SHOULD HAVE TOTALLY ENDED IN DEATH. BUT IT LOOKS LIKE THEIR FRIENDSHIP IS STRONGER THAN WE THOUGHT!
KSHAAANG
HA! YOU HELD BACK TOO. YOU KNEW THAT I WOULD BLOCK YOUR BLADE, SO YOU DELIBERATELY HIT MY ARM AND NOT MY HEART!
ALTHOUGH IT'S OBVIOUS WHO THE WINNER IS, I HOPE THAT YOU CHANGE YOUR MIND.
CHANGE DOES NOT COME EASILY TO THE HOLY VAGABOND!
BUT WHY MUST YOU INSIST ON LEAVING THE 8 IMMORTALS? I DON'T UNDER-STAND!
IF YOU UNDER-STOOD THIS, THERE WOULD BE NO REASON TO FIGHT.
VAGABOND...
RRRIIPPP

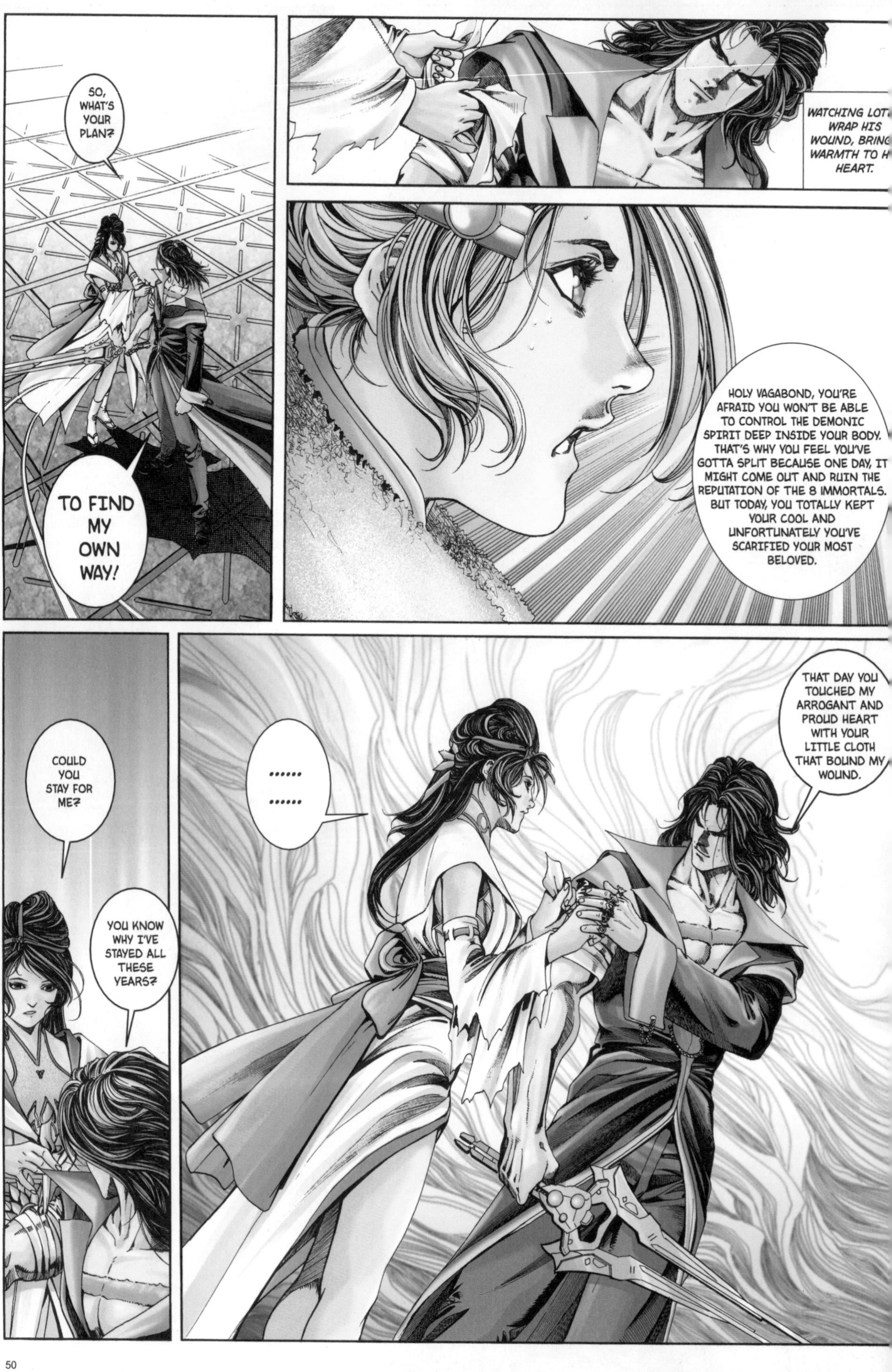
SO, WHAT'S YOUR PLAN?
TO FIND MY OWN WAY!
WATCHING LOT WRAP HIS WOUND, BRING WARMTH TO H HEART.
HOLY VAGABOND, YOU'RE AFRAID YOU WON'T BE ABLE TO CONTROL THE DEMONIC SPIRIT DEEP INSIDE YOUR BODY. THAT'S WHY YOU FEEL YOU'VE GOTTA SPLIT BECAUSE ONE DAY, IT MIGHT COME OUT AND RUIN THE REPUTATION OF THE 8 IMMORTALS. BUT TODAY, YOU TOTALLY KEPT YOUR COOL AND UNFORTUNATELY YOU'VE SCARIFIED YOUR MOST BELOVED.
COULD YOU STAY FOR ME?
YOU KNOW WHY I'VE STAYED ALL THESE YEARS?
....
THAT DAY YOU TOUCHED MY ARROGANT AND PROUD HEART WITH YOUR LITTLE CLOTH THAT BOUND MY WOUND.

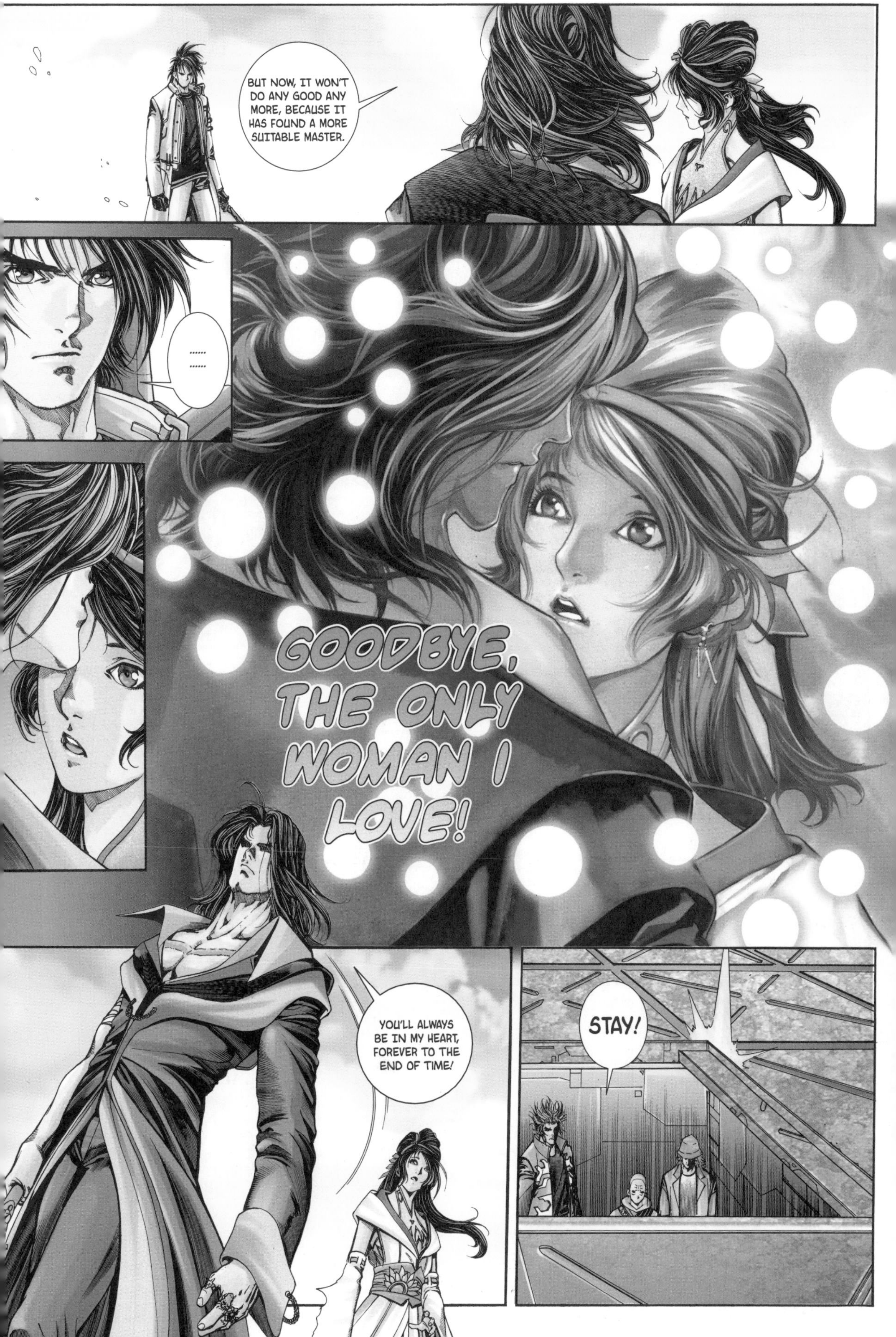
BUT NOW, IT WON'T DO ANY GOOD ANY MORE, BECAUSE IT HAS FOUND A MORE SUITABLE MASTER.
......
......
GOODBYE, THE ONLY WOMAN I LOVE!
YOU'LL ALWAYS BE IN MY HEART, FOREVER TO THE END OF TIME!
STAY!

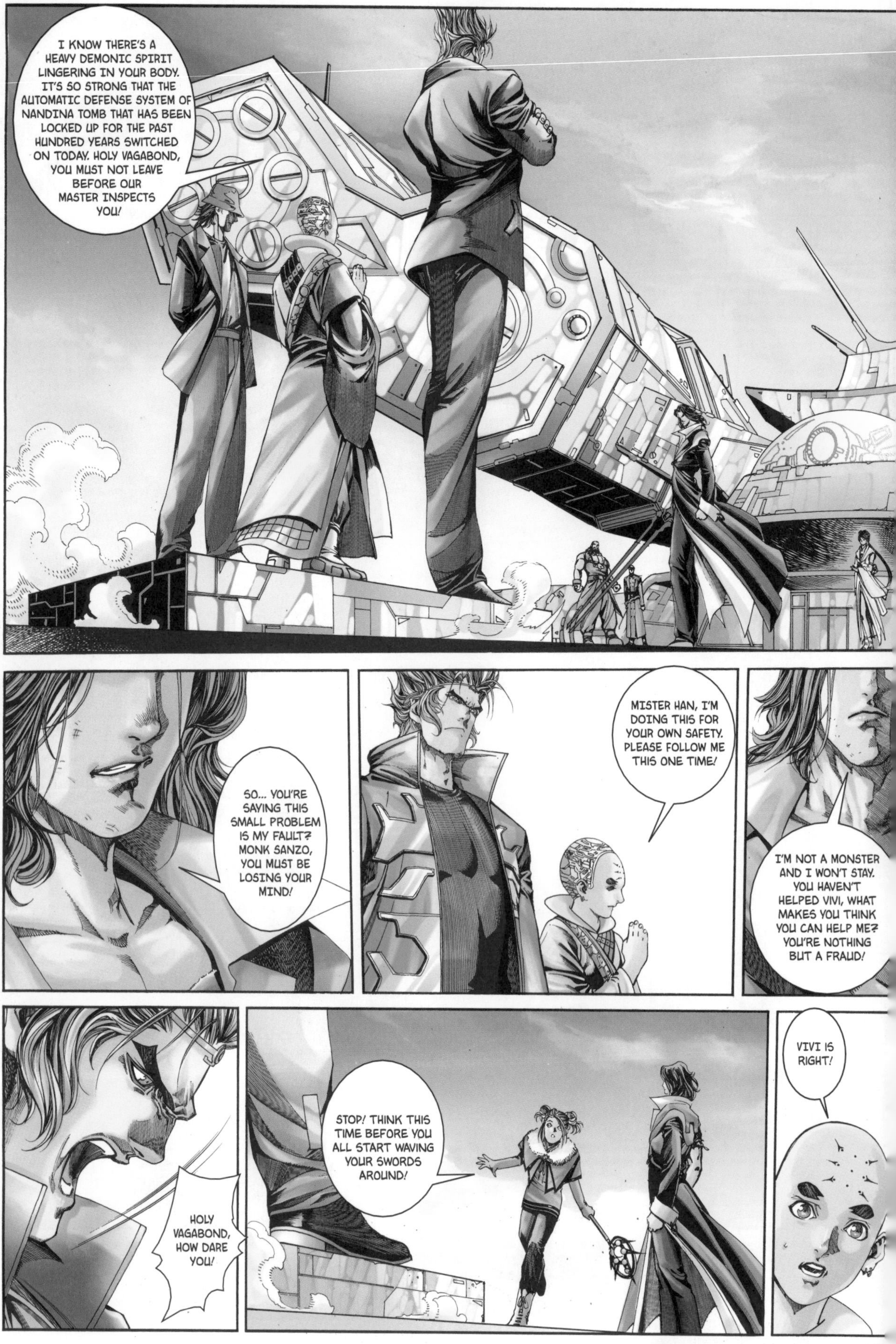

I KNOW THERE'S A HEAVY DEMONIC SPIRIT LINGERING IN YOUR BODY. IT'S SO STRONG THAT THE AUTOMATIC DEFENSE SYSTEM OF NANDINA TOMB THAT HAS BEEN LOCKED UP FOR THE PAST HUNDRED YEARS SWITCHED ON TODAY. HOLY VAGABOND, YOU MUST NOT LEAVE BEFORE OUR MASTER INSPECTS YOU!
SO... YOU'RE SAYING THIS SMALL PROBLEM IS MY FAULT? MONK SANZO, YOU MUST BE LOSING YOUR MIND!
MISTER HAN, I'M DOING THIS FOR YOUR OWN SAFETY. PLEASE FOLLOW ME THIS ONE TIME!
I'M NOT A MONSTER AND I WON'T STAY. YOU HAVEN'T HELPED VIVI, WHAT MAKES YOU THINK YOU CAN HELP ME? YOU'RE NOTHING BUT A FRAUD!
HOLY VAGABOND, HOW DARE YOU!
STOP! THINK THIS TIME BEFORE YOU ALL START WAVING YOUR SWORDS AROUND!
VIVI IS RIGHT!

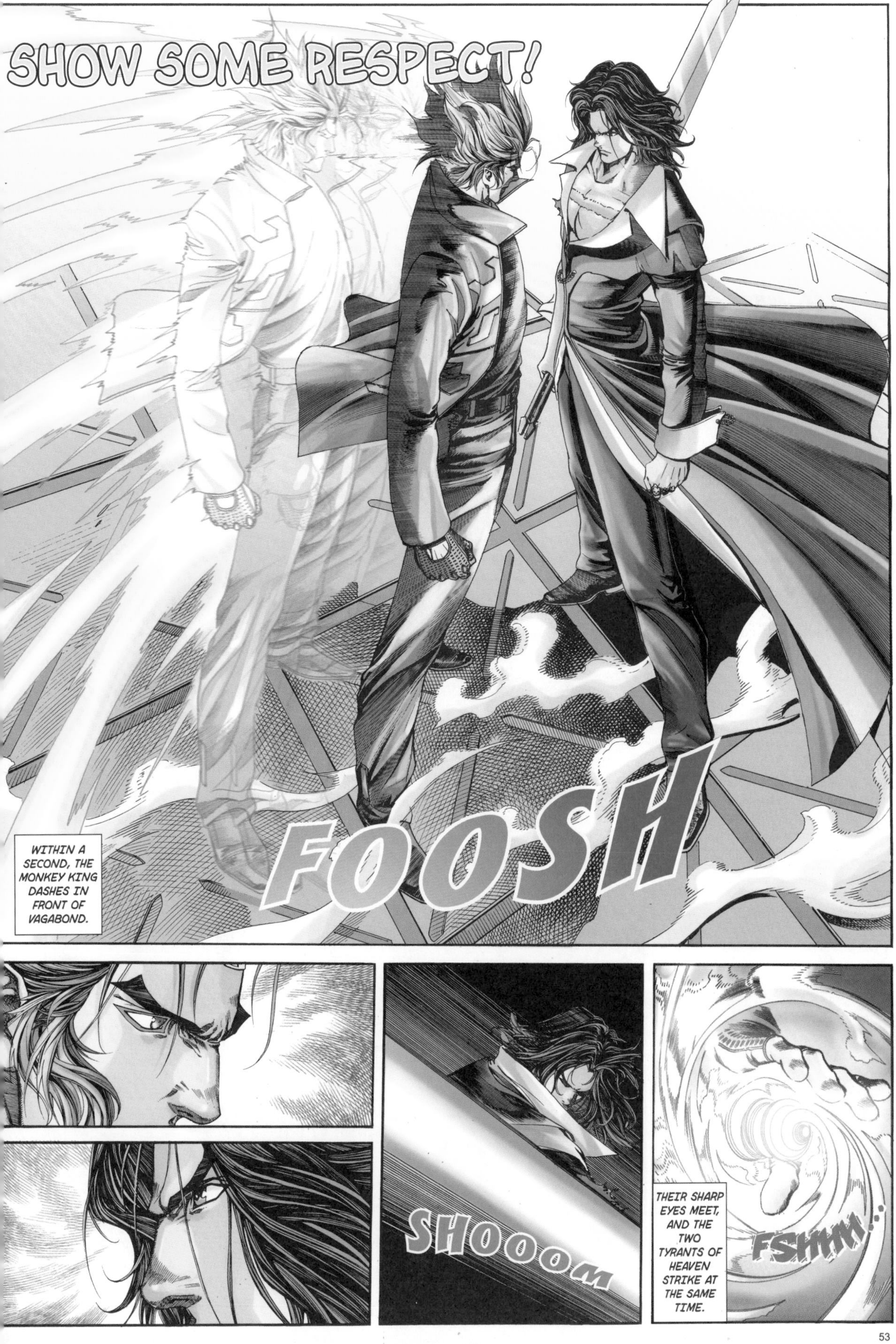
SHOW SOME RESPECT!
WITHIN A SECOND, THE MONKEY KING DASHES IN FRONT OF VAGABOND.
FOOSH
SHOOOOM
THEIR SHARP EYES MEET, AND THE TWO TYRANTS OF HEAVEN STRIKE AT THE SAME TIME.
FSHM..

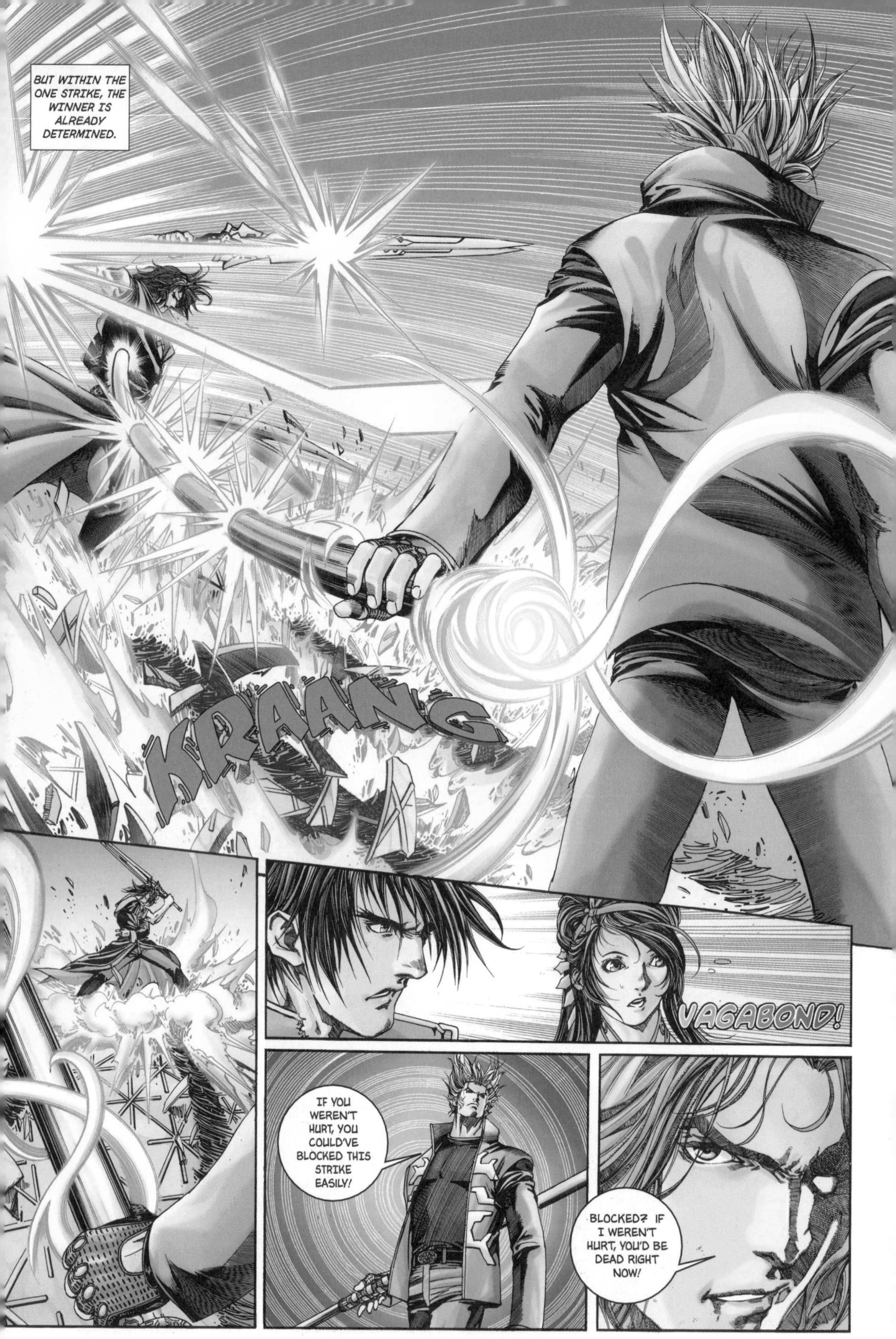
BUT WITHIN THE ONE STRIKE, THE WINNER IS ALREADY DETERMINED.
KRAANG
VAGABOND!
IF YOU WEREN'T HURT, YOU COULD'VE BLOCKED THIS STRIKE EASILY!
BLOCKED? IF I WEREN'T HURT, YOU'D BE DEAD RIGHT NOW!

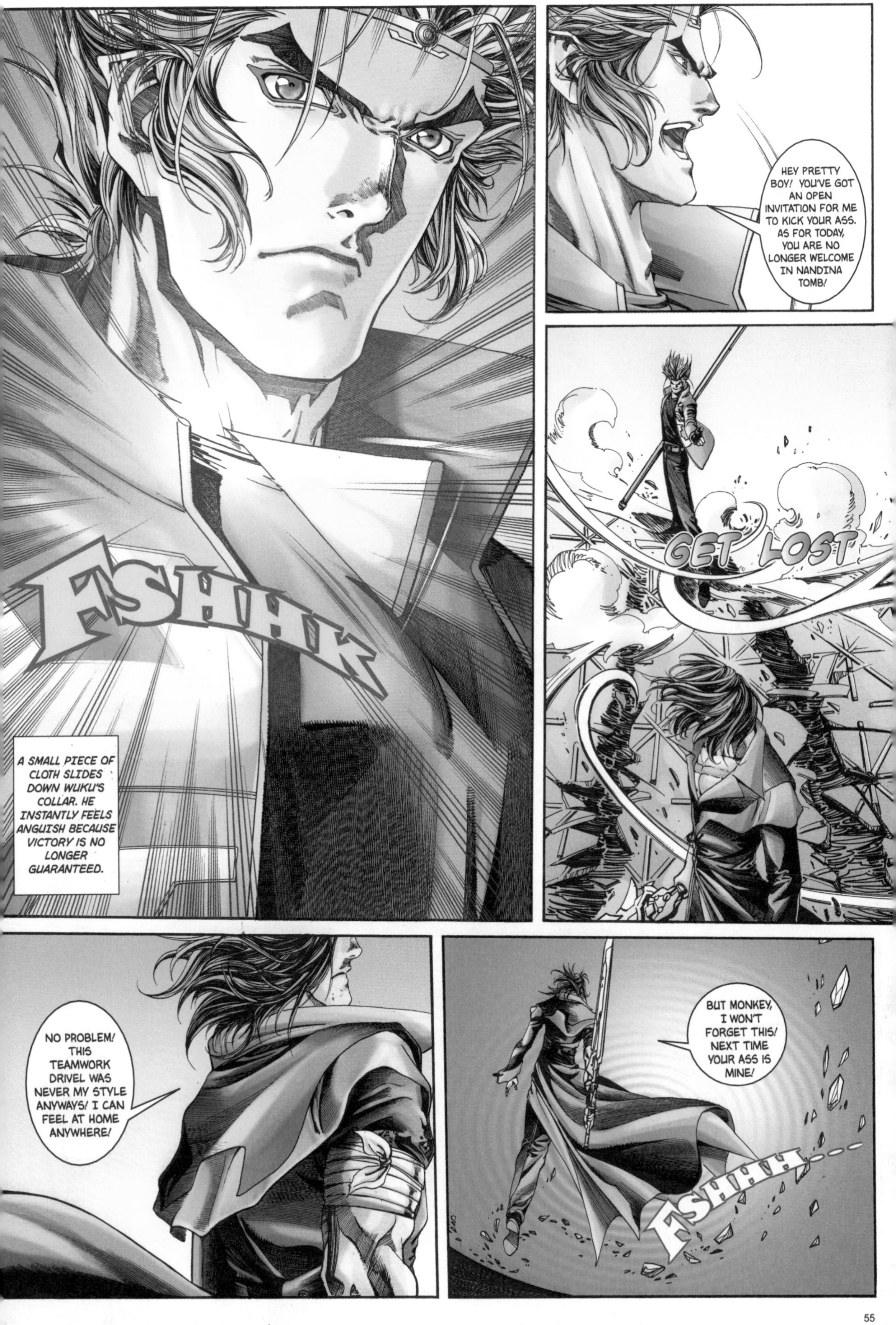
HEY PRETTY BOY! YOU'VE GOT AN OPEN INVITATION FOR ME TO KICK YOUR ASS. AS FOR TODAY, YOU ARE NO LONGER WELCOME IN NANDINA TOMB!
FSHHK
A SMALL PIECE OF CLOTH SLIDES DOWN WUKU'S COLLAR. HE INSTANTLY FEELS ANGUISH BECAUSE VICTORY IS NO LONGER GUARANTEED.
GET LOST
NO PROBLEM! THIS TEAMWORK DRIVEL WAS NEVER MY STYLE ANYWAYS! I CAN FEEL AT HOME ANYWHERE!
BUT MONKEY, I WON'T FORGET THIS! NEXT TIME YOUR ASS IS MINE!
FSHHH...

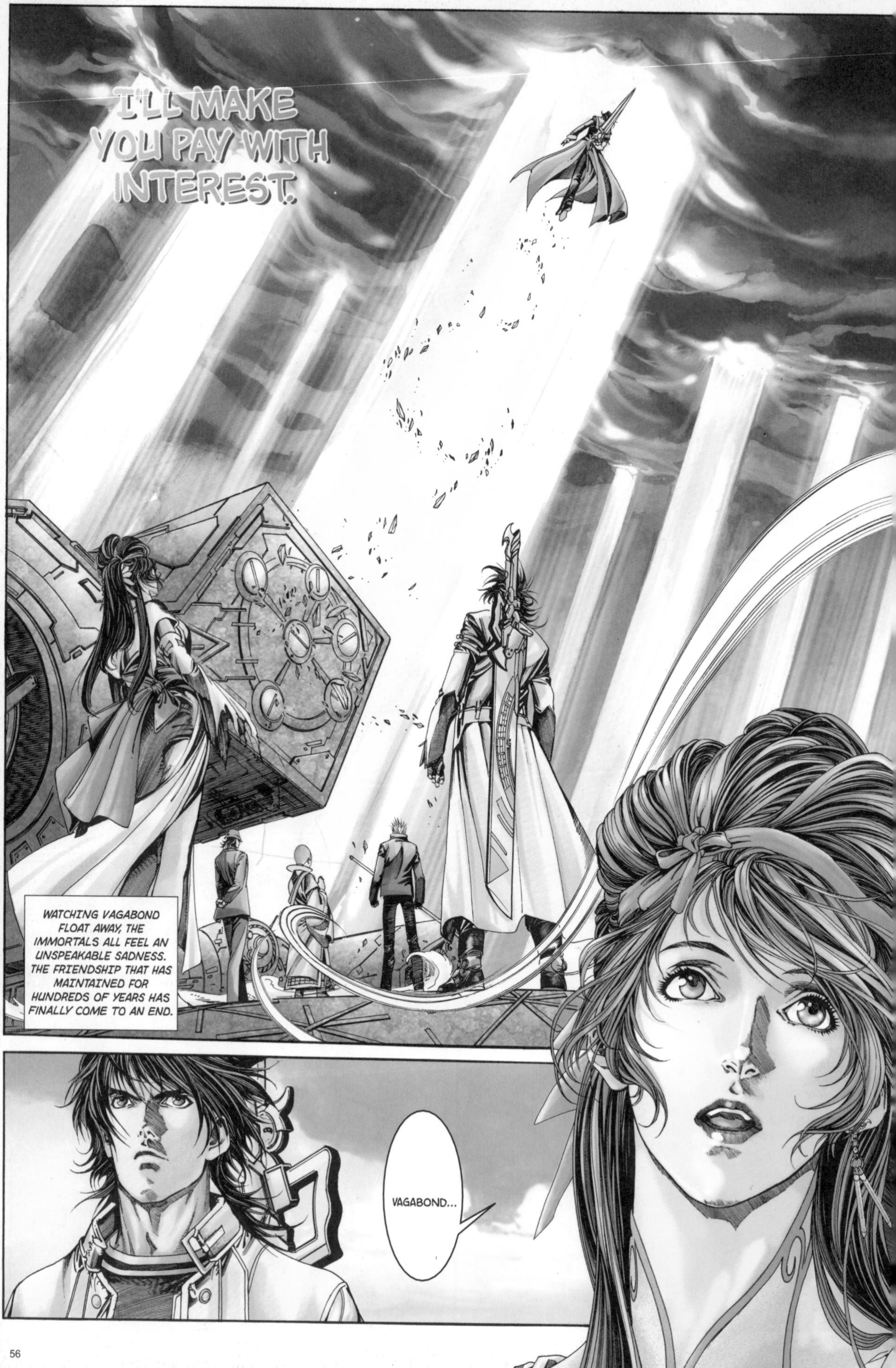
I'LL MAKE YOU PAY WITH INTEREST.
WATCHING VAGABOND FLOAT AWAY, THE IMMORTALS ALL FEEL AN UNSPEAKABLE SADNESS. THE FRIENDSHIP THAT HAS MAINTAINED FOR HUNDREDS OF YEARS HAS FINALLY COME TO AN END.
VAGABOND...

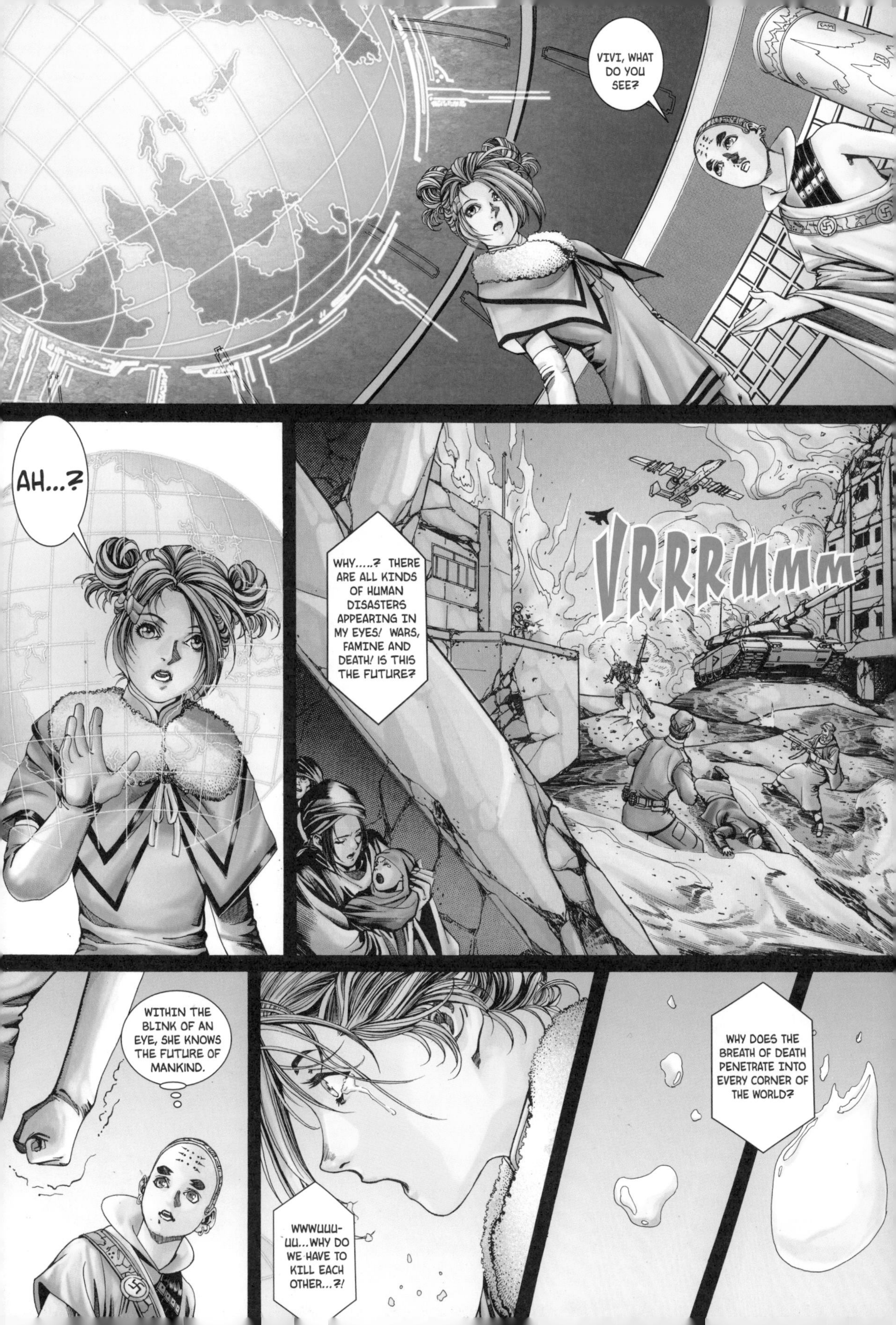
VIVI, WHAT DO YOU SEE?
AH...?
WHY.....? THERE ARE ALL KINDS OF HUMAN DISASTERS APPEARING IN MY EYES! WARS, FAMINE AND DEATH! IS THIS THE FUTURE?
VRRRMMM
WITHIN THE BLINK OF AN EYE, SHE KNOWS THE FUTURE OF MANKIND.
WWWUUU-UU...WHY DO WE HAVE TO KILL EACH OTHER...?!
WHY DOES THE BREATH OF DEATH PENETRATE INTO EVERY CORNER OF THE WORLD?

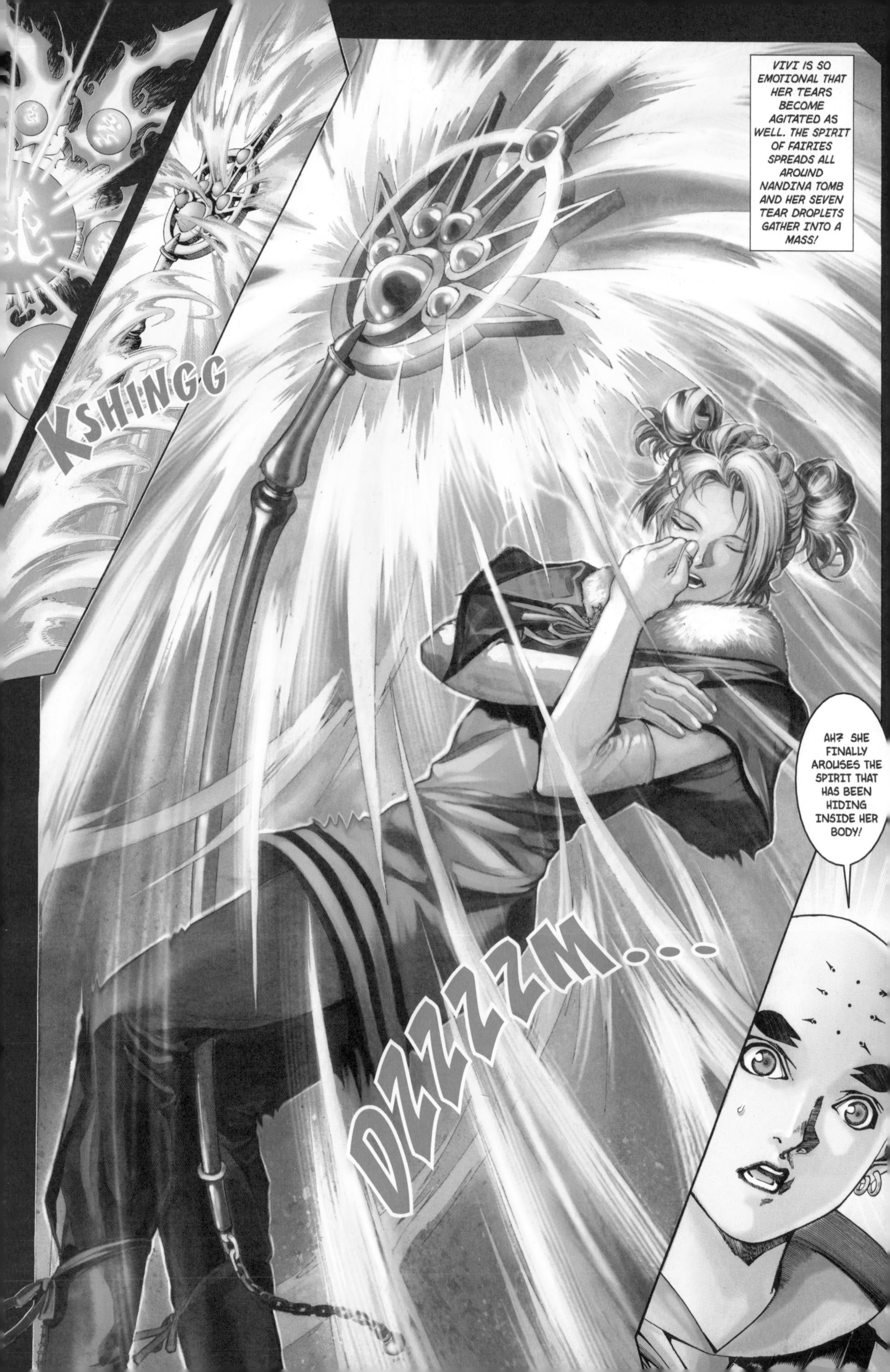
VIVI IS SO EMOTIONAL THAT HER TEARS BECOME AGITATED AS WELL. THE SPIRIT OF FAIRIES SPREADS ALL AROUND NANDINA TOMB AND HER SEVEN TEAR DROPLETS GATHER INTO A MASS!
KSHINGG
AH? SHE FINALLY AROUSES THE SPIRIT THAT HAS BEEN HIDING INSIDE HER BODY!
DZZZZM...

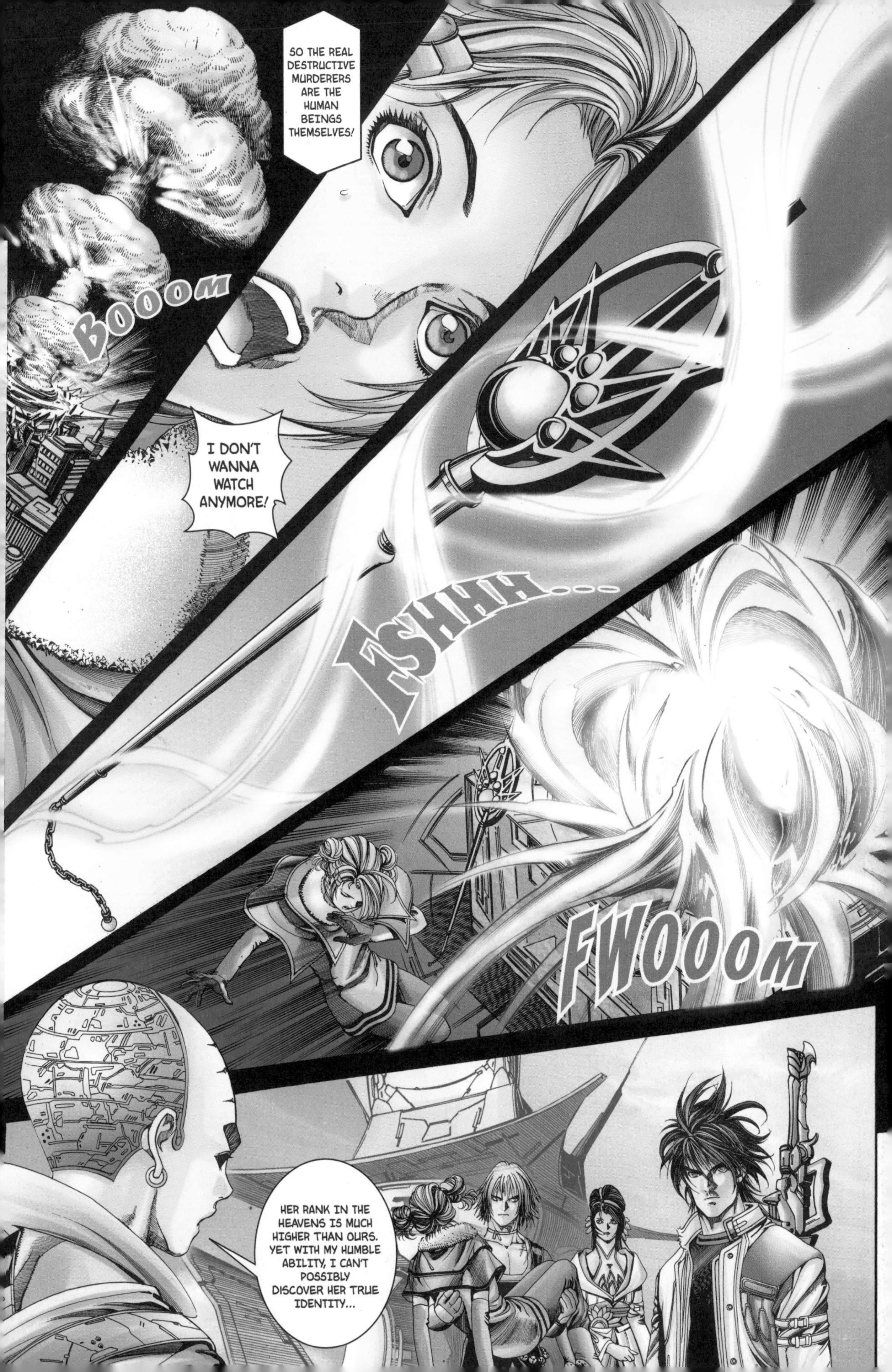

SO THE REAL DESTRUCTIVE MURDERERS ARE THE HUMAN BEINGS THEMSELVES!
BOOOM
I DON'T WANNA WATCH ANYMORE!
FSHHH...
FWOOOM
HER RANK IN THE HEAVENS IS MUCH HIGHER THAN OURS. YET WITH MY HUMBLE ABILITY, I CAN'T POSSIBLY DISCOVER HER TRUE IDENTITY...

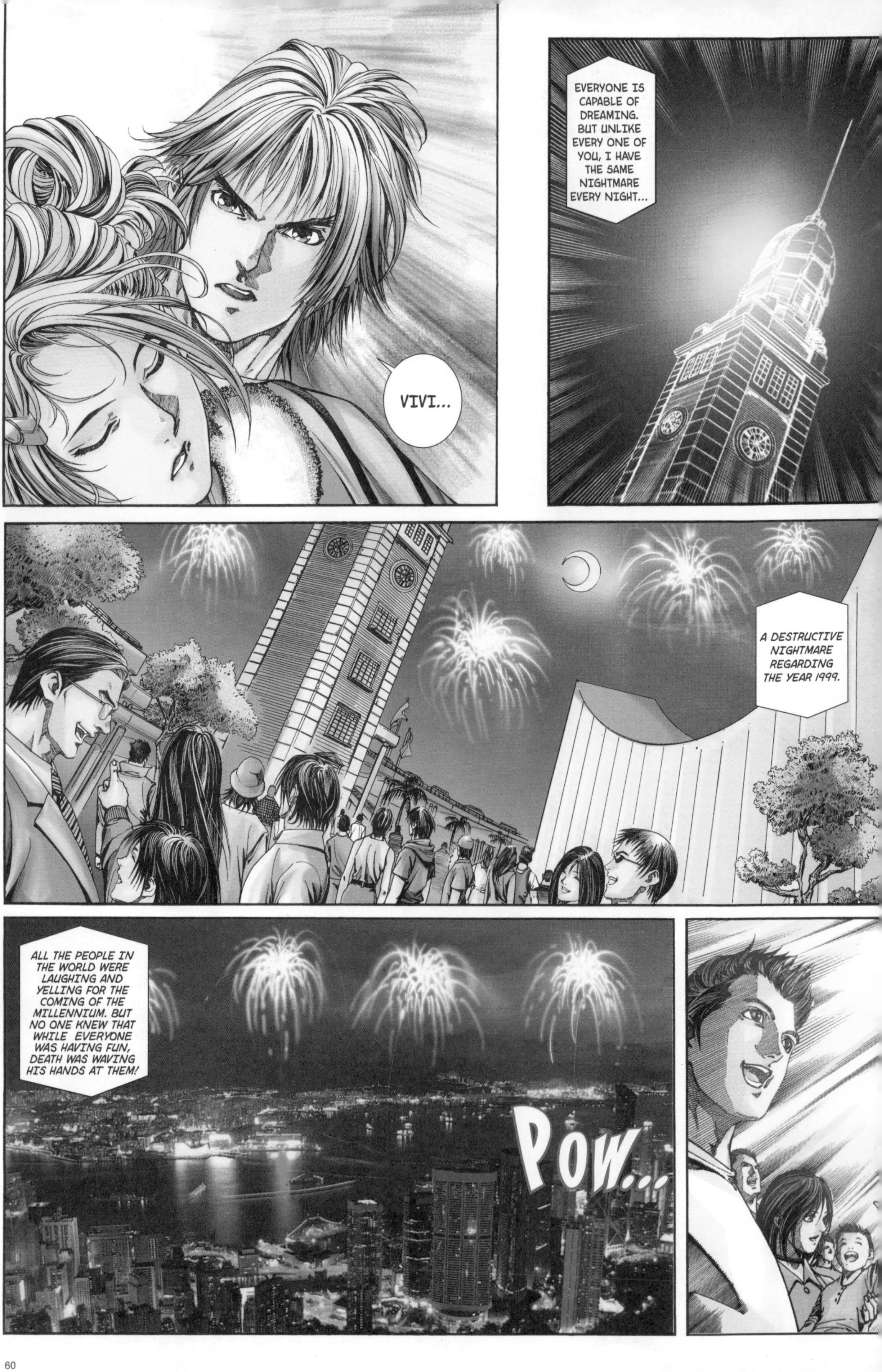

VIVI...
EVERYONE IS CAPABLE OF DREAMING. BUT UNLIKE EVERY ONE OF YOU, I HAVE THE SAME NIGHTMARE EVERY NIGHT...
A DESTRUCTIVE NIGHTMARE REGARDING THE YEAR 1999.
ALL THE PEOPLE IN THE WORLD WERE LAUGHING AND YELLING FOR THE COMING OF THE MILLENNIUM. BUT NO ONE KNEW THAT WHILE EVERYONE WAS HAVING FUN, DEATH WAS WAVING HIS HANDS AT THEM!
POW...

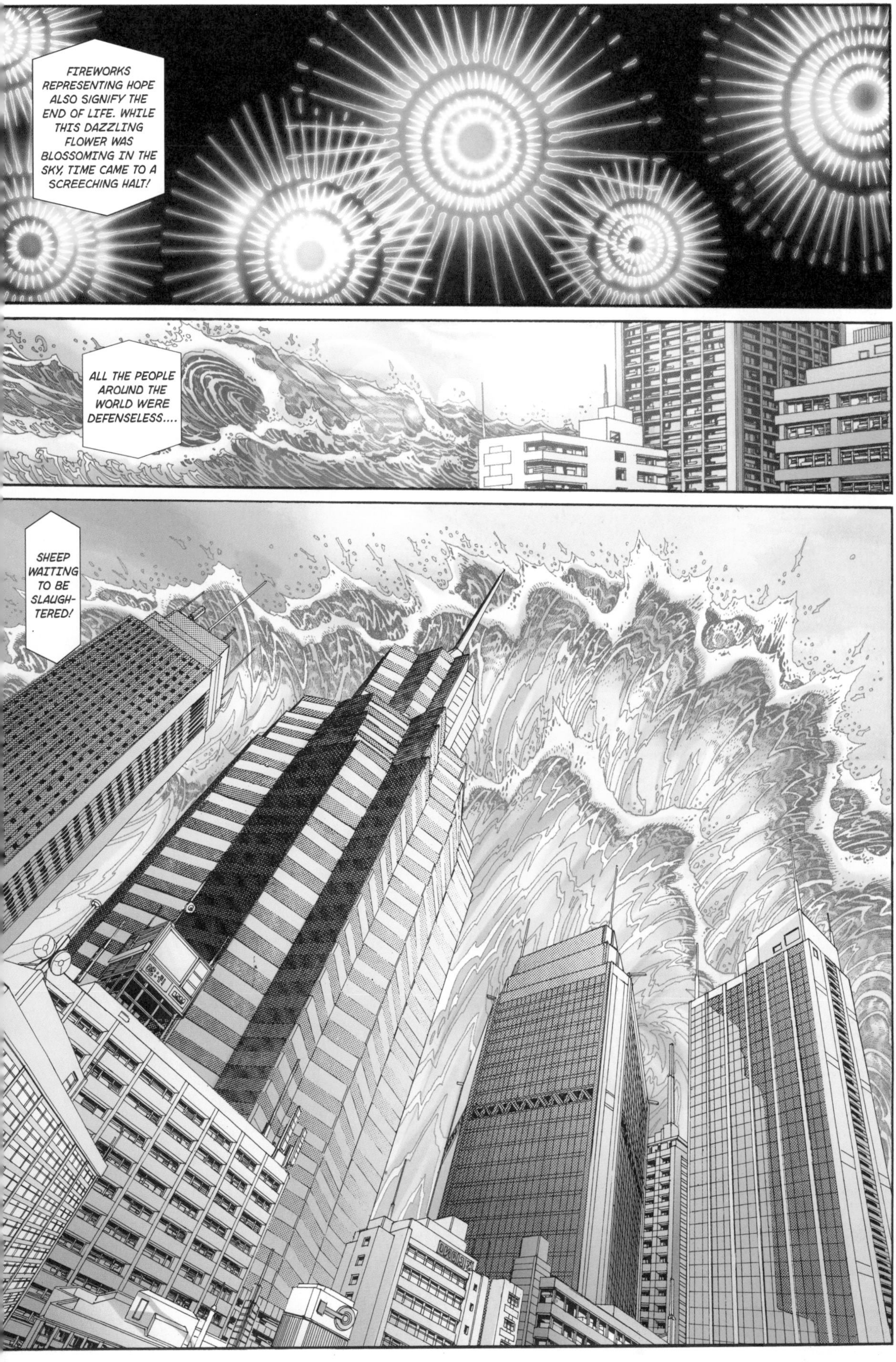
FIREWORKS REPRESENTING HOPE ALSO SIGNIFY THE END OF LIFE. WHILE THIS DAZZLING FLOWER WAS BLOSSOMING IN THE SKY, TIME CAME TO A SCREECHING HALT!
ALL THE PEOPLE AROUND THE WORLD WERE DEFENSELESS....
SHEEP WAITING TO BE SLAUGH-TERED!

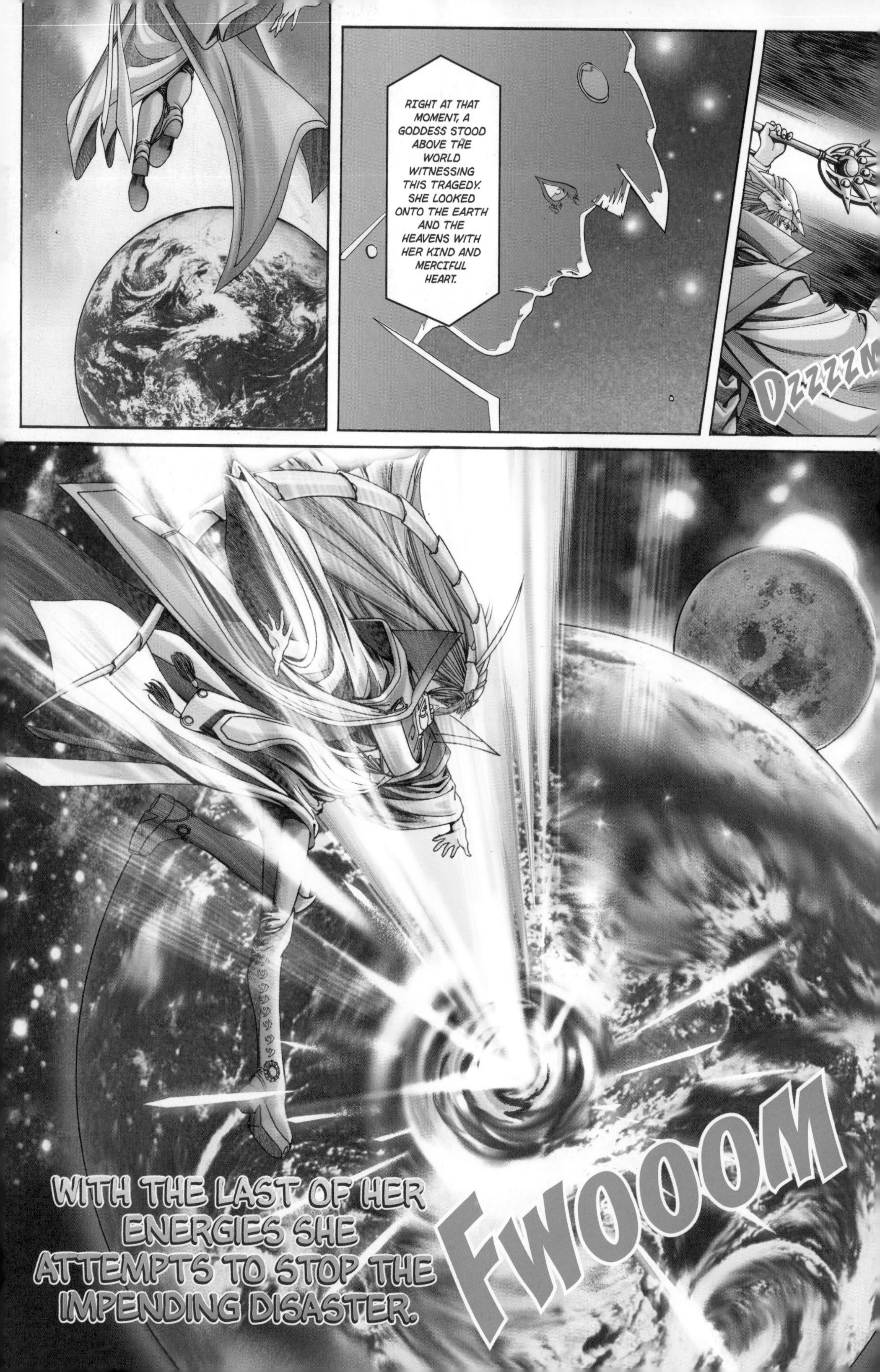
RIGHT AT THAT MOMENT, A GODDESS STOOD ABOVE THE WORLD WITNESSING THIS TRAGEDY. SHE LOOKED ONTO THE EARTH AND THE HEAVENS WITH HER KIND AND MERCIFUL HEART.
DZZZZM
WITH THE LAST OF HER ENERGIES SHE ATTEMPTS TO STOP THE IMPENDING DISASTER.
FWOOOM

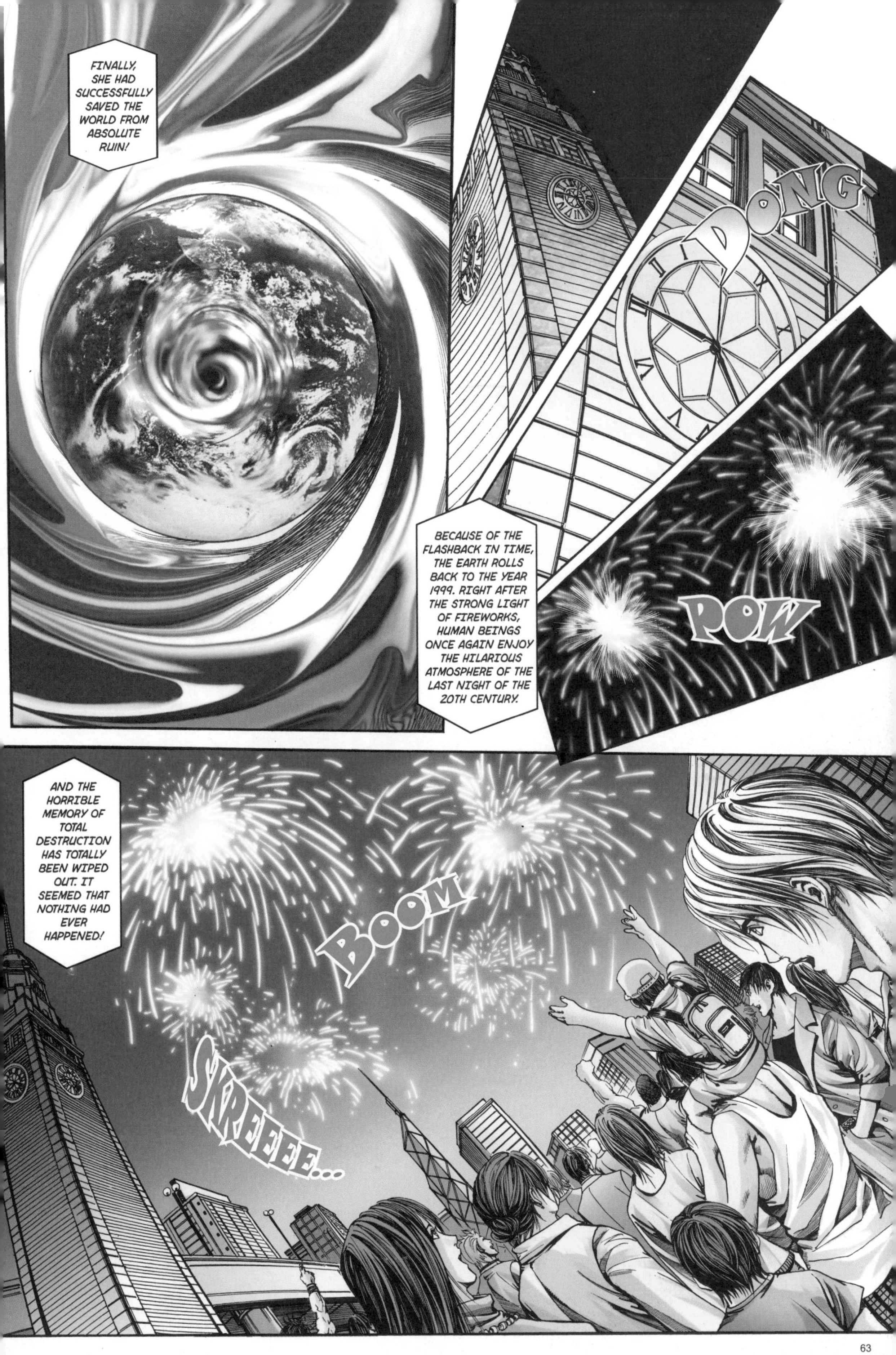
FINALLY, SHE HAD SUCCESSFULLY SAVED THE WORLD FROM ABSOLUTE RUIN!
DONG
BECAUSE OF THE FLASHBACK IN TIME, THE EARTH ROLLS BACK TO THE YEAR 1999. RIGHT AFTER THE STRONG LIGHT OF FIREWORKS, HUMAN BEINGS ONCE AGAIN ENJOY THE HILARIOUS ATMOSPHERE OF THE LAST NIGHT OF THE 20TH CENTURY.
POW
AND THE HORRIBLE MEMORY OF TOTAL DESTRUCTION HAS TOTALLY BEEN WIPED OUT. IT SEEMED THAT NOTHING HAD EVER HAPPENED!
BOOM
SKREEEEE...

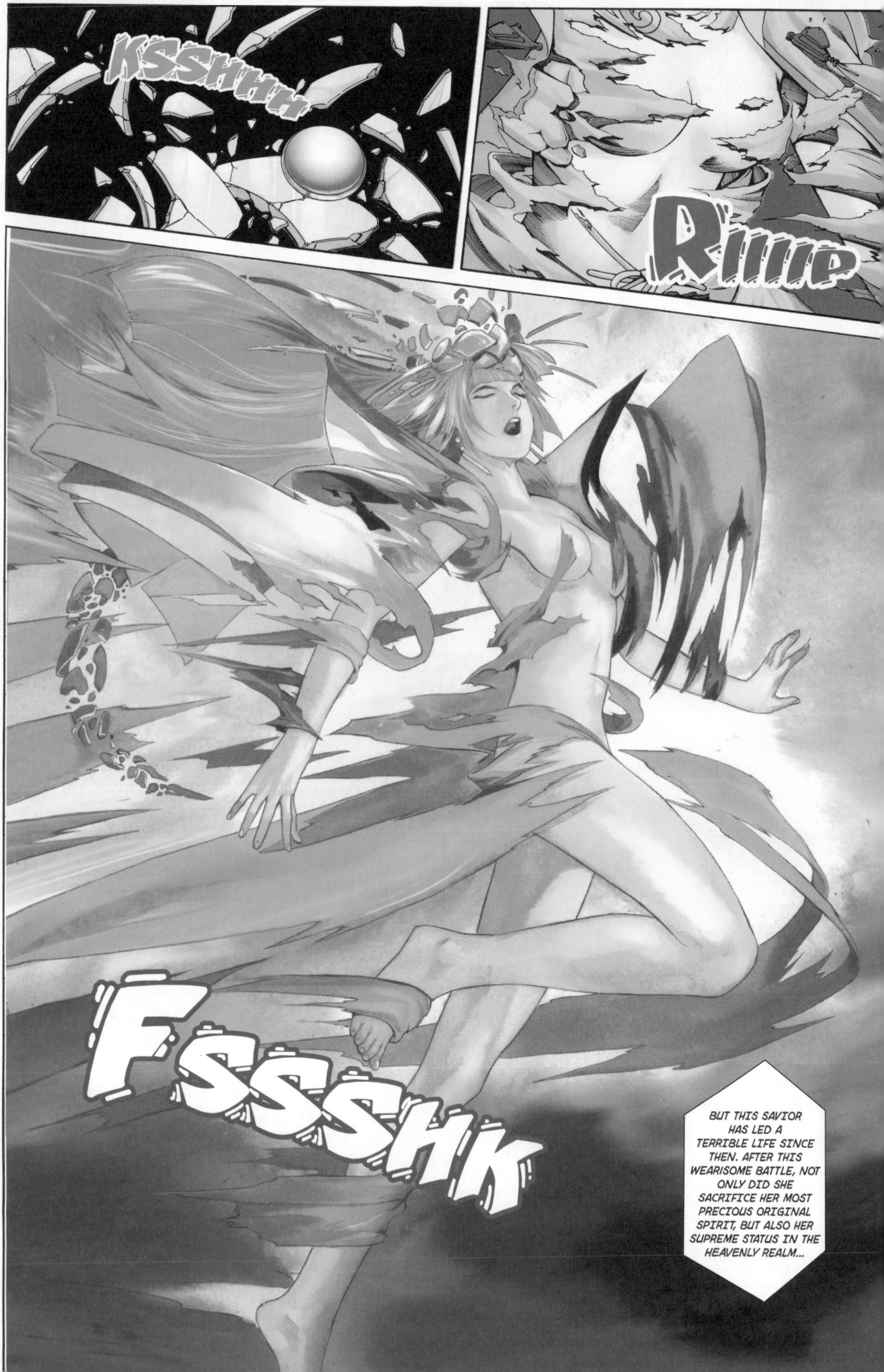
KSSHHH
RIIIIP
FSSSHK
BUT THIS SAVIOR HAS LED A TERRIBLE LIFE SINCE THEN. AFTER THIS WEARISOME BATTLE, NOT ONLY DID SHE SACRIFICE HER MOST PRECIOUS ORIGINAL SPIRIT, BUT ALSO HER SUPREME STATUS IN THE HEAVENLY REALM...

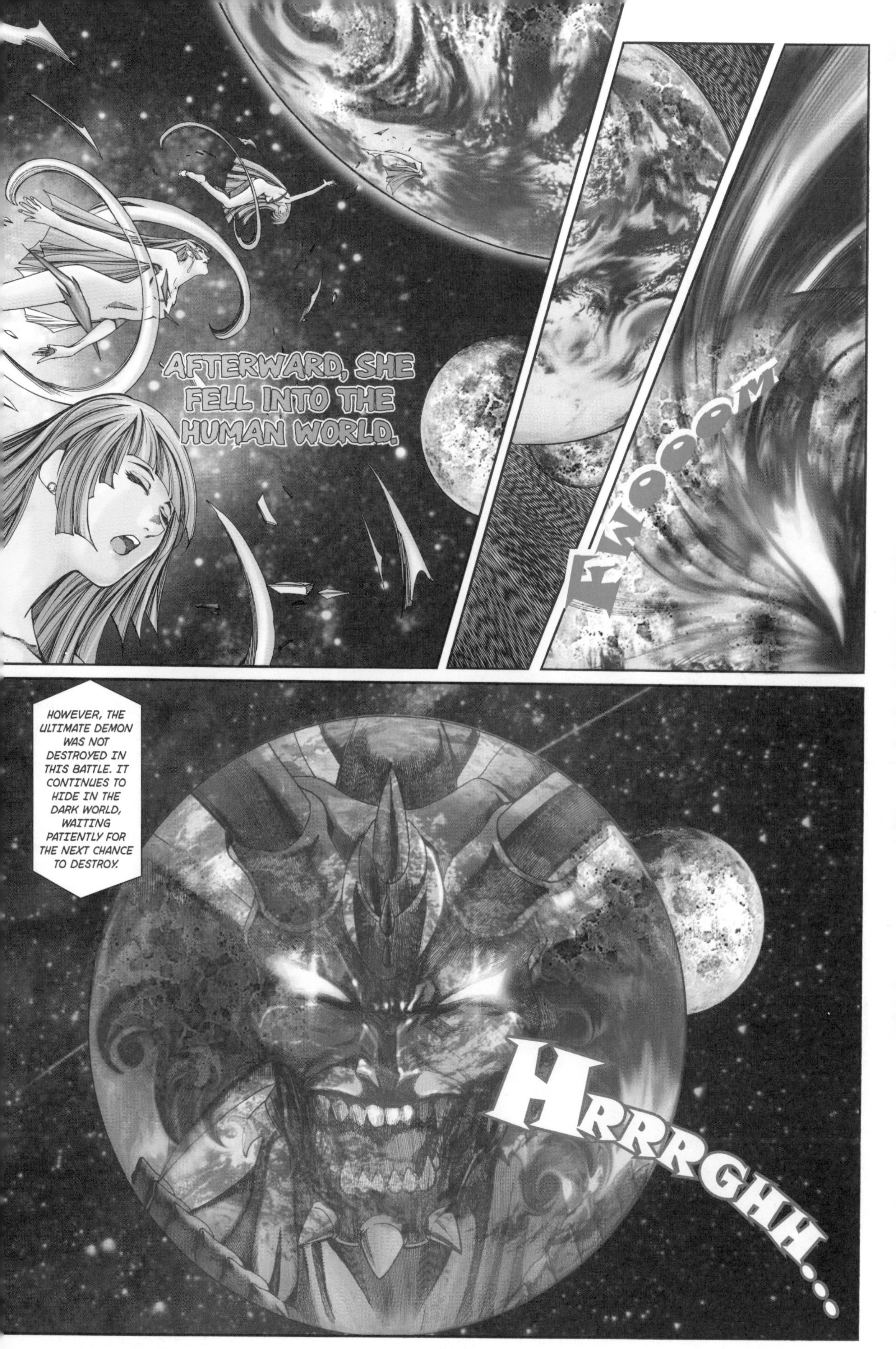
AFTERWARD, SHE FELL INTO THE HUMAN WORLD.
FWOOOOM
HOWEVER, THE ULTIMATE DEMON WAS NOT DESTROYED IN THIS BATTLE. IT CONTINUES TO HIDE IN THE DARK WORLD, WAITING PATIENTLY FOR THE NEXT CHANCE TO DESTROY.
HRRRGHH...

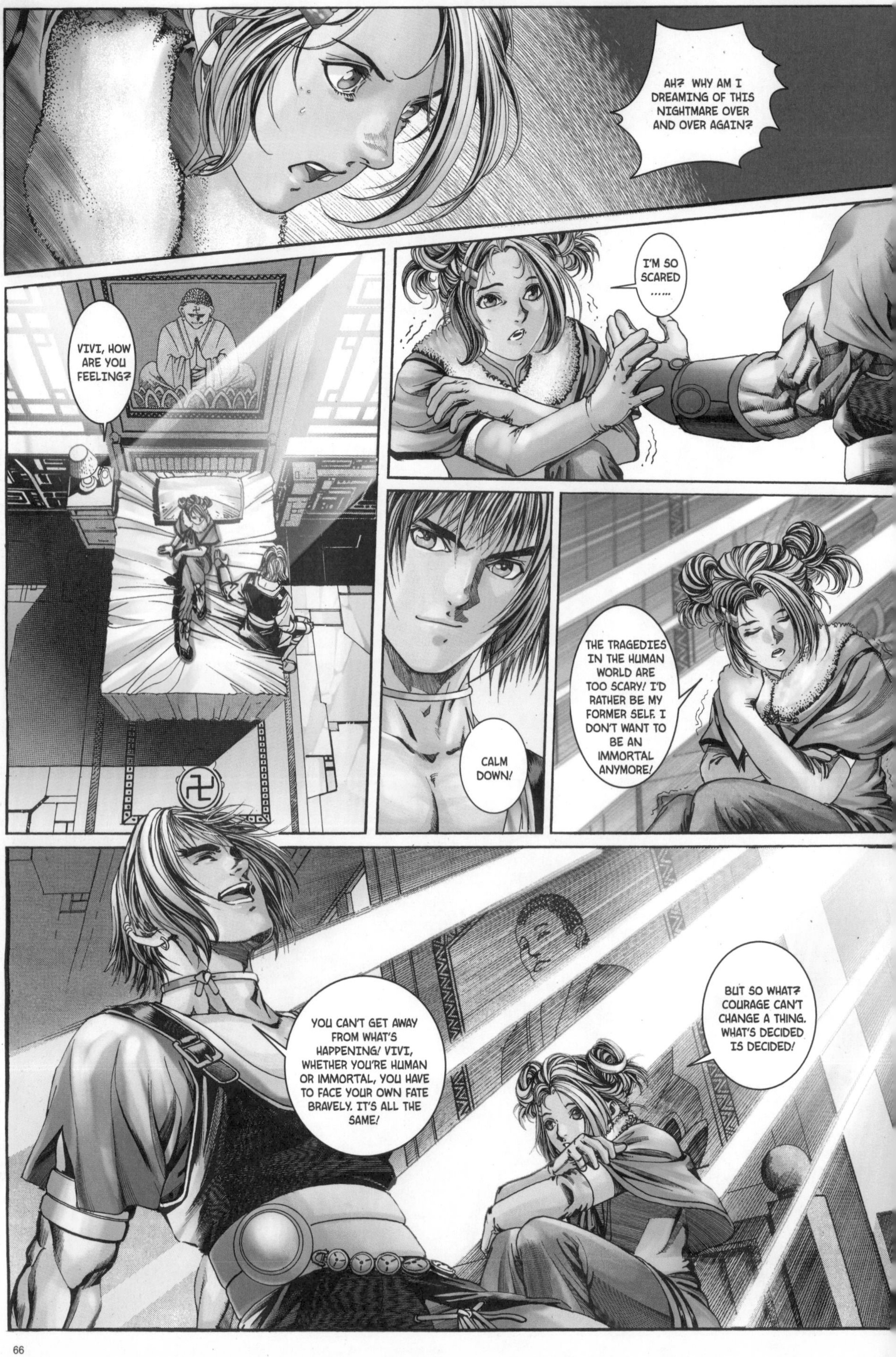
AH? WHY AM I DREAMING OF THIS NIGHTMARE OVER AND OVER AGAIN?
VIVI, HOW ARE YOU FEELING?
I'M SO SCARED ......
CALM DOWN!
THE TRAGEDIES IN THE HUMAN WORLD ARE TOO SCARY! I'D RATHER BE MY FORMER SELF. I DON'T WANT TO BE AN IMMORTAL ANYMORE!
YOU CAN'T GET AWAY FROM WHAT'S HAPPENING! VIVI, WHETHER YOU'RE HUMAN OR IMMORTAL, YOU HAVE TO FACE YOUR OWN FATE BRAVELY. IT'S ALL THE SAME!
BUT SO WHAT? COURAGE CAN'T CHANGE A THING. WHAT'S DECIDED IS DECIDED!

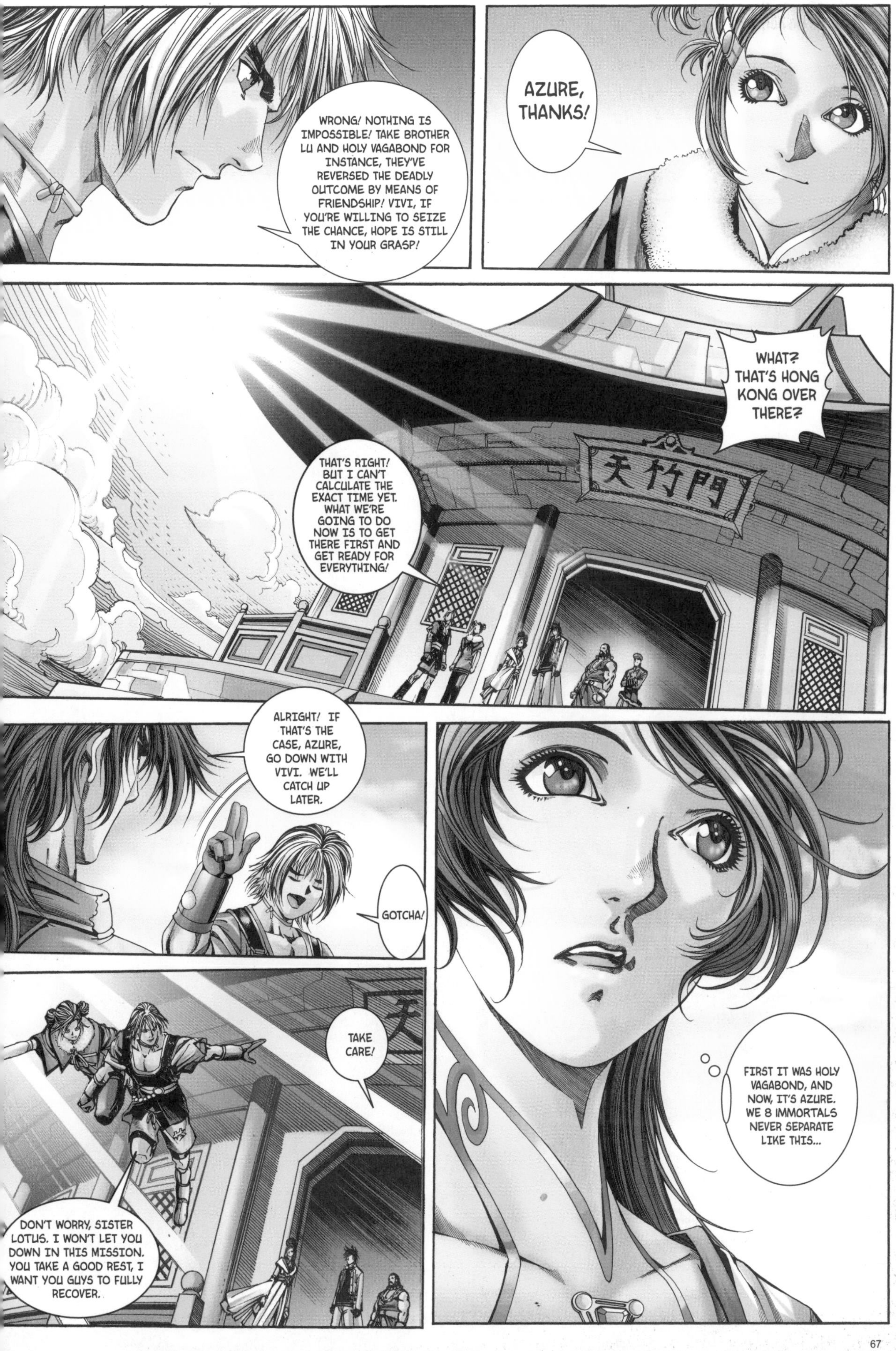
WRONG! NOTHING IS IMPOSSIBLE! TAKE BROTHER LU AND HOLY VAGABOND FOR INSTANCE, THEY'VE REVERSED THE DEADLY OUTCOME BY MEANS OF FRIENDSHIP! VIVI, IF YOU'RE WILLING TO SEIZE THE CHANCE, HOPE IS STILL IN YOUR GRASP!
AZURE, THANKS!
WHAT? THAT'S HONG KONG OVER THERE?
天竹門
THAT'S RIGHT! BUT I CAN'T CALCULATE THE EXACT TIME YET. WHAT WE'RE GOING TO DO NOW IS TO GET THERE FIRST AND GET READY FOR EVERYTHING!
ALRIGHT! IF THAT'S THE CASE, AZURE, GO DOWN WITH VIVI. WE'LL CATCH UP LATER.
GOTCHA!
TAKE CARE!
DON'T WORRY, SISTER LOTUS. I WON'T LET YOU DOWN IN THIS MISSION. YOU TAKE A GOOD REST, I WANT YOU GUYS TO FULLY RECOVER.
FIRST IT WAS HOLY VAGABOND, AND NOW, IT'S AZURE. WE 8 IMMORTALS NEVER SEPARATE LIKE THIS...

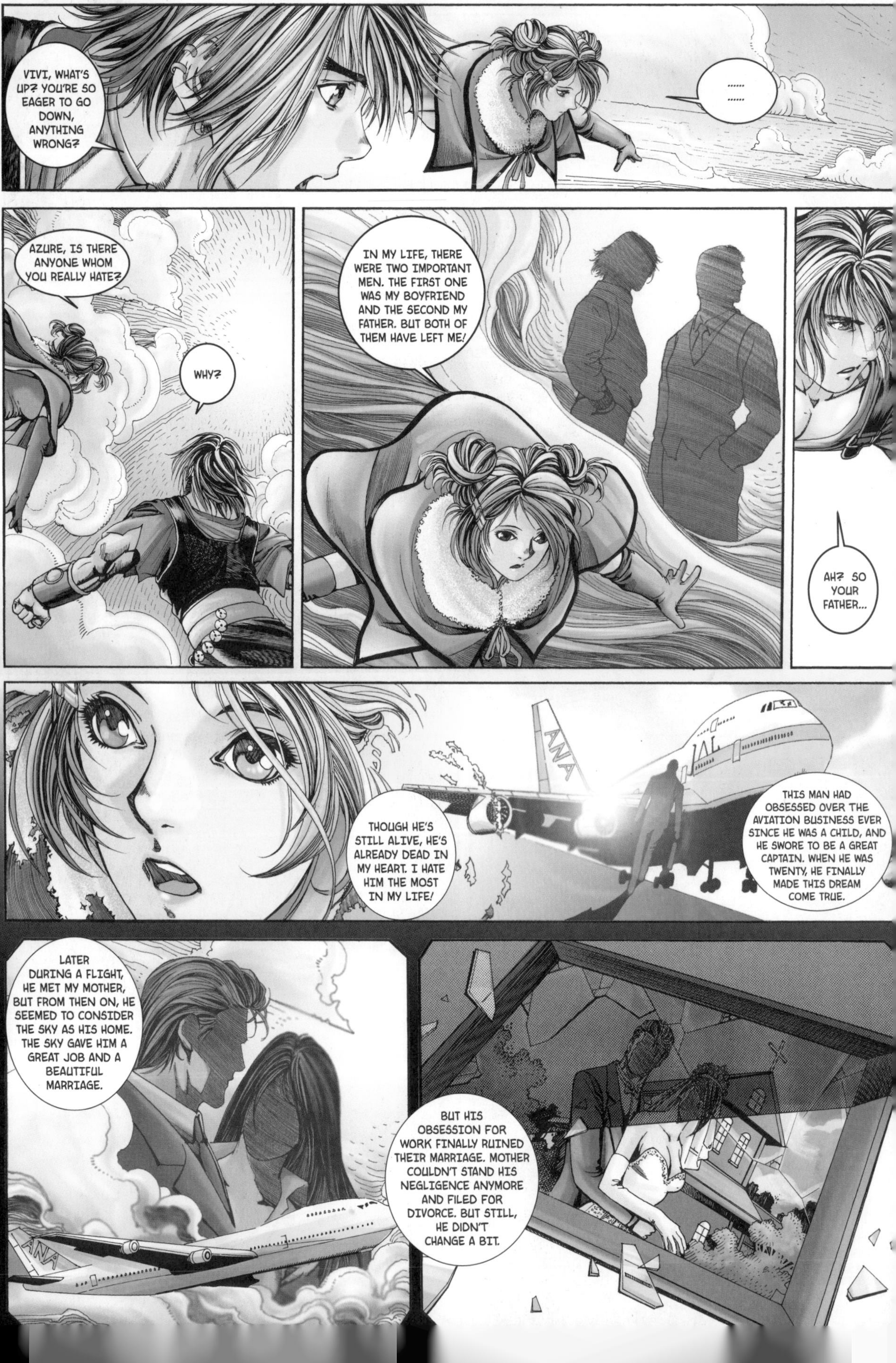
VIVI, WHAT'S UP? YOU'RE SO EAGER TO GO DOWN, ANYTHING WRONG?
......
......
AZURE, IS THERE ANYONE WHOM YOU REALLY HATE?
WHY?
IN MY LIFE, THERE WERE TWO IMPORTANT MEN. THE FIRST ONE WAS MY BOYFRIEND AND THE SECOND MY FATHER. BUT BOTH OF THEM HAVE LEFT ME!
AH? SO YOUR FATHER...
THOUGH HE'S STILL ALIVE, HE'S ALREADY DEAD IN MY HEART. I HATE HIM THE MOST IN MY LIFE!
ANA
THIS MAN HAD OBSESSED OVER THE AVIATION BUSINESS EVER SINCE HE WAS A CHILD, AND HE SWORE TO BE A GREAT CAPTAIN. WHEN HE WAS TWENTY, HE FINALLY MADE THIS DREAM COME TRUE.
LATER DURING A FLIGHT, HE MET MY MOTHER, BUT FROM THEN ON, HE SEEMED TO CONSIDER THE SKY AS HIS HOME. THE SKY GAVE HIM A GREAT JOB AND A BEAUTIFUL MARRIAGE.
ANA
BUT HIS OBSESSION FOR WORK FINALLY RUINED THEIR MARRIAGE. MOTHER COULDN'T STAND HIS NEGLIGENCE ANYMORE AND FILED FOR DIVORCE. BUT STILL, HE DIDN'T CHANGE A BIT.

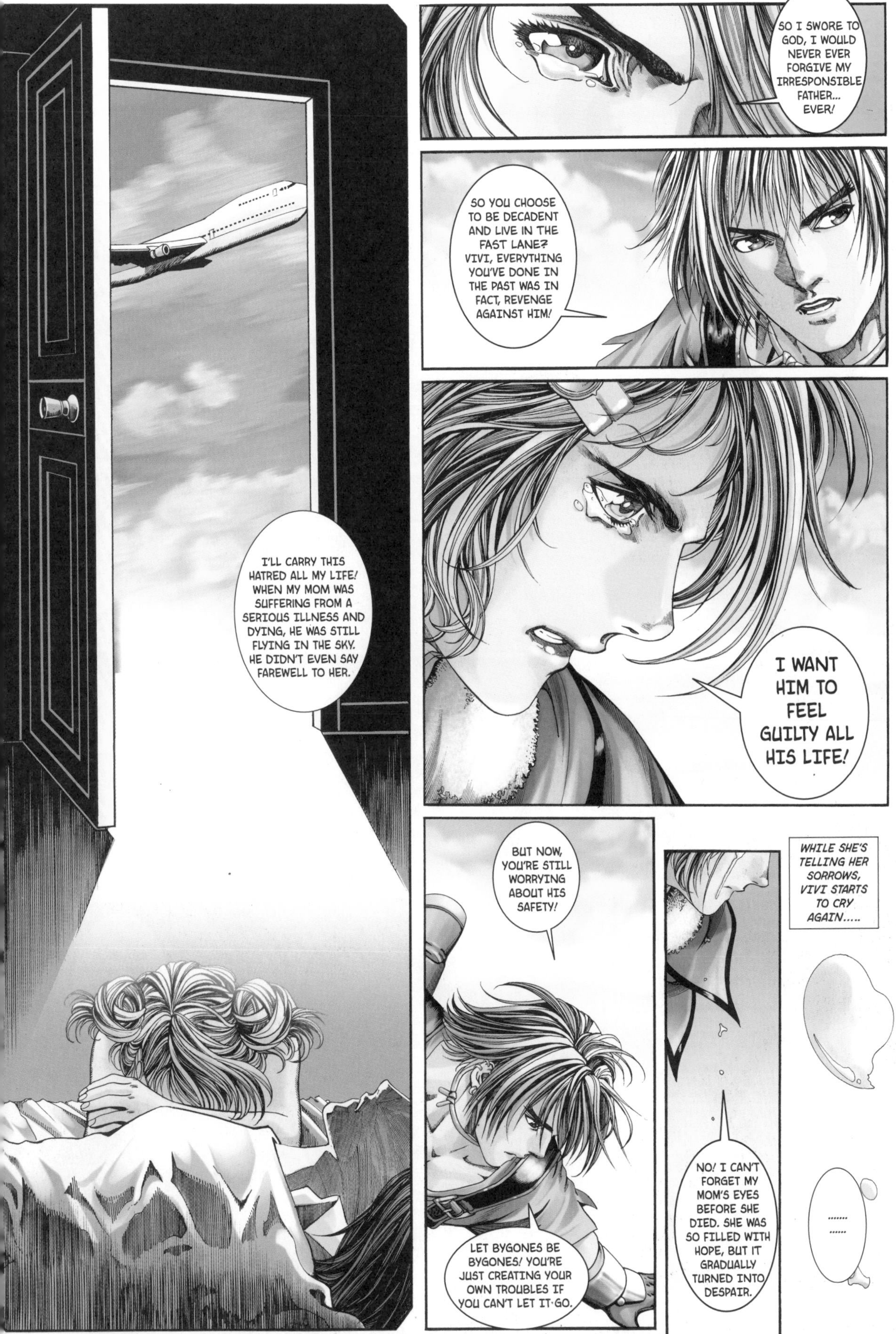
I'LL CARRY THIS HATRED ALL MY LIFE! WHEN MY MOM WAS SUFFERING FROM A SERIOUS ILLNESS AND DYING, HE WAS STILL FLYING IN THE SKY. HE DIDN'T EVEN SAY FAREWELL TO HER.
SO I SWORE TO GOD, I WOULD NEVER EVER FORGIVE MY IRRESPONSIBLE FATHER... EVER!
SO YOU CHOOSE TO BE DECADENT AND LIVE IN THE FAST LANE? VIVI, EVERYTHING YOU'VE DONE IN THE PAST WAS IN FACT, REVENGE AGAINST HIM!
I WANT HIM TO FEEL GUILTY ALL HIS LIFE!
BUT NOW, YOU'RE STILL WORRYING ABOUT HIS SAFETY!
LET BYGONES BE BYGONES! YOU'RE JUST CREATING YOUR OWN TROUBLES IF YOU CAN'T LET IT GO.
NO! I CAN'T FORGET MY MOM'S EYES BEFORE SHE DIED. SHE WAS SO FILLED WITH HOPE, BUT IT GRADUALLY TURNED INTO DESPAIR.
WHILE SHE'S TELLING HER SORROWS, VIVI STARTS TO CRY AGAIN.....
......
......

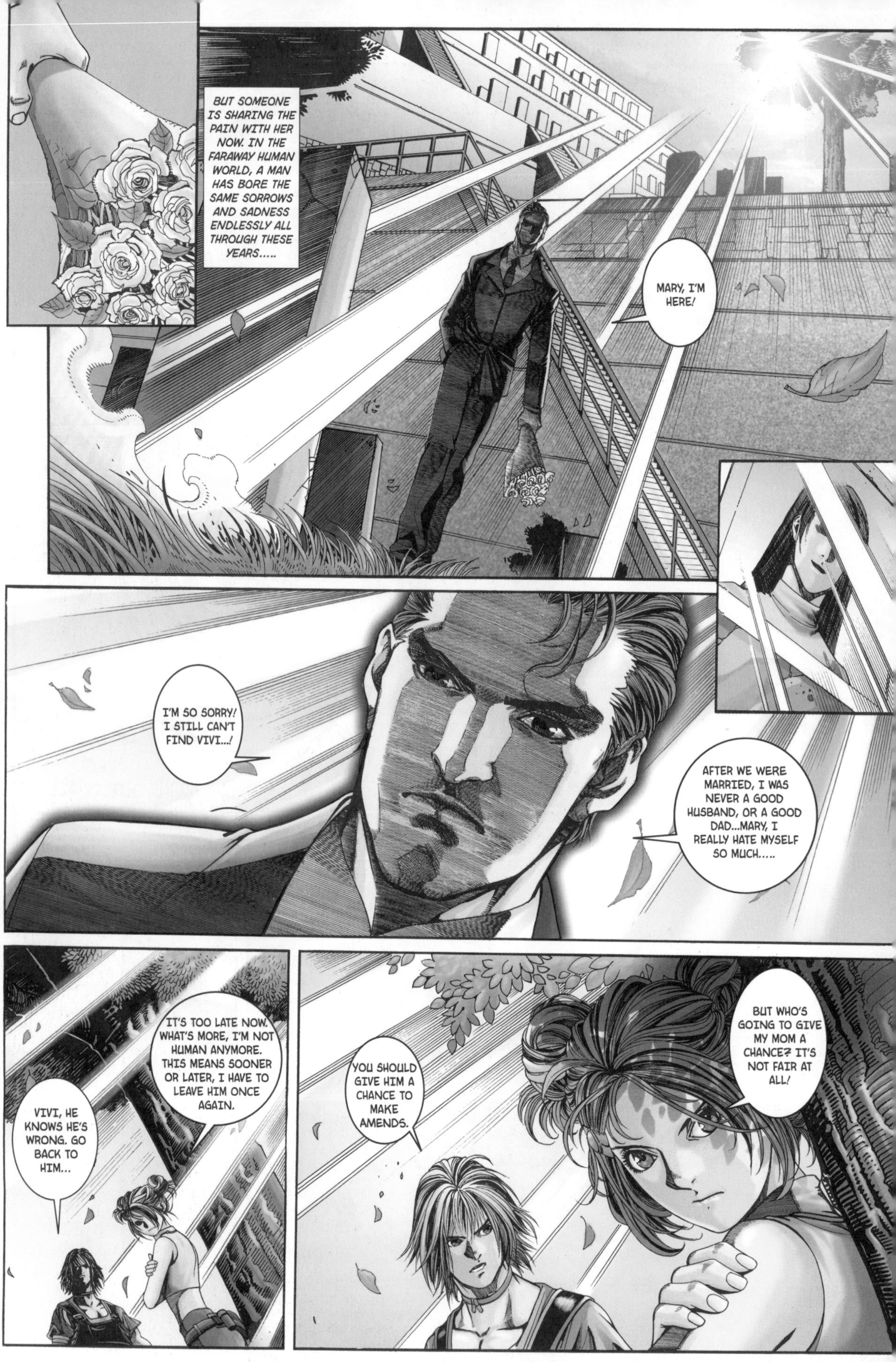
BUT SOMEONE IS SHARING THE PAIN WITH HER NOW. IN THE FARAWAY HUMAN WORLD, A MAN HAS BORE THE SAME SORROWS AND SADNESS ENDLESSLY ALL THROUGH THESE YEARS.....
MARY, I'M HERE!
I'M SO SORRY! I STILL CAN'T FIND VIVI...!
AFTER WE WERE MARRIED, I WAS NEVER A GOOD HUSBAND, OR A GOOD DAD...MARY, I REALLY HATE MYSELF SO MUCH.....
VIVI, HE KNOWS HE'S WRONG. GO BACK TO HIM...
IT'S TOO LATE NOW. WHAT'S MORE, I'M NOT HUMAN ANYMORE. THIS MEANS SOONER OR LATER, I HAVE TO LEAVE HIM ONCE AGAIN.
YOU SHOULD GIVE HIM A CHANCE TO MAKE AMENDS.
BUT WHO'S GOING TO GIVE MY MOM A CHANCE? IT'S NOT FAIR AT ALL!

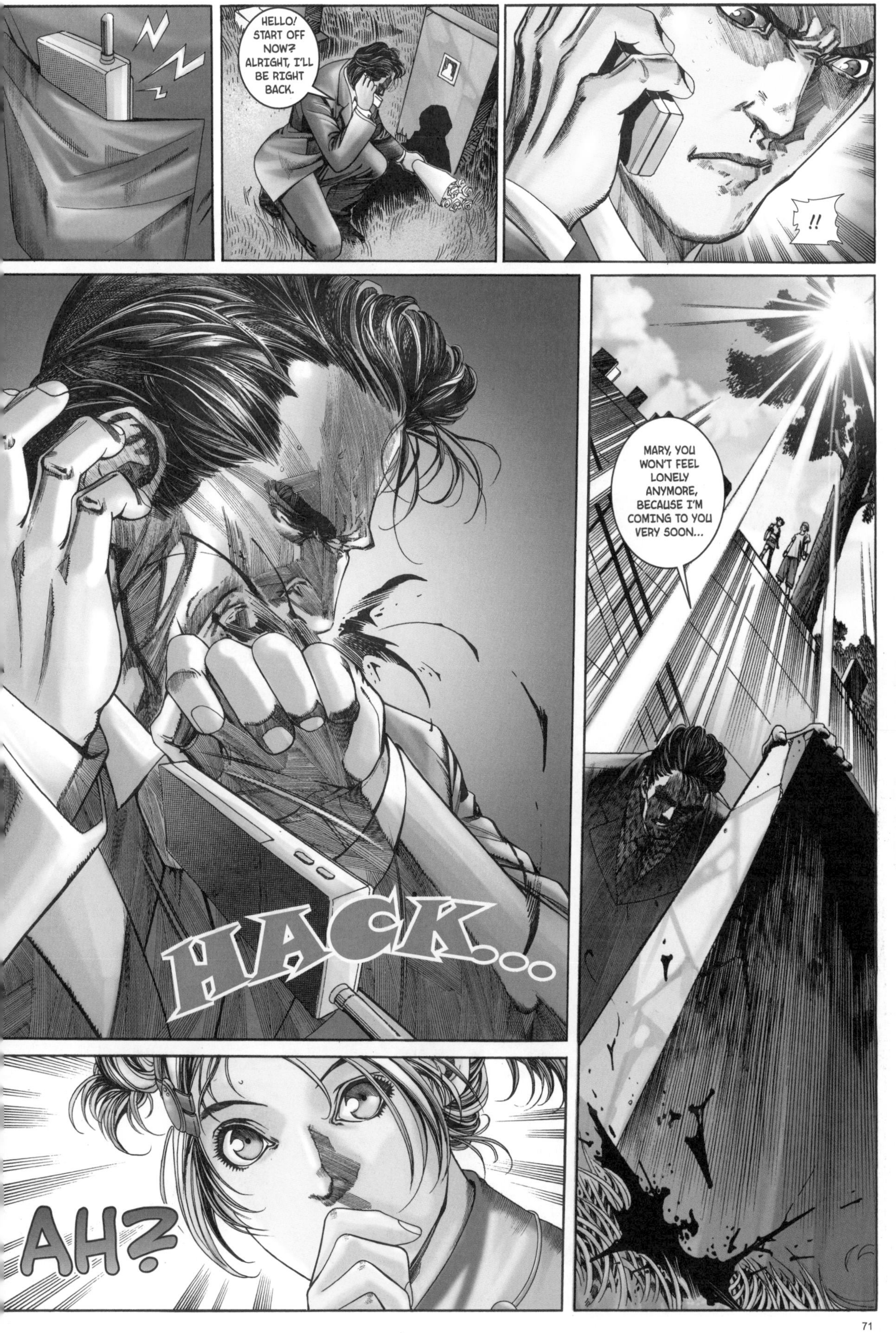
HELLO! START OFF NOW? ALRIGHT, I'LL BE RIGHT BACK.
!!
HACK...
MARY, YOU WON'T FEEL LONELY ANYMORE, BECAUSE I'M COMING TO YOU VERY SOON...
AH?

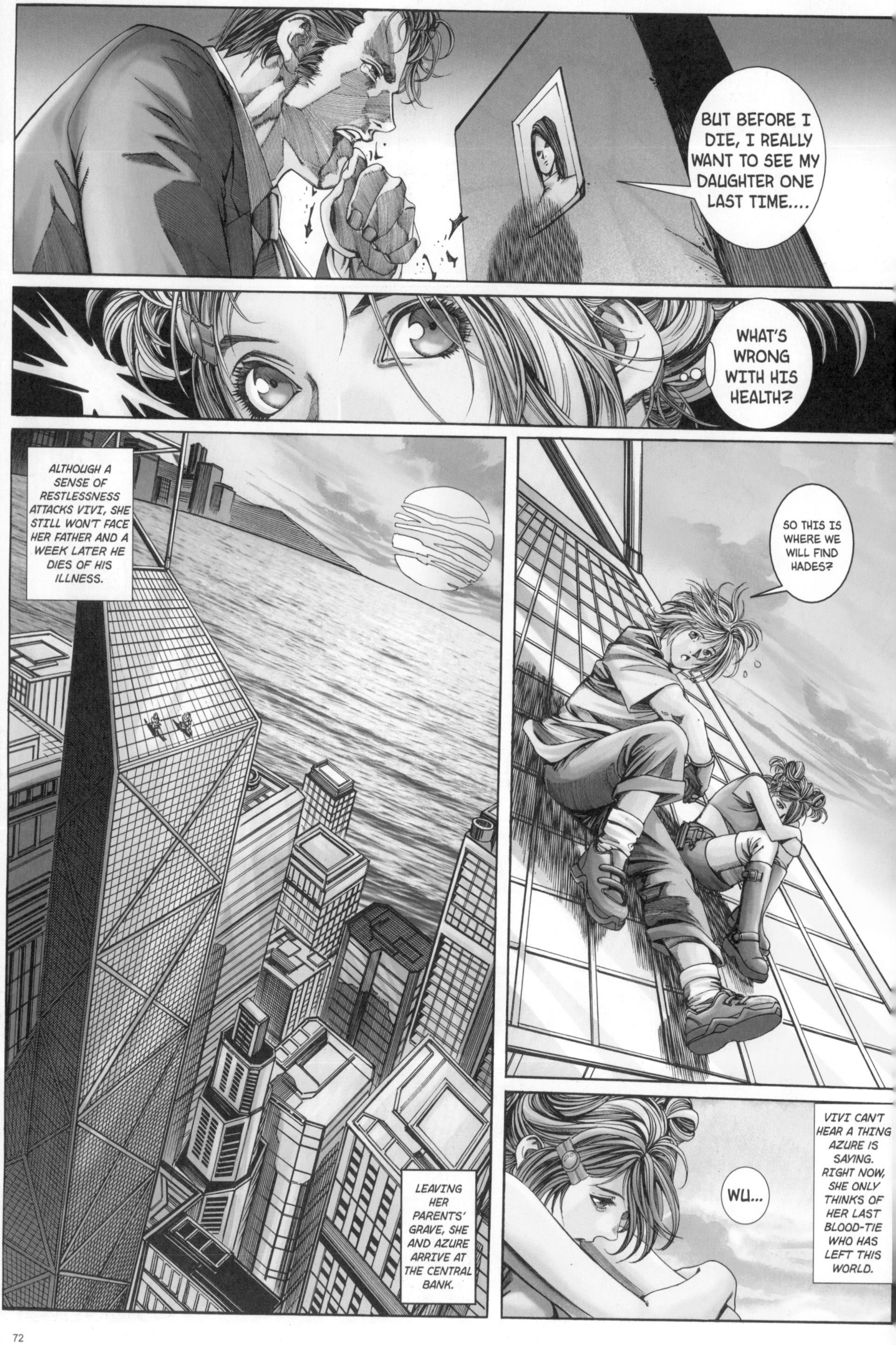
BUT BEFORE I DIE, I REALLY WANT TO SEE MY DAUGHTER ONE LAST TIME....
WHAT'S WRONG WITH HIS HEALTH?
ALTHOUGH A SENSE OF RESTLESSNESS ATTACKS VIVI, SHE STILL WON'T FACE HER FATHER AND A WEEK LATER HE DIES OF HIS ILLNESS.
LEAVING HER PARENTS' GRAVE, SHE AND AZURE ARRIVE AT THE CENTRAL BANK.
SO THIS IS WHERE WE WILL FIND HADES?
WU...
VIVI CAN'T HEAR A THING AZURE IS SAYING. RIGHT NOW, SHE ONLY THINKS OF HER LAST BLOOD-TIE WHO HAS LEFT THIS WORLD.

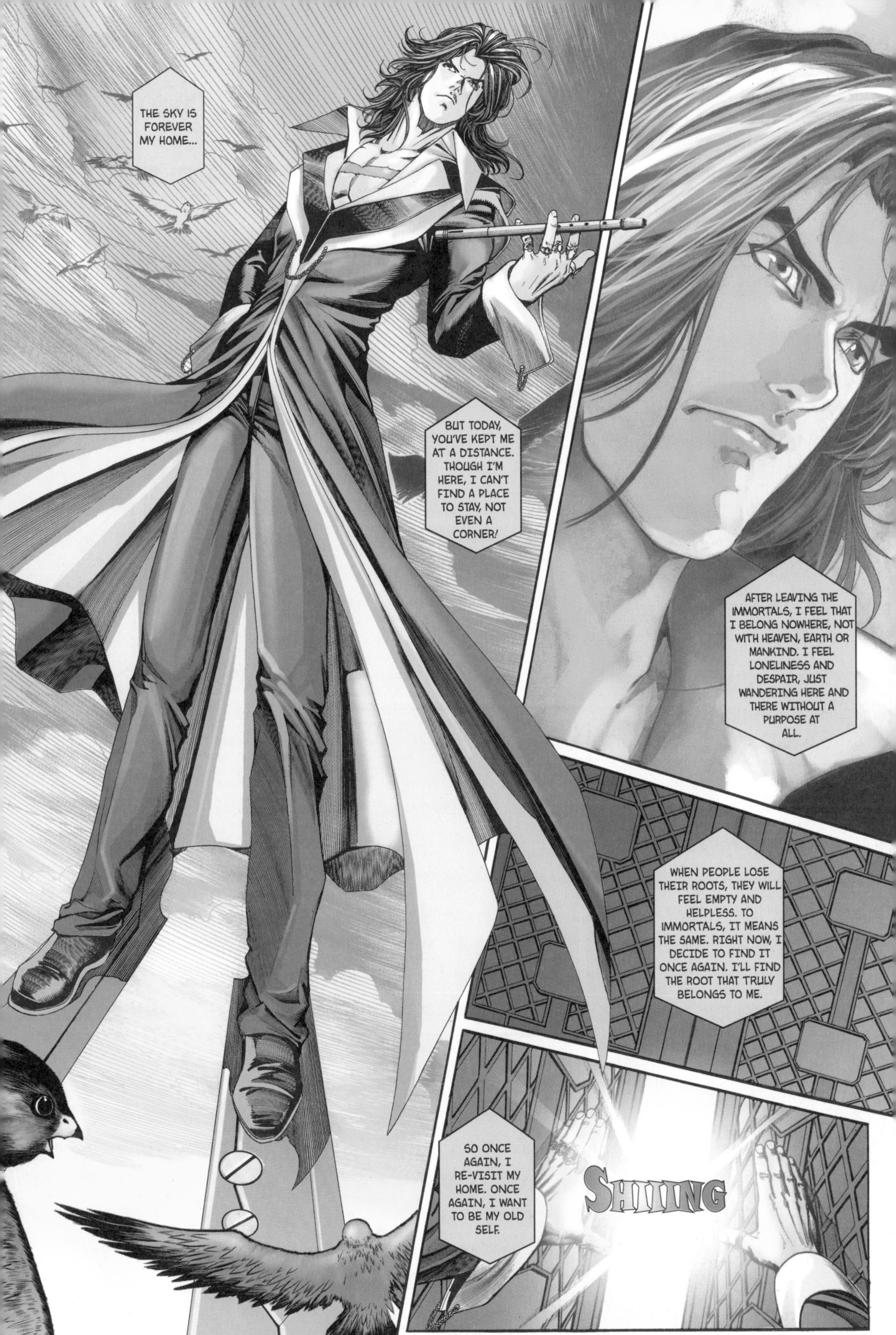
THE SKY IS FOREVER MY HOME...
BUT TODAY, YOU'VE KEPT ME AT A DISTANCE. THOUGH I'M HERE, I CAN'T FIND A PLACE TO STAY, NOT EVEN A CORNER!
AFTER LEAVING THE IMMORTALS, I FEEL THAT I BELONG NOWHERE, NOT WITH HEAVEN, EARTH OR MANKIND. I FEEL LONELINESS AND DESPAIR, JUST WANDERING HERE AND THERE WITHOUT A PURPOSE AT ALL.
WHEN PEOPLE LOSE THEIR ROOTS, THEY WILL FEEL EMPTY AND HELPLESS. TO IMMORTALS, IT MEANS THE SAME. RIGHT NOW, I DECIDE TO FIND IT ONCE AGAIN. I'LL FIND THE ROOT THAT TRULY BELONGS TO ME.
SO ONCE AGAIN, I RE-VISIT MY HOME. ONCE AGAIN, I WANT TO BE MY OLD SELF.
SHIIING

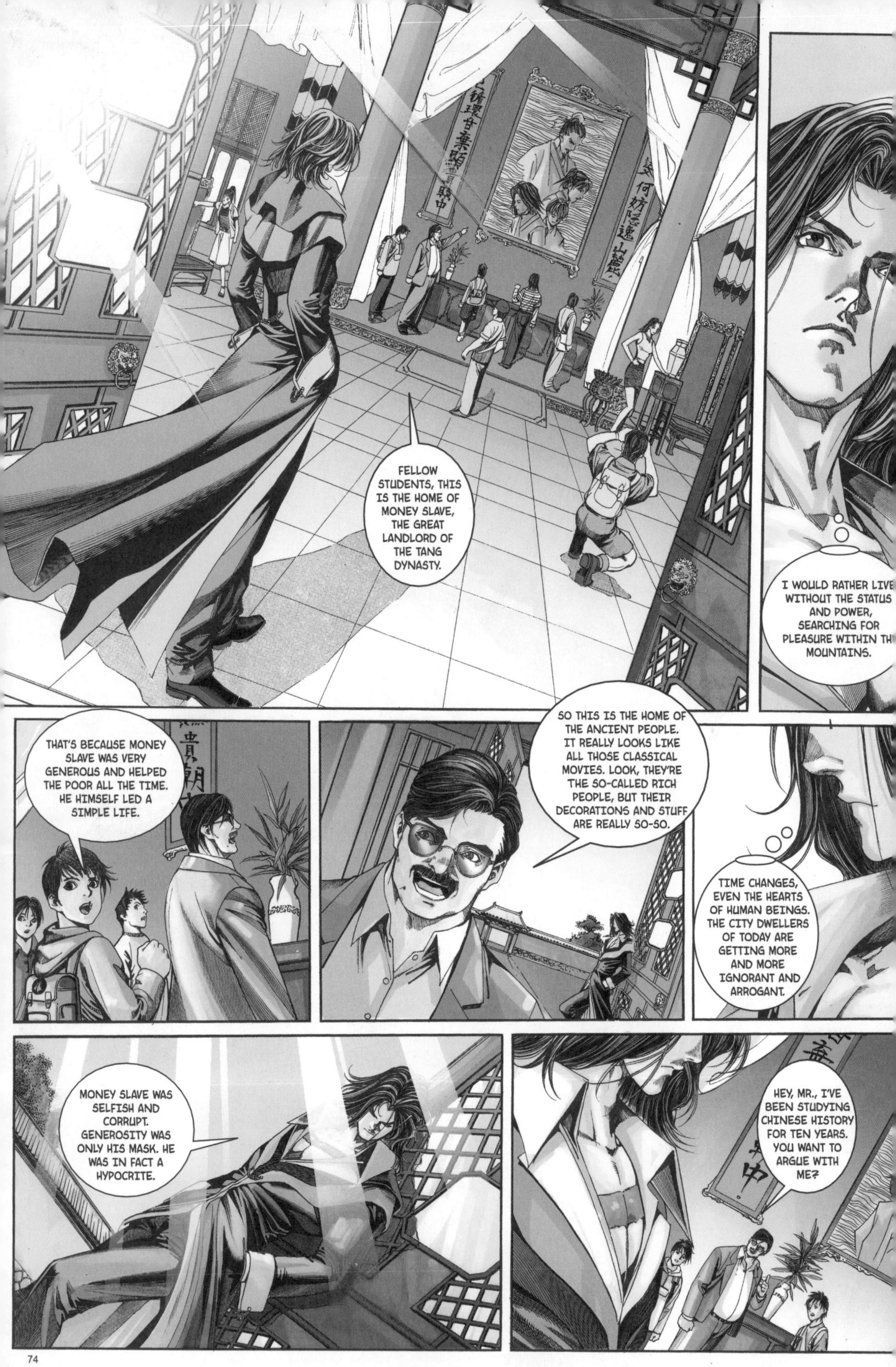
FELLOW STUDENTS, THIS IS THE HOME OF MONEY SLAVE, THE GREAT LANDLORD OF THE TANG DYNASTY.
I WOULD RATHER LIVE WITHOUT THE STATUS AND POWER, SEARCHING FOR PLEASURE WITHIN THE MOUNTAINS.
THAT'S BECAUSE MONEY SLAVE WAS VERY GENEROUS AND HELPED THE POOR ALL THE TIME. HE HIMSELF LED A SIMPLE LIFE.
SO THIS IS THE HOME OF THE ANCIENT PEOPLE. IT REALLY LOOKS LIKE ALL THOSE CLASSICAL MOVIES. LOOK, THEY'RE THE SO-CALLED RICH PEOPLE, BUT THEIR DECORATIONS AND STUFF ARE REALLY SO-SO.
TIME CHANGES, EVEN THE HEARTS OF HUMAN BEINGS. THE CITY DWELLERS OF TODAY ARE GETTING MORE AND MORE IGNORANT AND ARROGANT.
MONEY SLAVE WAS SELFISH AND CORRUPT. GENEROSITY WAS ONLY HIS MASK. HE WAS IN FACT A HYPOCRITE.
HEY, MR., I'VE BEEN STUDYING CHINESE HISTORY FOR TEN YEARS. YOU WANT TO ARGUE WITH ME?

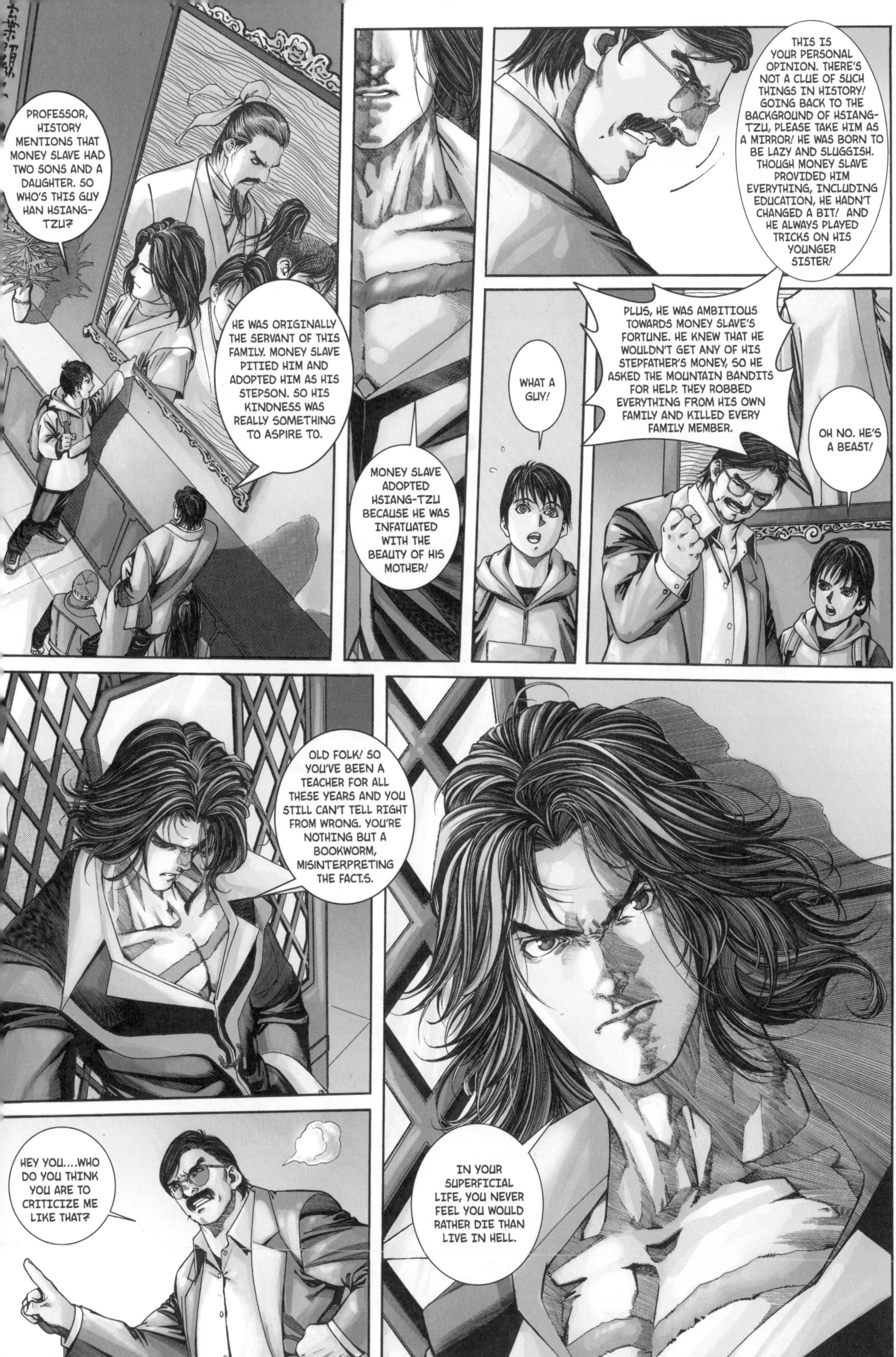
PROFESSOR, HISTORY MENTIONS THAT MONEY SLAVE HAD TWO SONS AND A DAUGHTER. SO WHO'S THIS GUY HAN HSIANG-TZU?
HE WAS ORIGINALLY THE SERVANT OF THIS FAMILY. MONEY SLAVE PITIED HIM AND ADOPTED HIM AS HIS STEPSON. SO HIS KINDNESS WAS REALLY SOMETHING TO ASPIRE TO.
MONEY SLAVE ADOPTED HSIANG-TZU BECAUSE HE WAS INFATUATED WITH THE BEAUTY OF HIS MOTHER!
THIS IS YOUR PERSONAL OPINION. THERE'S NOT A CLUE OF SUCH THINGS IN HISTORY! GOING BACK TO THE BACKGROUND OF HSIANG-TZU, PLEASE TAKE HIM AS A MIRROR! HE WAS BORN TO BE LAZY AND SLUGGISH. THOUGH MONEY SLAVE PROVIDED HIM EVERYTHING, INCLUDING EDUCATION, HE HADN'T CHANGED A BIT! AND HE ALWAYS PLAYED TRICKS ON HIS YOUNGER SISTER!
WHAT A GUY!
PLUS, HE WAS AMBITIOUS TOWARDS MONEY SLAVE'S FORTUNE. HE KNEW THAT HE WOULDN'T GET ANY OF HIS STEPFATHER'S MONEY, SO HE ASKED THE MOUNTAIN BANDITS FOR HELP. THEY ROBBED EVERYTHING FROM HIS OWN FAMILY AND KILLED EVERY FAMILY MEMBER.
OH NO. HE'S A BEAST!
OLD FOLK! SO YOU'VE BEEN A TEACHER FOR ALL THESE YEARS AND YOU STILL CAN'T TELL RIGHT FROM WRONG. YOU'RE NOTHING BUT A BOOKWORM, MISINTERPRETING THE FACT.S.
HEY YOU....WHO DO YOU THINK YOU ARE TO CRITICIZE ME LIKE THAT?
IN YOUR SUPERFICIAL LIFE, YOU NEVER FEEL YOU WOULD RATHER DIE THAN LIVE IN HELL.

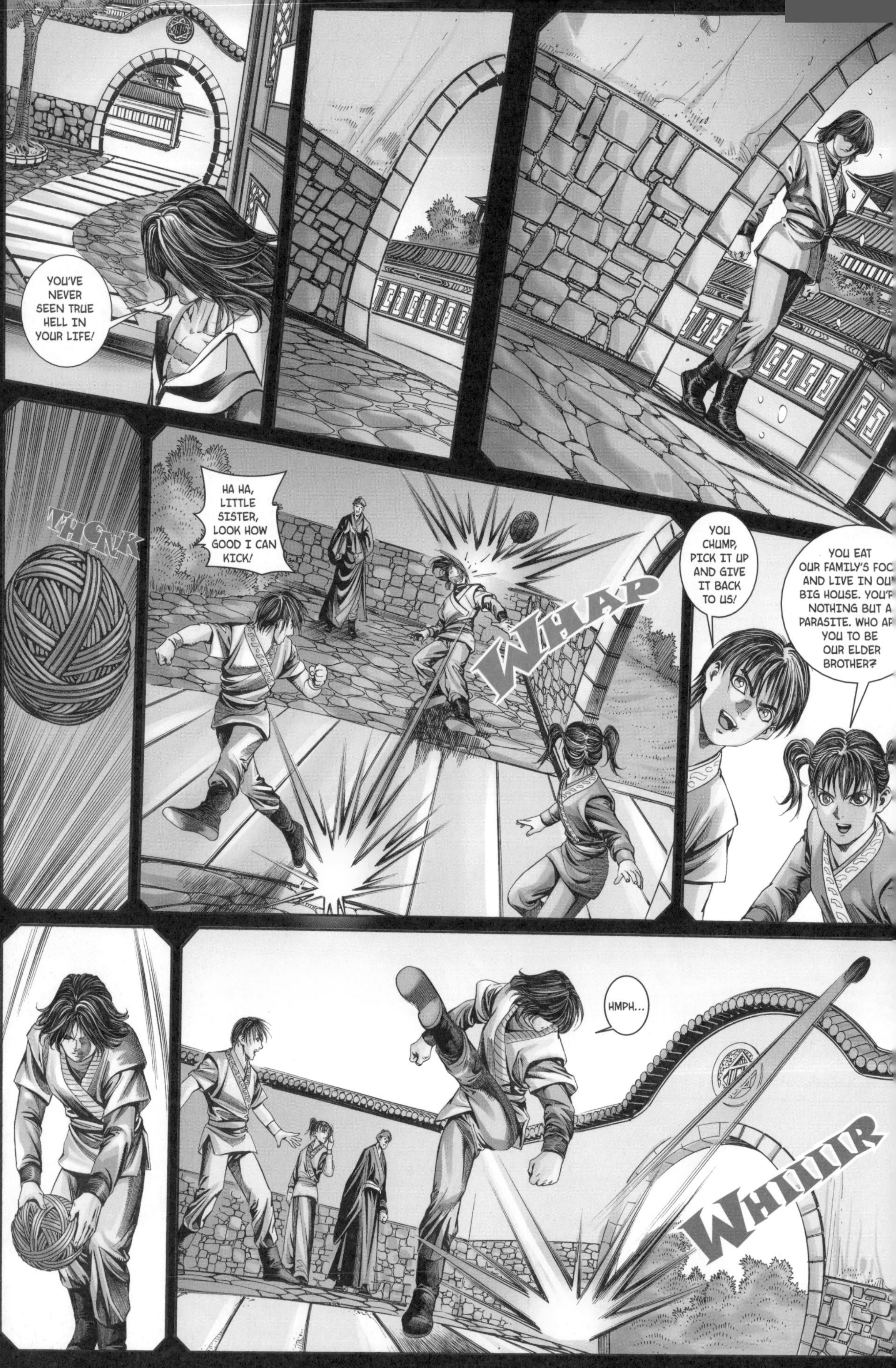
YOU'VE NEVER SEEN TRUE HELL IN YOUR LIFE!
THONK
HA HA, LITTLE SISTER, LOOK HOW GOOD I CAN KICK!
WHAP
YOU CHUMP, PICK IT UP AND GIVE IT BACK TO US!
HMPH...
WHIIIR

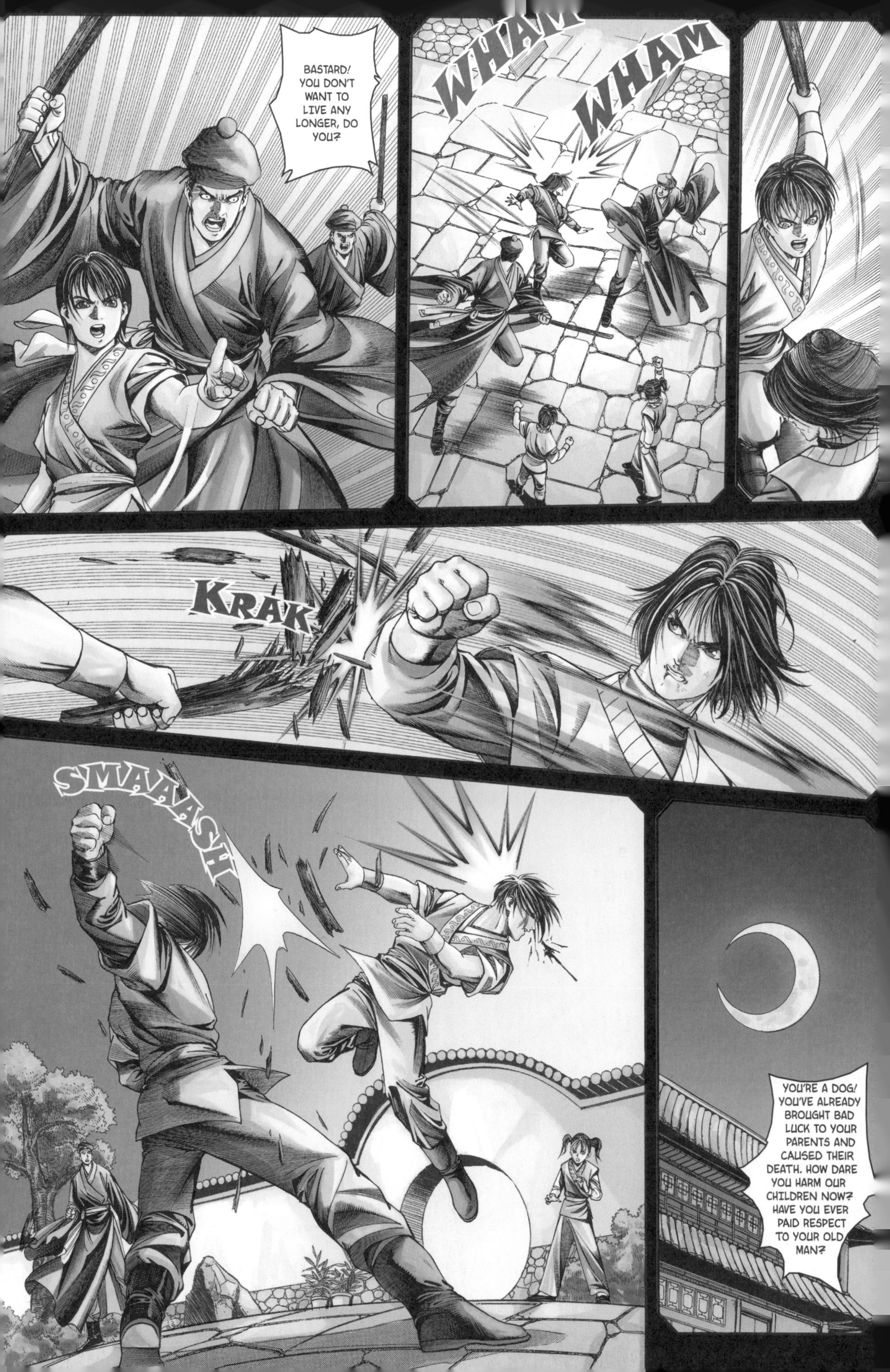
BASTARD! YOU DON'T WANT TO LIVE ANY LONGER, DO YOU?
WHAM
WHAM
KRAK
SMAAASH
YOU'RE A DOG! YOU'VE ALREADY BROUGHT BAD LUCK TO YOUR PARENTS AND CAUSED THEIR DEATH. HOW DARE YOU HARM OUR CHILDREN NOW? HAVE YOU EVER PAID RESPECT TO YOUR OLD MAN?

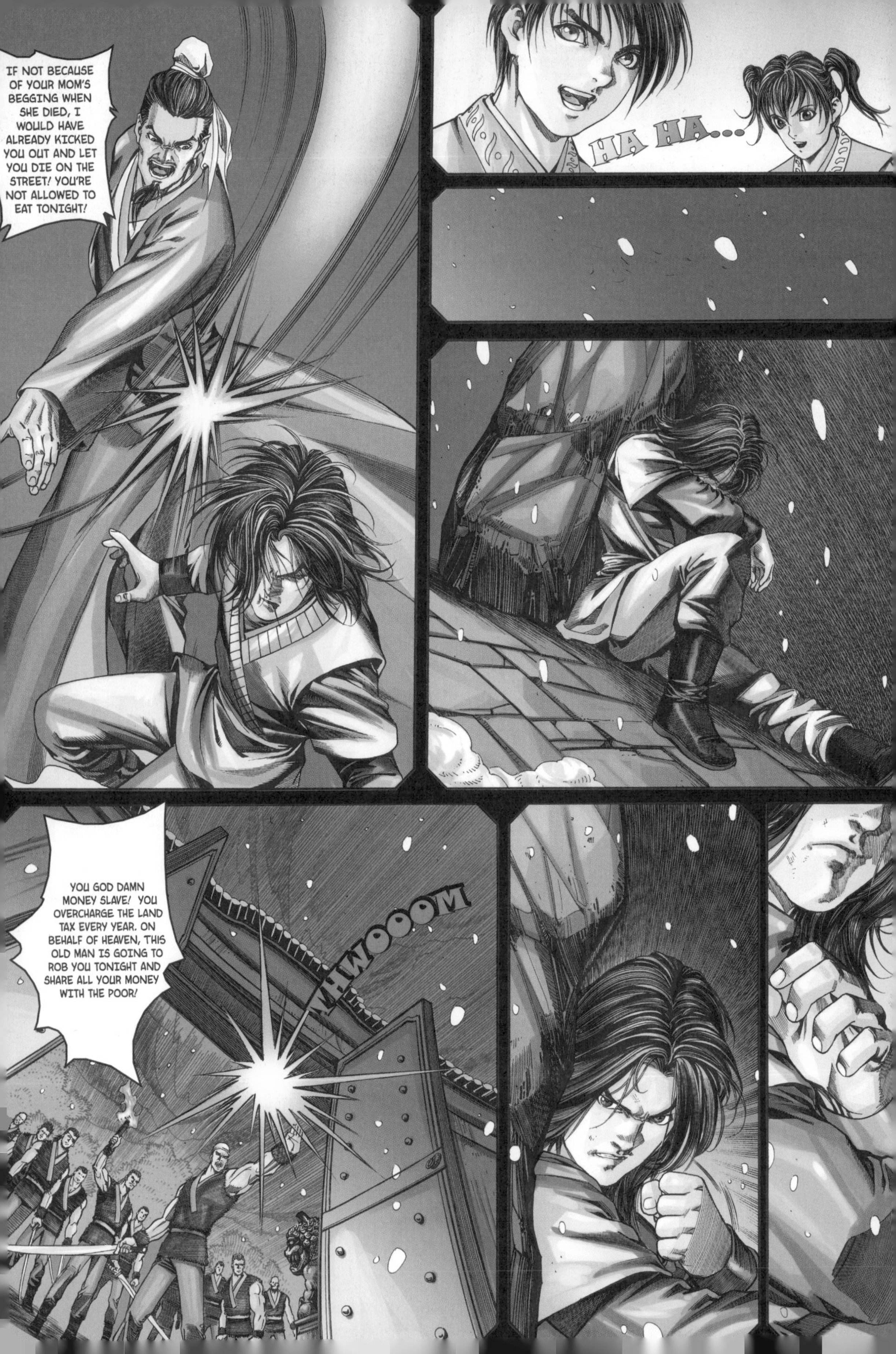
IF NOT BECAUSE OF YOUR MOM'S BEGGING WHEN SHE DIED, I WOULD HAVE ALREADY KICKED YOU OUT AND LET YOU DIE ON THE STREET! YOU'RE NOT ALLOWED TO EAT TONIGHT!
HA HA...
YOU GOD DAMN MONEY SLAVE! YOU OVERCHARGE THE LAND TAX EVERY YEAR. ON BEHALF OF HEAVEN, THIS OLD MAN IS GOING TO ROB YOU TONIGHT AND SHARE ALL YOUR MONEY WITH THE POOR!
WHWOOOM

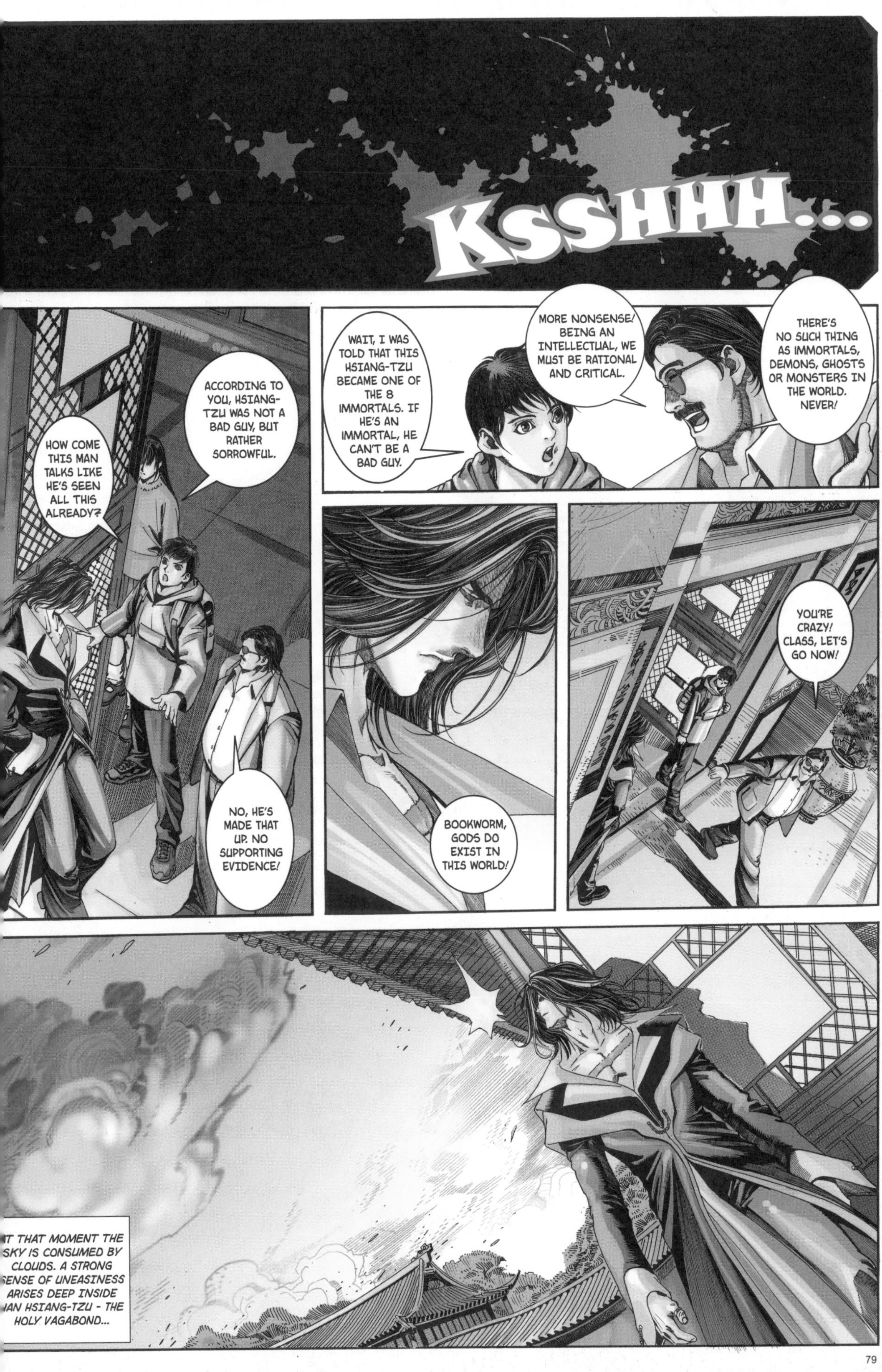
KSSHHH...
ACCORDING TO YOU, HSIANG-TZU WAS NOT A BAD GUY, BUT RATHER SORROWFUL.
HOW COME THIS MAN TALKS LIKE HE'S SEEN ALL THIS ALREADY?
NO, HE'S MADE THAT UP. NO SUPPORTING EVIDENCE!
WAIT, I WAS TOLD THAT THIS HSIANG-TZU BECAME ONE OF THE 8 IMMORTALS. IF HE'S AN IMMORTAL, HE CAN'T BE A BAD GUY.
MORE NONSENSE! BEING AN INTELLECTUAL, WE MUST BE RATIONAL AND CRITICAL.
THERE'S NO SUCH THING AS IMMORTALS, DEMONS, GHOSTS OR MONSTERS IN THE WORLD. NEVER!
BOOKWORM, GODS DO EXIST IN THIS WORLD!
YOU'RE CRAZY! CLASS, LET'S GO NOW!
T THAT MOMENT THE SKY IS CONSUMED BY CLOUDS. A STRONG SENSE OF UNEASINESS ARISES DEEP INSIDE AN HSIANG-TZU - THE HOLY VAGABOND...

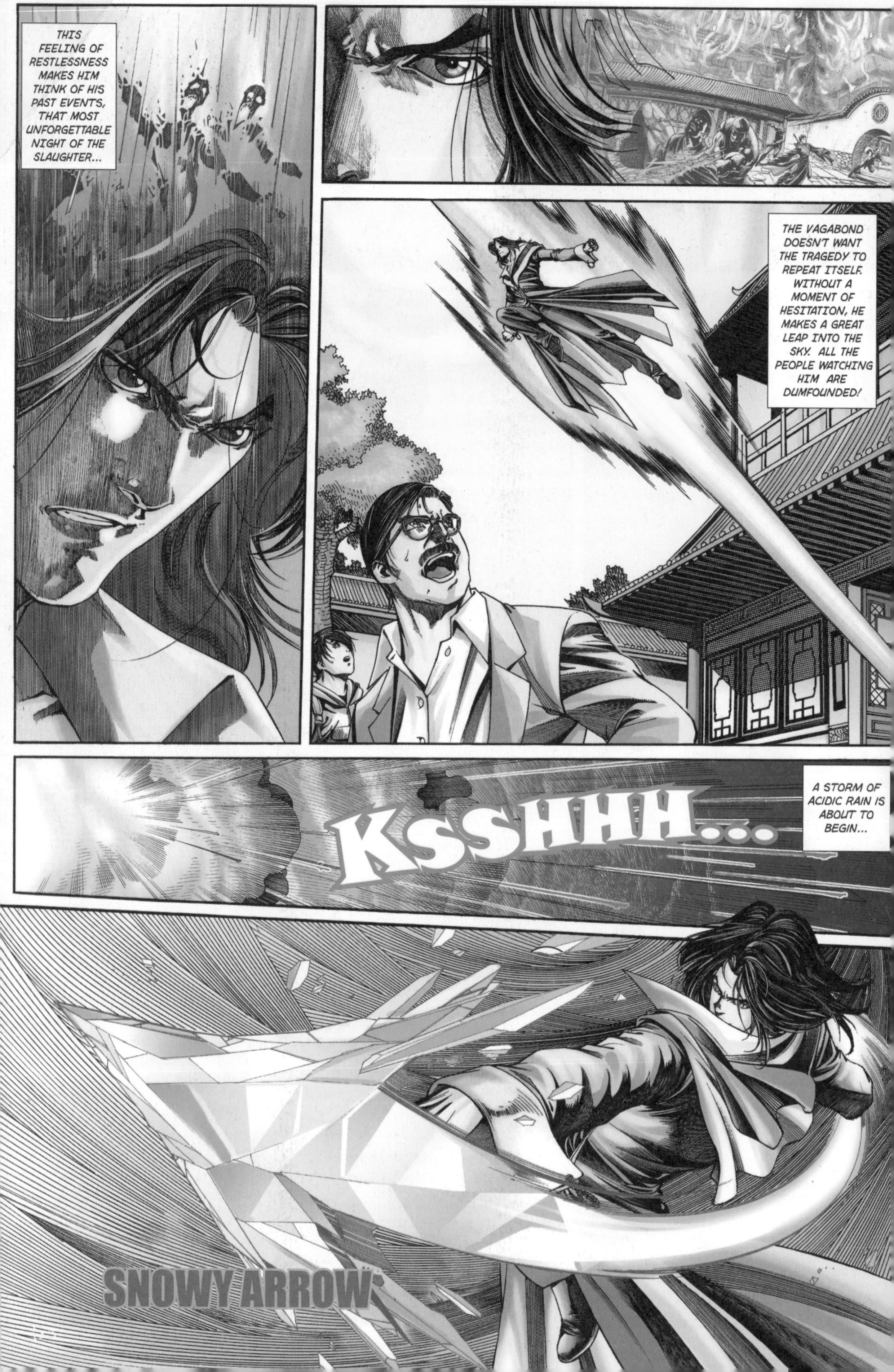
THIS FEELING OF RESTLESSNESS MAKES HIM THINK OF HIS PAST EVENTS, THAT MOST UNFORGETTABLE NIGHT OF THE SLAUGHTER...
THE VAGABOND DOESN'T WANT THE TRAGEDY TO REPEAT ITSELF. WITHOUT A MOMENT OF HESITATION, HE MAKES A GREAT LEAP INTO THE SKY. ALL THE PEOPLE WATCHING HIM ARE DUMFOUNDED!
KSSHHH...
A STORM OF ACIDIC RAIN IS ABOUT TO BEGIN...
SNOWY ARROW!

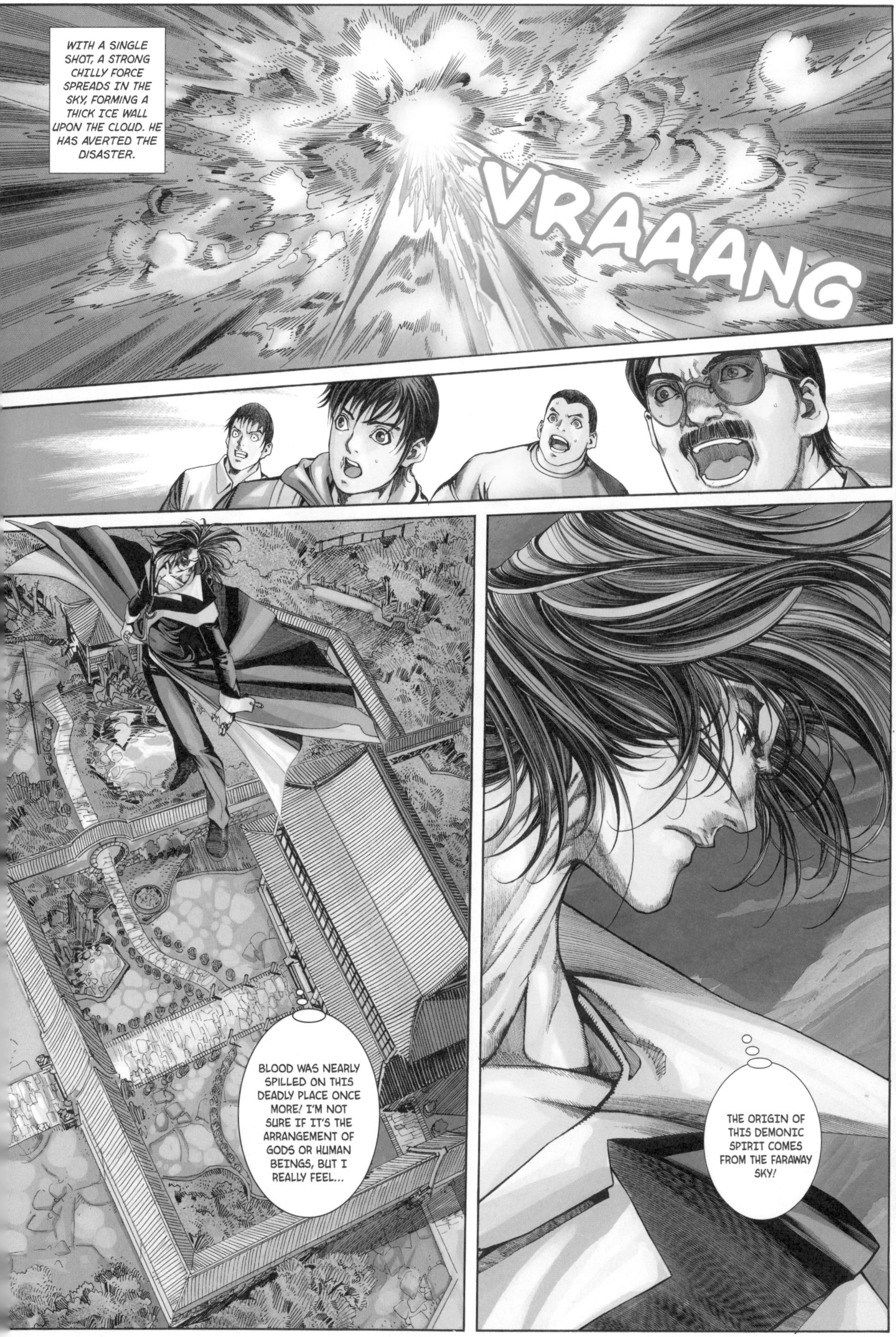
WITH A SINGLE SHOT, A STRONG CHILLY FORCE SPREADS IN THE SKY, FORMING A THICK ICE WALL UPON THE CLOUD. HE HAS AVERTED THE DISASTER.
VRAAANG
BLOOD WAS NEARLY SPILLED ON THIS DEADLY PLACE ONCE MORE! I'M NOT SURE IF IT'S THE ARRANGEMENT OF GODS OR HUMAN BEINGS, BUT I REALLY FEEL...
THE ORIGIN OF THIS DEMONIC SPIRIT COMES FROM THE FARAWAY SKY!

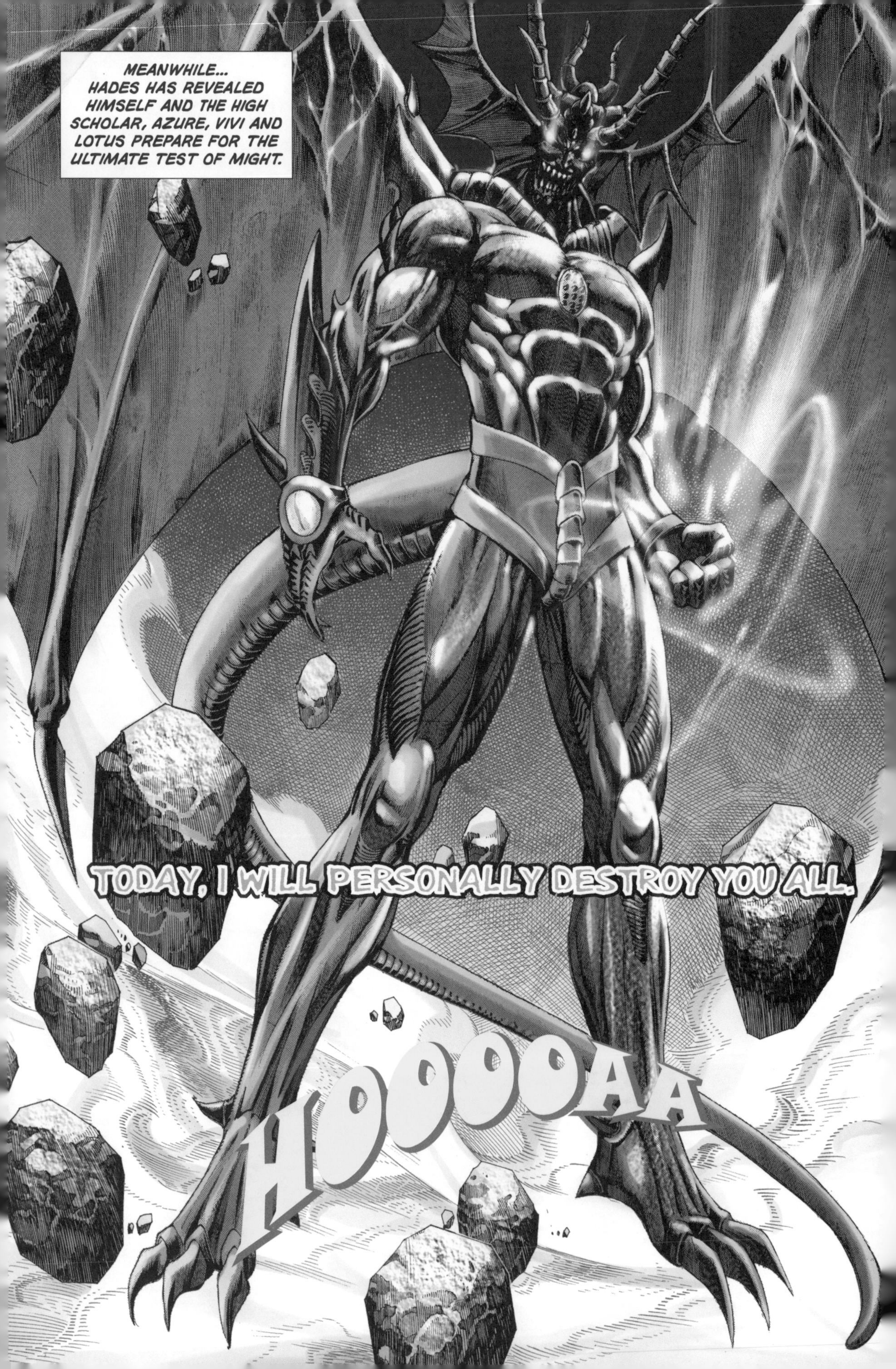
MEANWHILE... HADES HAS REVEALED HIMSELF AND THE HIGH SCHOLAR, AZURE, VIVI AND LOTUS PREPARE FOR THE ULTIMATE TEST OF MIGHT.
TODAY, I WILL PERSONALLY DESTROY YOU ALL.
HOOOOAA

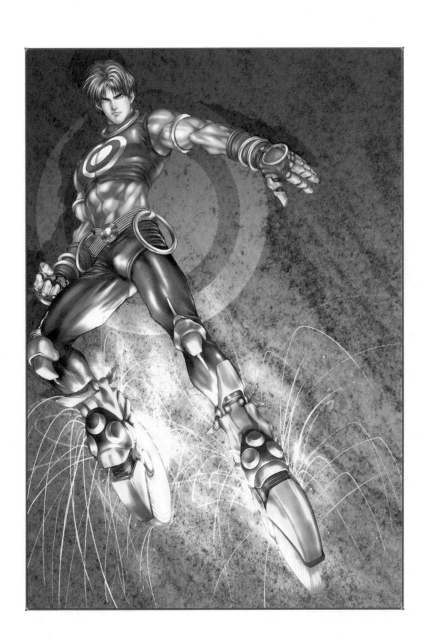

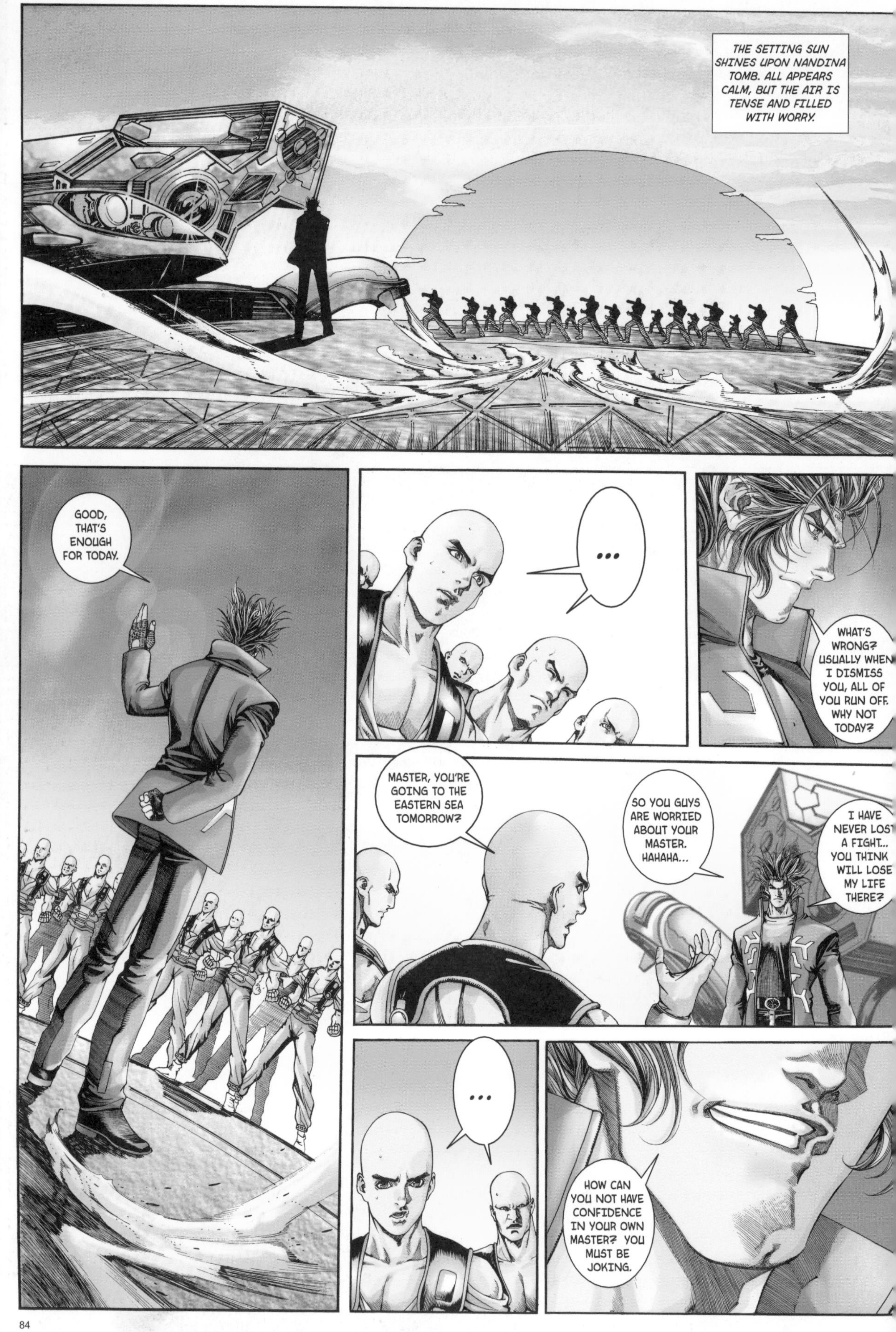
THE SETTING SUN SHINES UPON NANDINA TOMB. ALL APPEARS CALM, BUT THE AIR IS TENSE AND FILLED WITH WORRY.
GOOD, THAT'S ENOUGH FOR TODAY.
...
WHAT'S WRONG? USUALLY WHEN I DISMISS YOU, ALL OF YOU RUN OFF. WHY NOT TODAY?
MASTER, YOU'RE GOING TO THE EASTERN SEA TOMORROW?
SO YOU GUYS ARE WORRIED ABOUT YOUR MASTER. HAHAHA...
I HAVE NEVER LOST A FIGHT... YOU THINK WILL LOSE MY LIFE THERE?
...
HOW CAN YOU NOT HAVE CONFIDENCE IN YOUR OWN MASTER? YOU MUST BE JOKING.

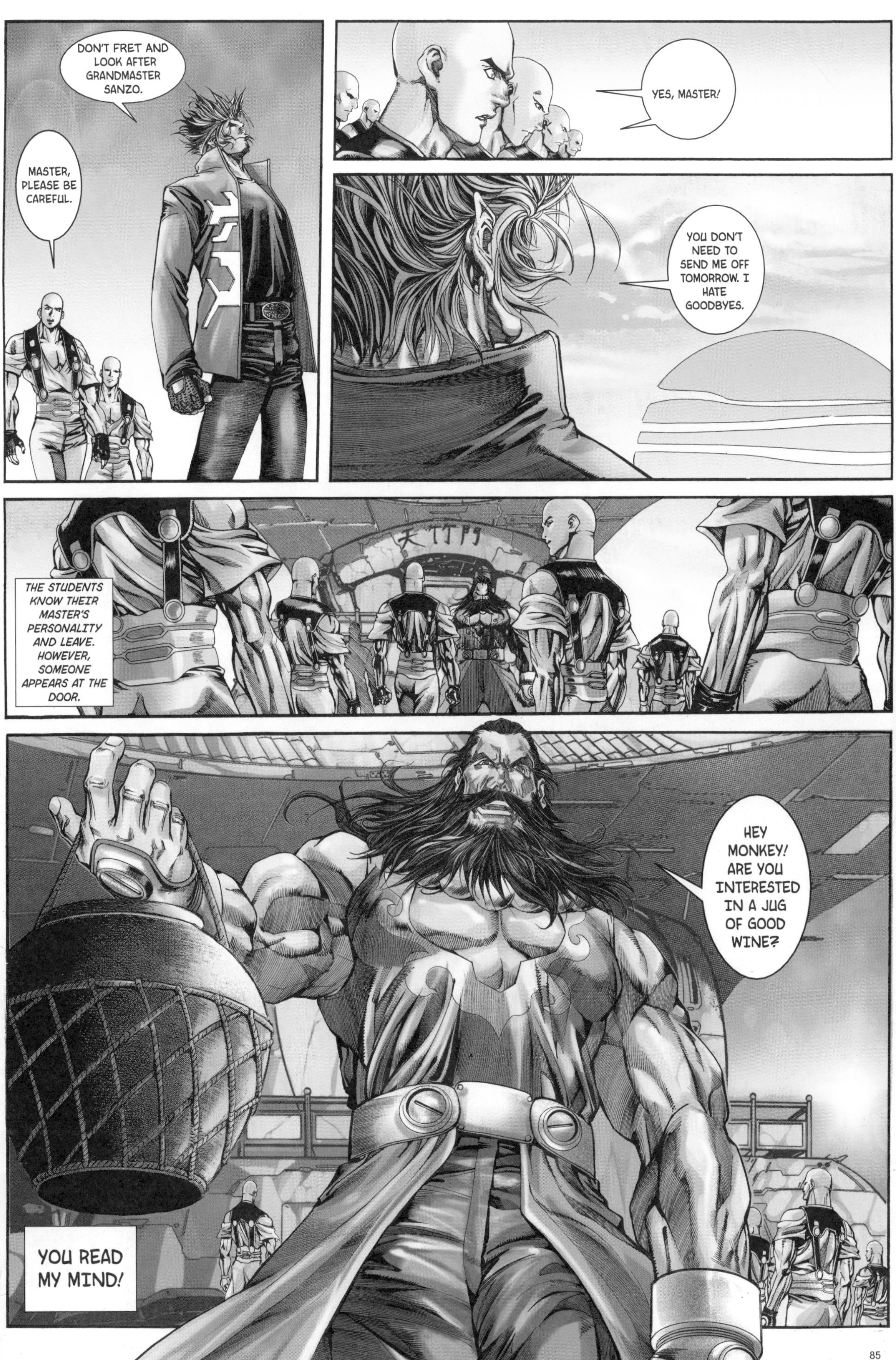
DON'T FRET AND LOOK AFTER GRANDMASTER SANZO.
MASTER, PLEASE BE CAREFUL.
YES, MASTER!
YOU DON'T NEED TO SEND ME OFF TOMORROW. I HATE GOODBYES.
THE STUDENTS KNOW THEIR MASTER'S PERSONALITY AND LEAVE. HOWEVER, SOMEONE APPEARS AT THE DOOR.
HEY MONKEY! ARE YOU INTERESTED IN A JUG OF GOOD WINE?
YOU READ MY MIND!

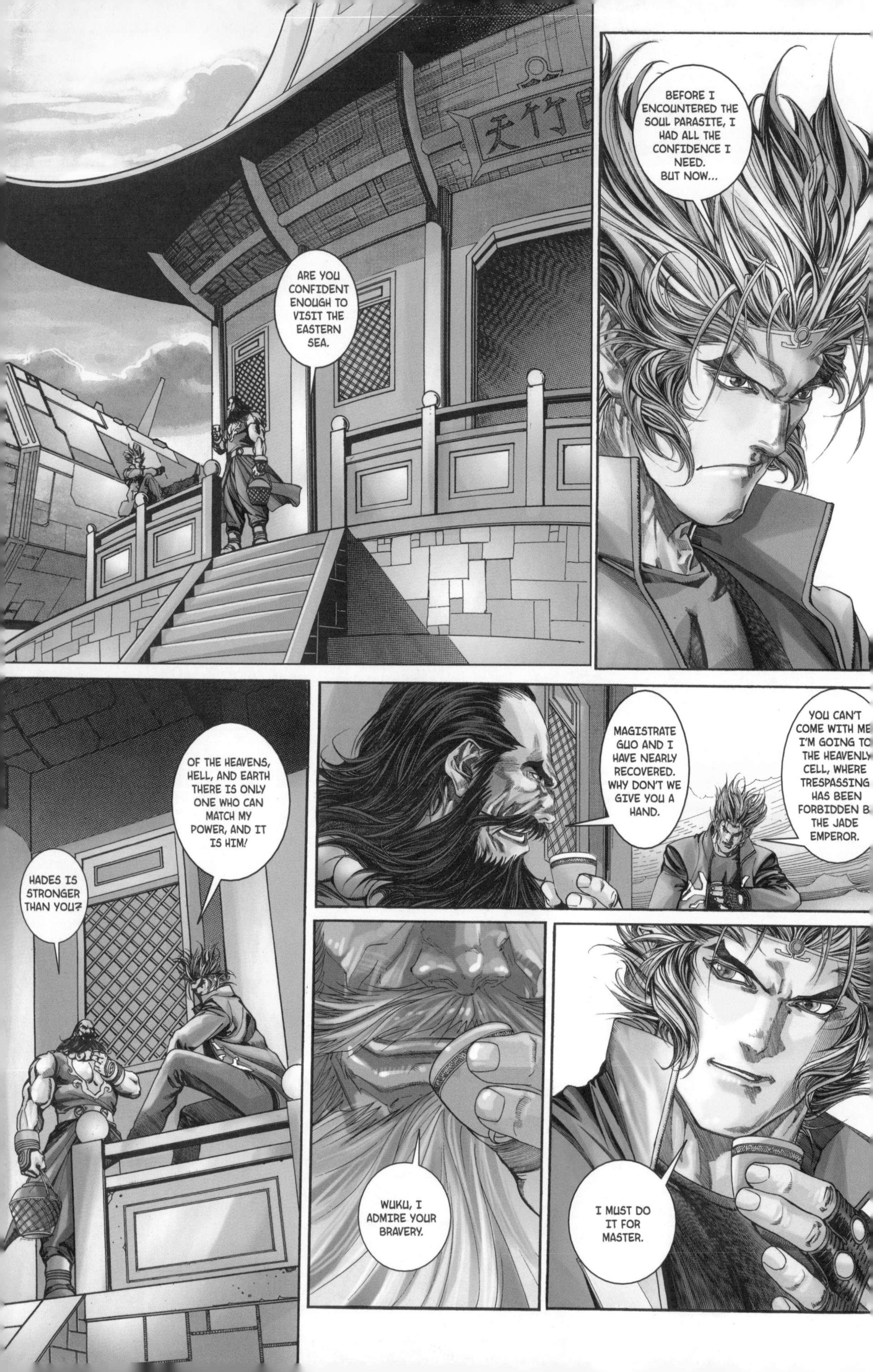
天竹
ARE YOU CONFIDENT ENOUGH TO VISIT THE EASTERN SEA.
BEFORE I ENCOUNTERED THE SOUL PARASITE, I HAD ALL THE CONFIDENCE I NEED. BUT NOW...
OF THE HEAVENS, HELL, AND EARTH THERE IS ONLY ONE WHO CAN MATCH MY POWER, AND IT IS HIM!
HADES IS STRONGER THAN YOU?
MAGISTRATE GUO AND I HAVE NEARLY RECOVERED. WHY DON'T WE GIVE YOU A HAND.
YOU CAN'T COME WITH ME I'M GOING TO THE HEAVENLY CELL, WHERE TRESPASSING HAS BEEN FORBIDDEN B THE JADE EMPEROR.
WUKU, I ADMIRE YOUR BRAVERY.
I MUST DO IT FOR MASTER.

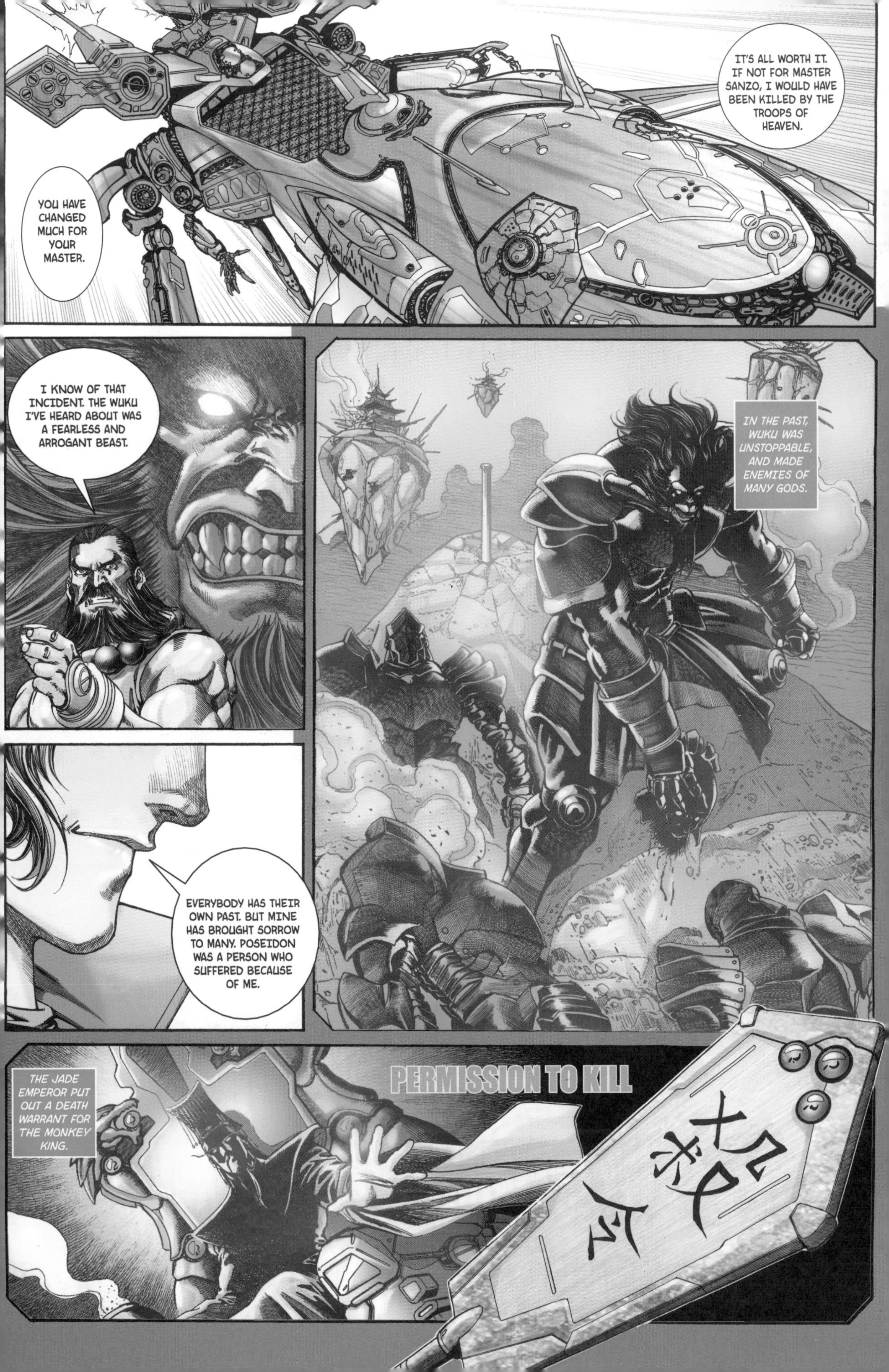
IT'S ALL WORTH IT. IF NOT FOR MASTER SANZO, I WOULD HAVE BEEN KILLED BY THE TROOPS OF HEAVEN.
YOU HAVE CHANGED MUCH FOR YOUR MASTER.
I KNOW OF THAT INCIDENT. THE WUKU I'VE HEARD ABOUT WAS A FEARLESS AND ARROGANT BEAST.
EVERYBODY HAS THEIR OWN PAST. BUT MINE HAS BROUGHT SORROW TO MANY. POSEIDON WAS A PERSON WHO SUFFERED BECAUSE OF ME.
IN THE PAST, WUKU WAS UNSTOPPABLE, AND MADE ENEMIES OF MANY GODS.
THE JADE EMPEROR PUT OUT A DEATH WARRANT FOR THE MONKEY KING.
PERMISSION TO KILL

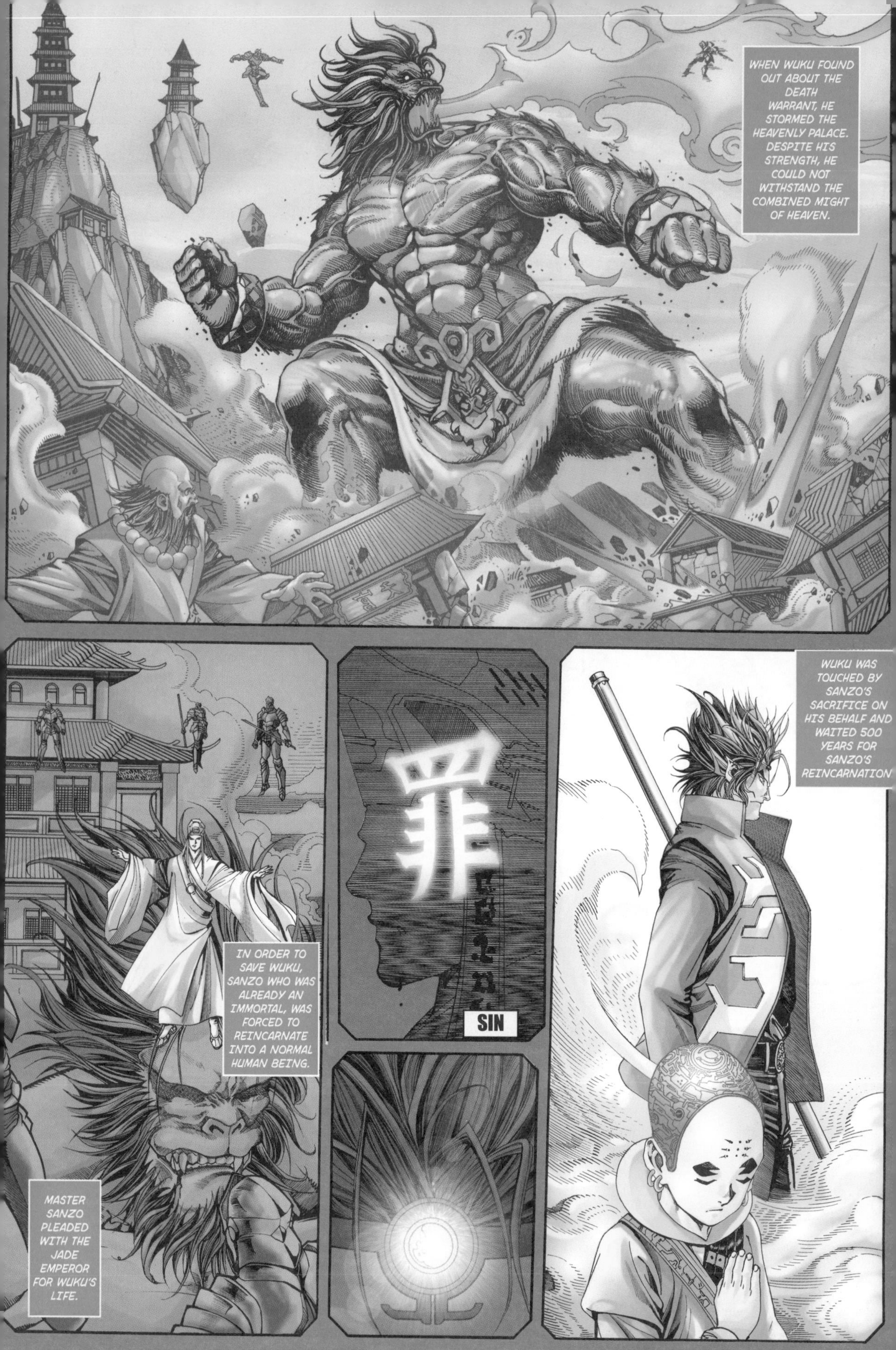
WHEN WUKU FOUND OUT ABOUT THE DEATH WARRANT, HE STORMED THE HEAVENLY PALACE. DESPITE HIS STRENGTH, HE COULD NOT WITHSTAND THE COMBINED MIGHT OF HEAVEN.
MASTER SANZO PLEADED WITH THE JADE EMPEROR FOR WUKU'S LIFE.
IN ORDER TO SAVE WUKU, SANZO WHO WAS ALREADY AN IMMORTAL, WAS FORCED TO REINCARNATE INTO A NORMAL HUMAN BEING.
罪
SIN
WUKU WAS TOUCHED BY SANZO'S SACRIFICE ON HIS BEHALF AND WAITED 500 YEARS FOR SANZO'S REINCARNATION

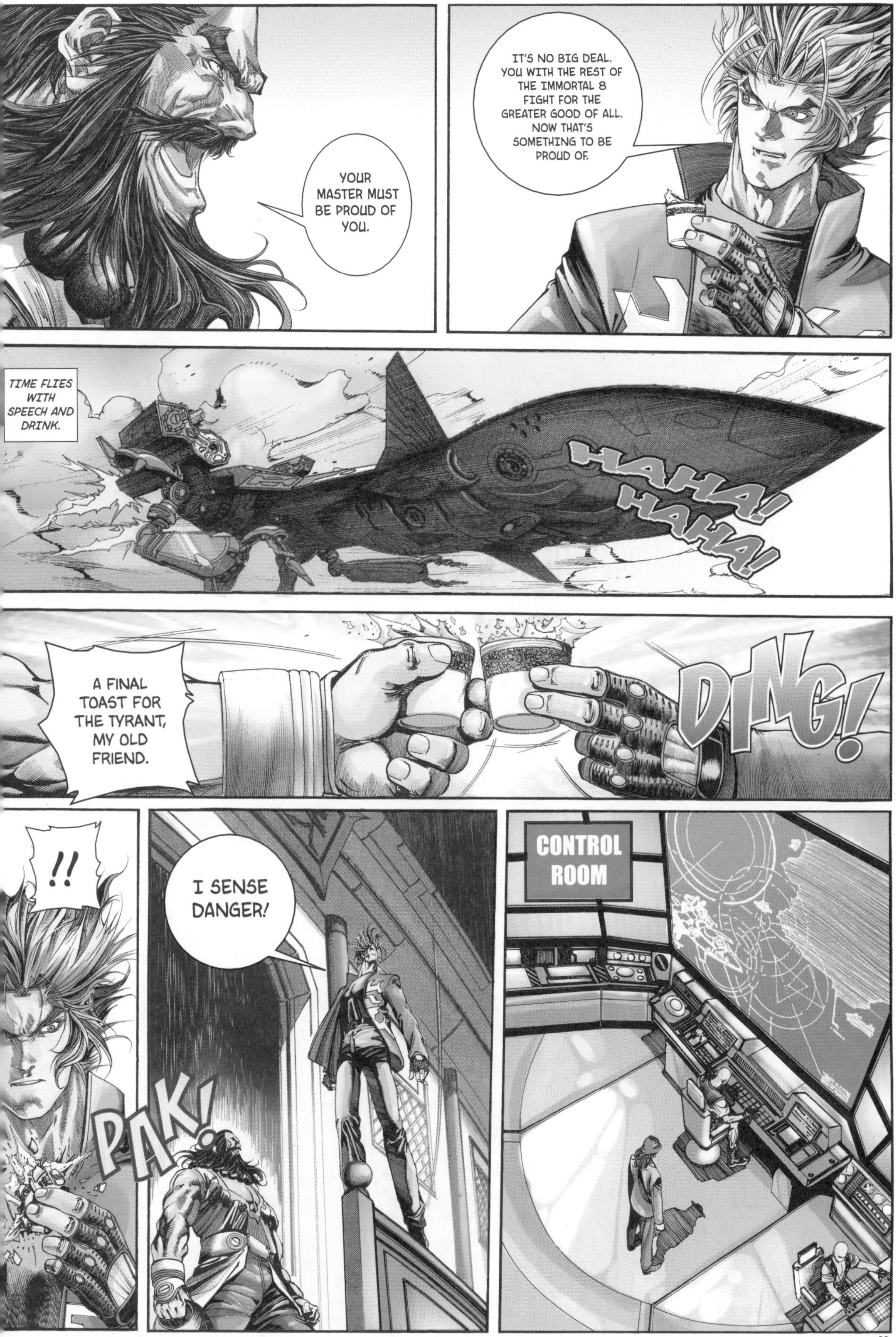
YOUR MASTER MUST BE PROUD OF YOU.
IT'S NO BIG DEAL. YOU WITH THE REST OF THE IMMORTAL 8 FIGHT FOR THE GREATER GOOD OF ALL. NOW THAT'S SOMETHING TO BE PROUD OF.
TIME FLIES WITH SPEECH AND DRINK.
HAHA! HAHA!
A FINAL TOAST FOR THE TYRANT, MY OLD FRIEND.
DING!
!!
PAK!
I SENSE DANGER!
CONTROL ROOM

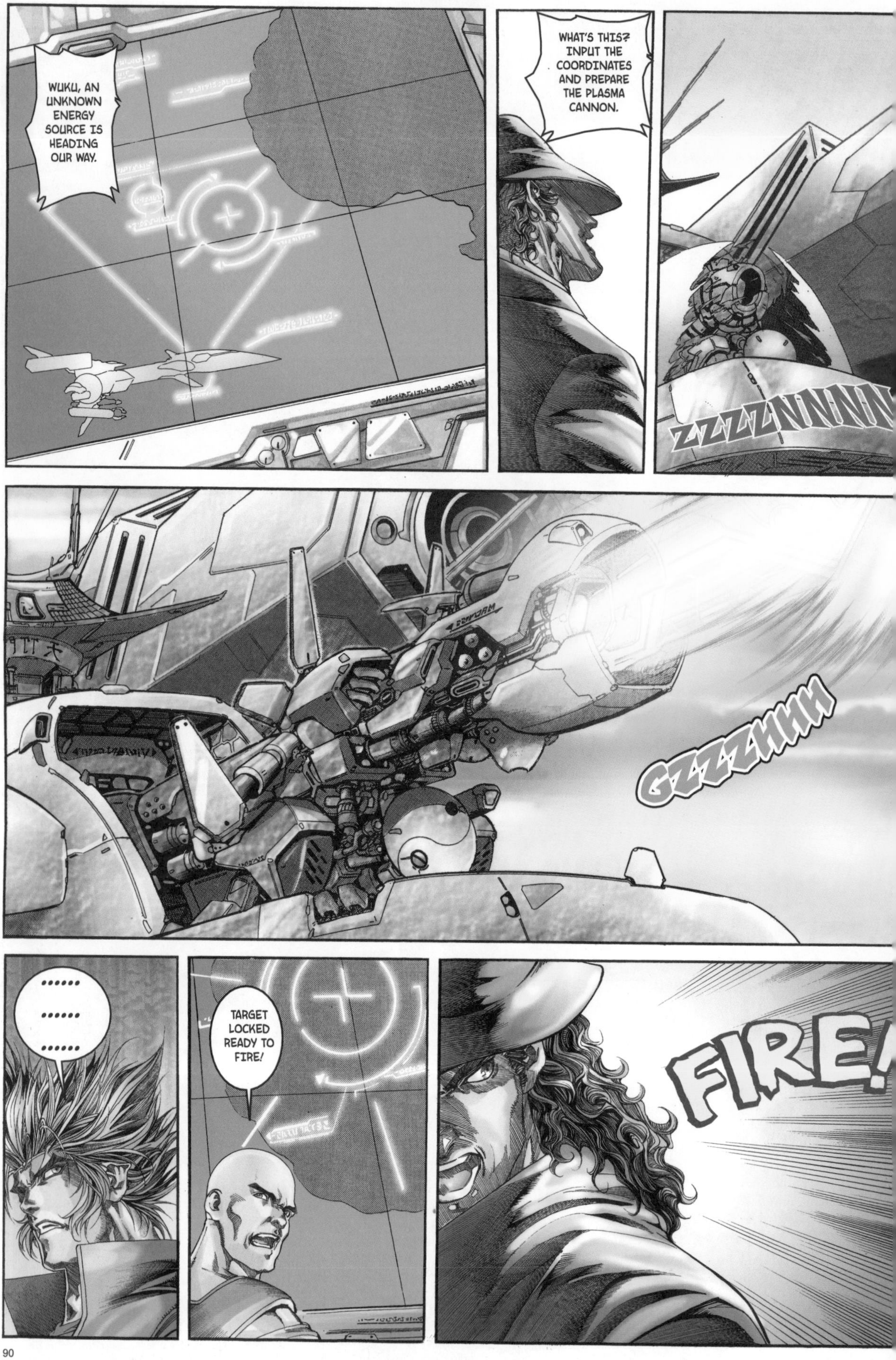
WUKU, AN UNKNOWN ENERGY SOURCE IS HEADING OUR WAY.
WHAT'S THIS? INPUT THE COORDINATES AND PREPARE THE PLASMA CANNON.
ZZZZNNNN
GZZZHHH
......
......
......
TARGET LOCKED READY TO FIRE!
FIRE!

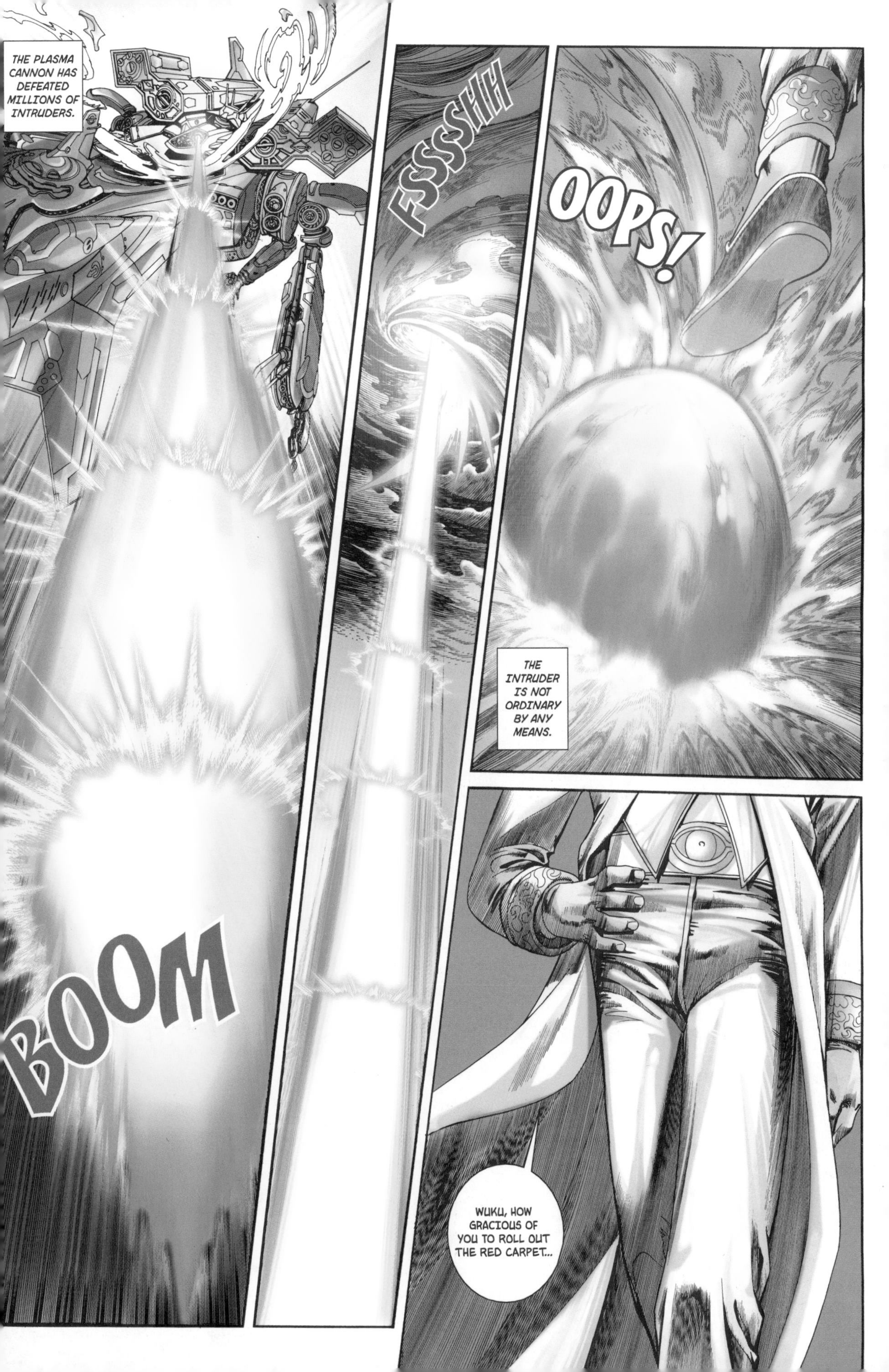
THE PLASMA CANNON HAS DEFEATED MILLIONS OF INTRUDERS.
BOOM
FSSSSHH
OOPS!
THE INTRUDER IS NOT ORDINARY BY ANY MEANS.
WUKU, HOW GRACIOUS OF YOU TO ROLL OUT THE RED CARPET...

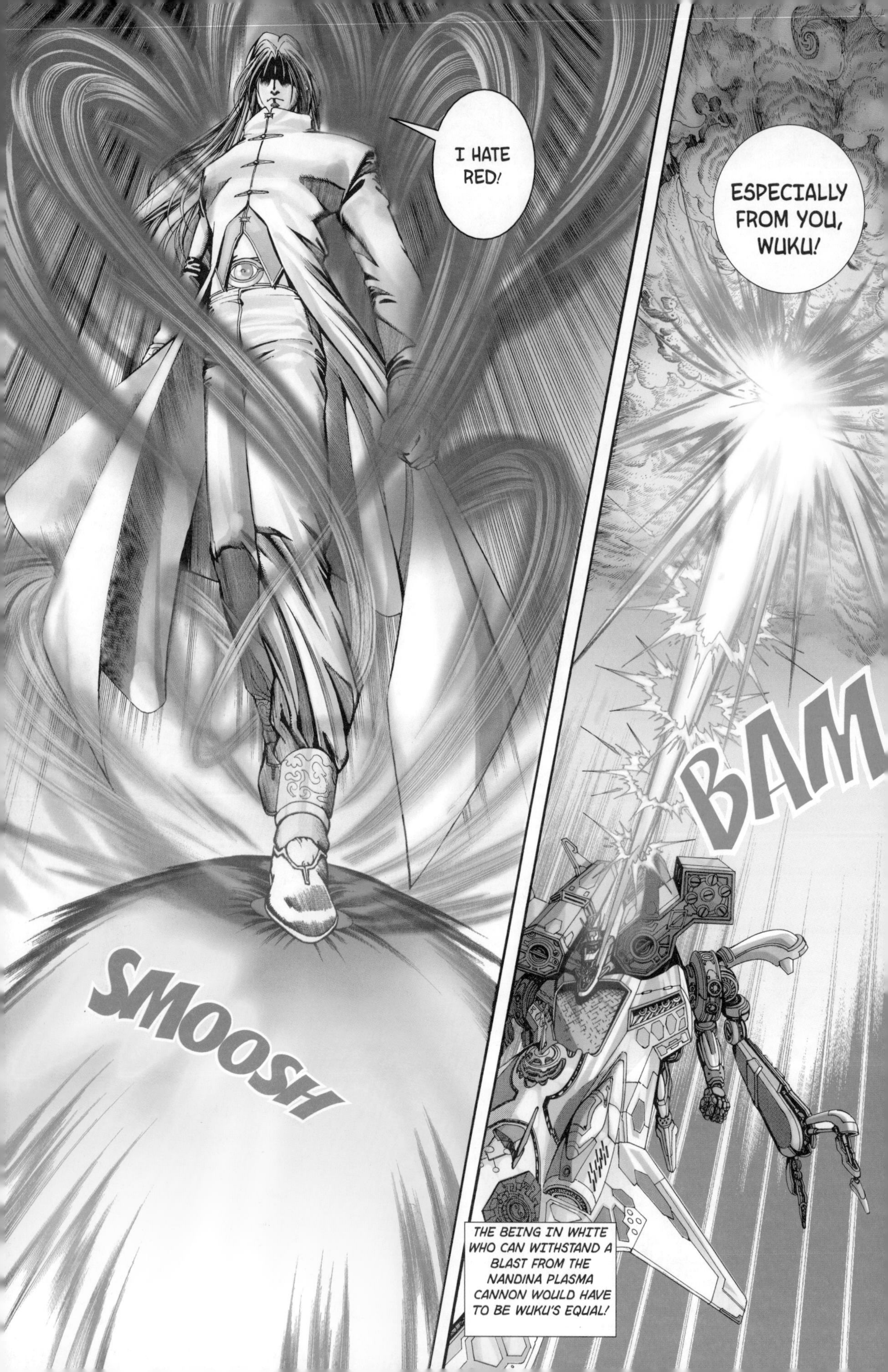
I HATE RED!
ESPECIALLY FROM YOU, WUKU!
BAM
SMOOSH
THE BEING IN WHITE WHO CAN WITHSTAND A BLAST FROM THE NANDINA PLASMA CANNON WOULD HAVE TO BE WUKU'S EQUAL!

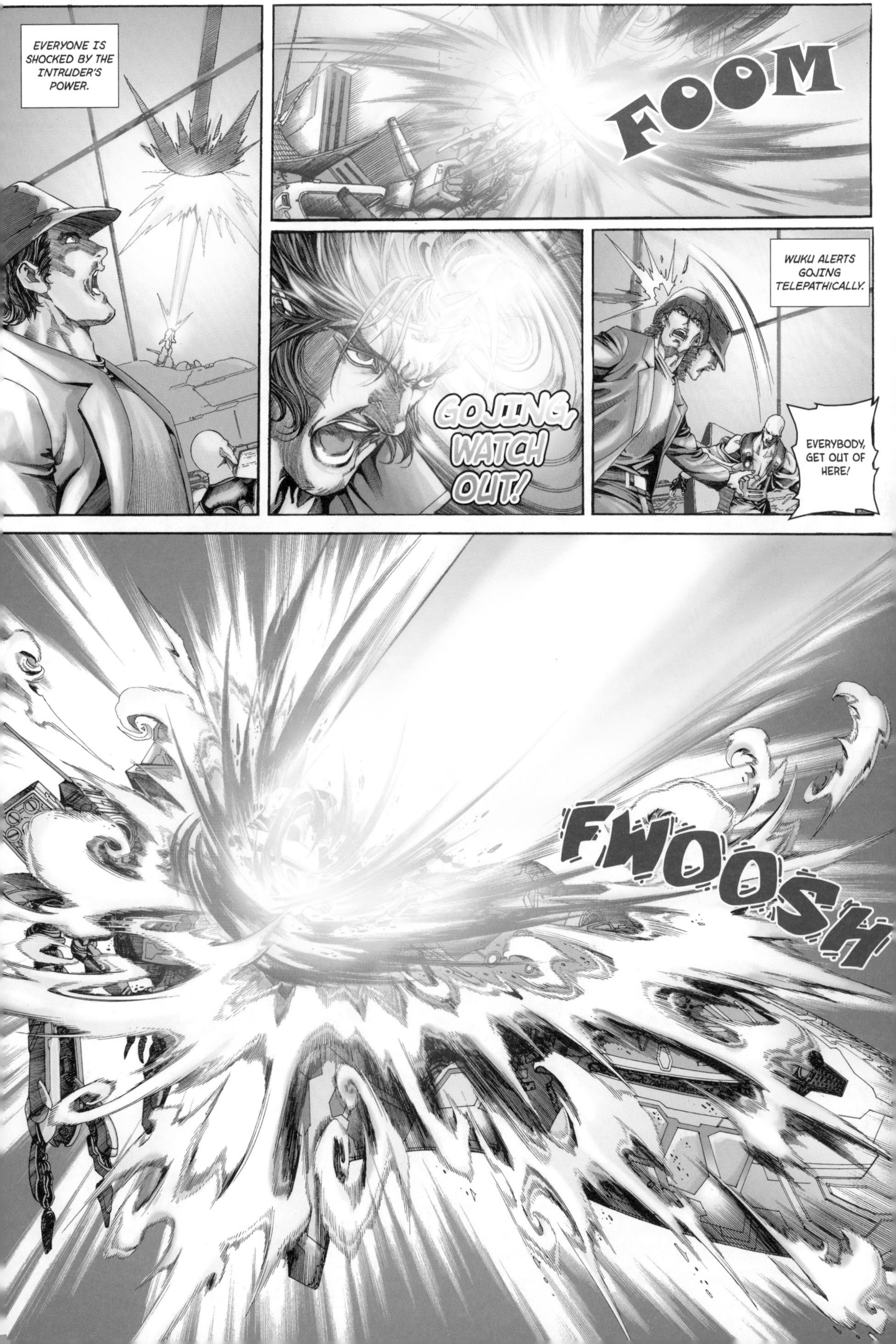
EVERYONE IS SHOCKED BY THE INTRUDER'S POWER.
FOOM
GOJING, WATCH OUT!
WUKU ALERTS GOJING TELEPATHICALLY.
EVERYBODY, GET OUT OF HERE!
FWOOSH

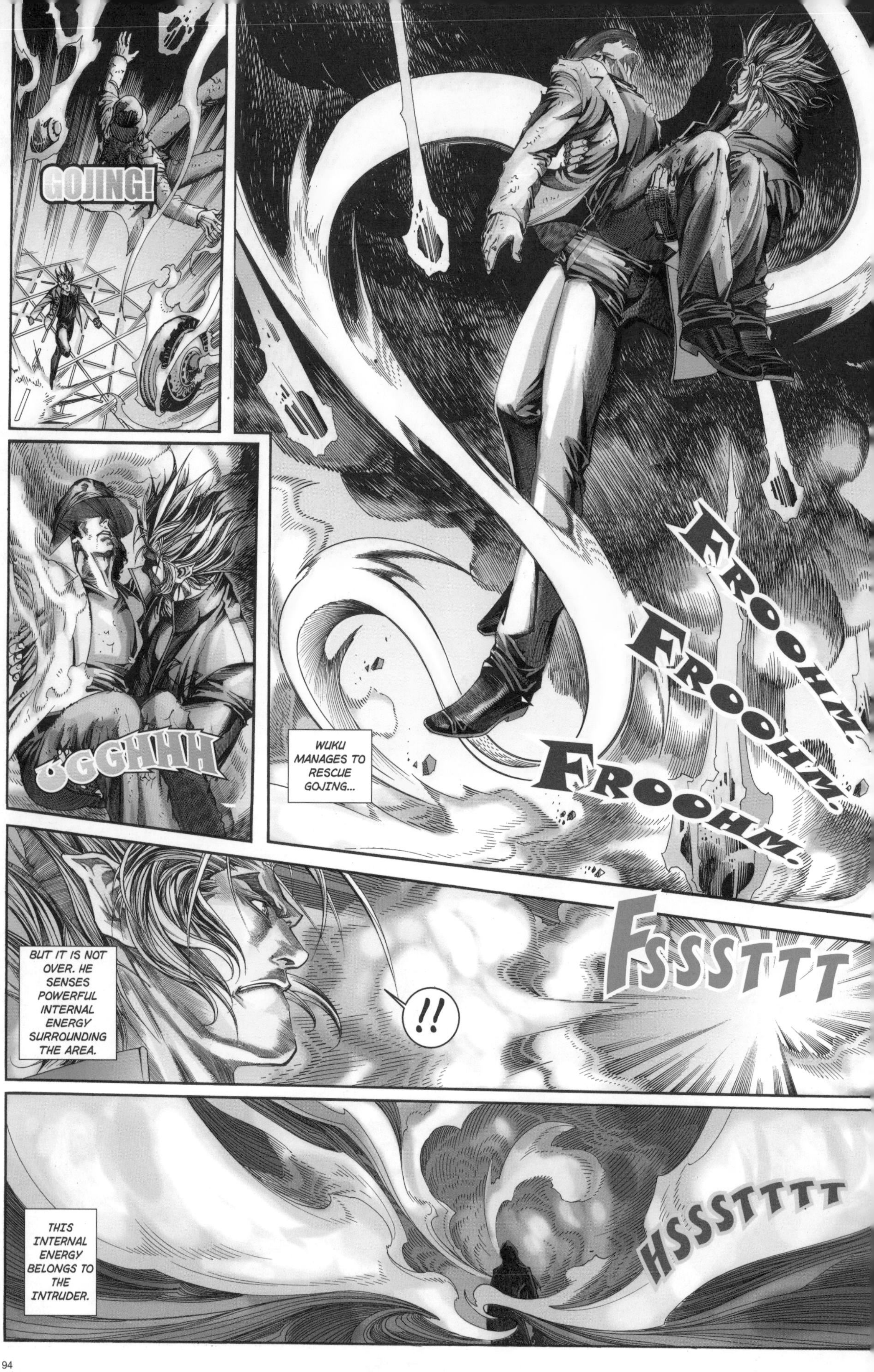
GOJING!
UGGHHH
WUKU MANAGES TO RESCUE GOJING...
FROOHM!
FROOHM!
FROOHM!
BUT IT IS NOT OVER. HE SENSES POWERFUL INTERNAL ENERGY SURROUNDING THE AREA.
!!
FSSSTTTT
THIS INTERNAL ENERGY BELONGS TO THE INTRUDER.
HSSSTTTTT

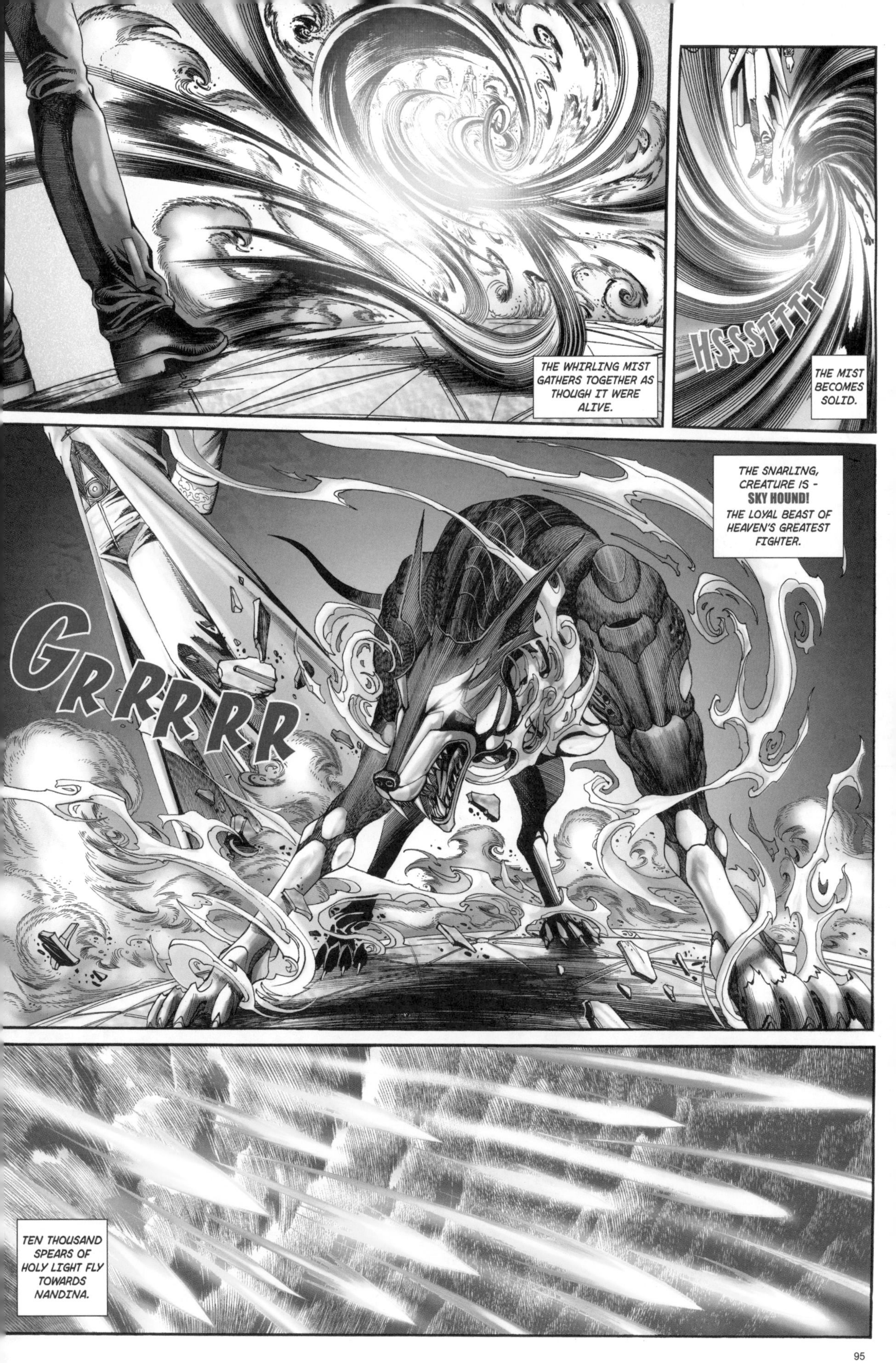
THE WHIRLING MIST GATHERS TOGETHER AS THOUGH IT WERE ALIVE.
HSSSTTTT
THE MIST BECOMES SOLID.
THE SNARLING, CREATURE IS - SKY HOUND! THE LOYAL BEAST OF HEAVEN'S GREATEST FIGHTER.
GRRRRRR
TEN THOUSAND SPEARS OF HOLY LIGHT FLY TOWARDS NANDINA.

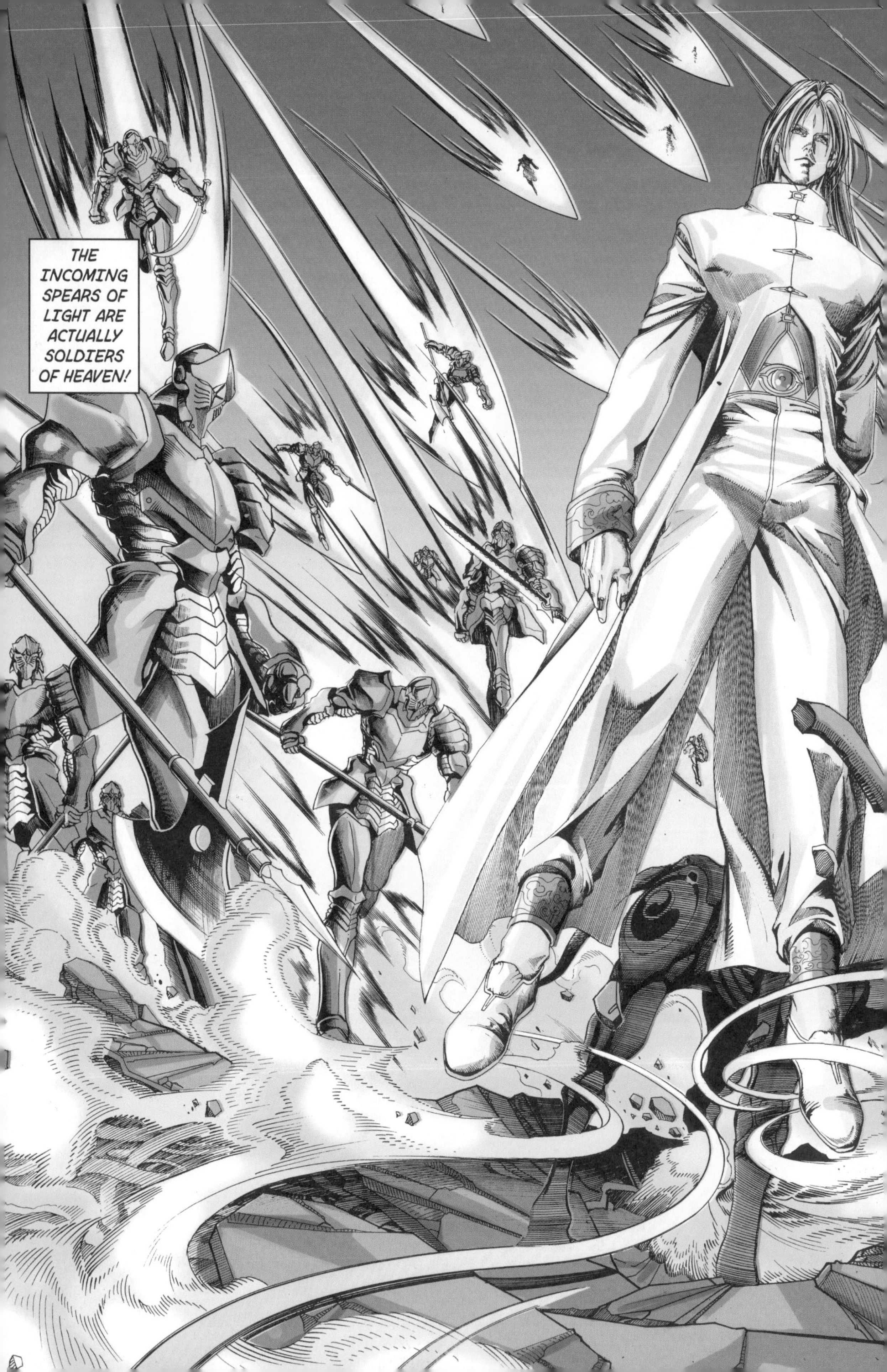
THE INCOMING SPEARS OF LIGHT ARE ACTUALLY SOLDIERS OF HEAVEN!

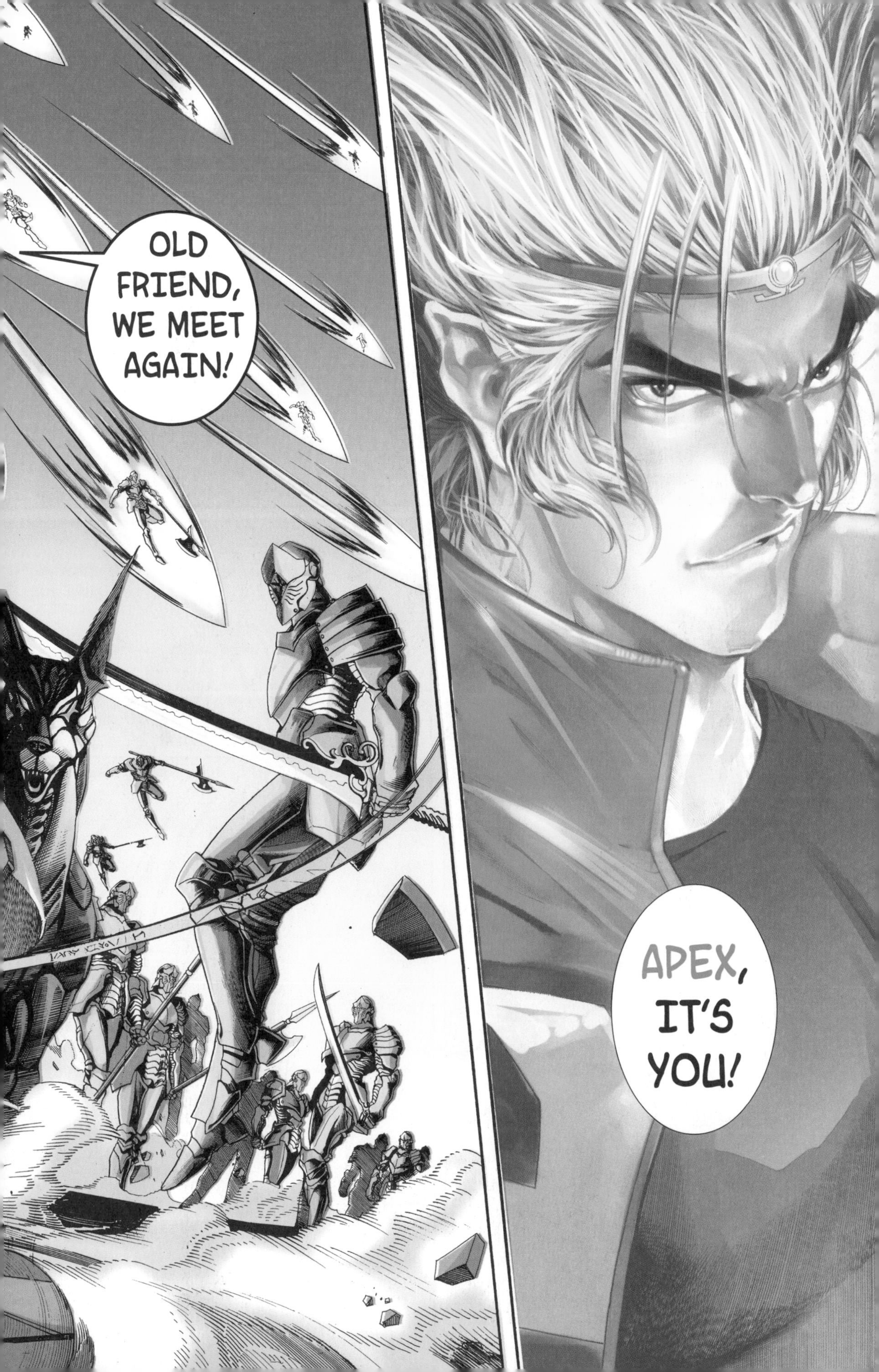
APEX, IT'S YOU!
OLD FRIEND, WE MEET AGAIN!

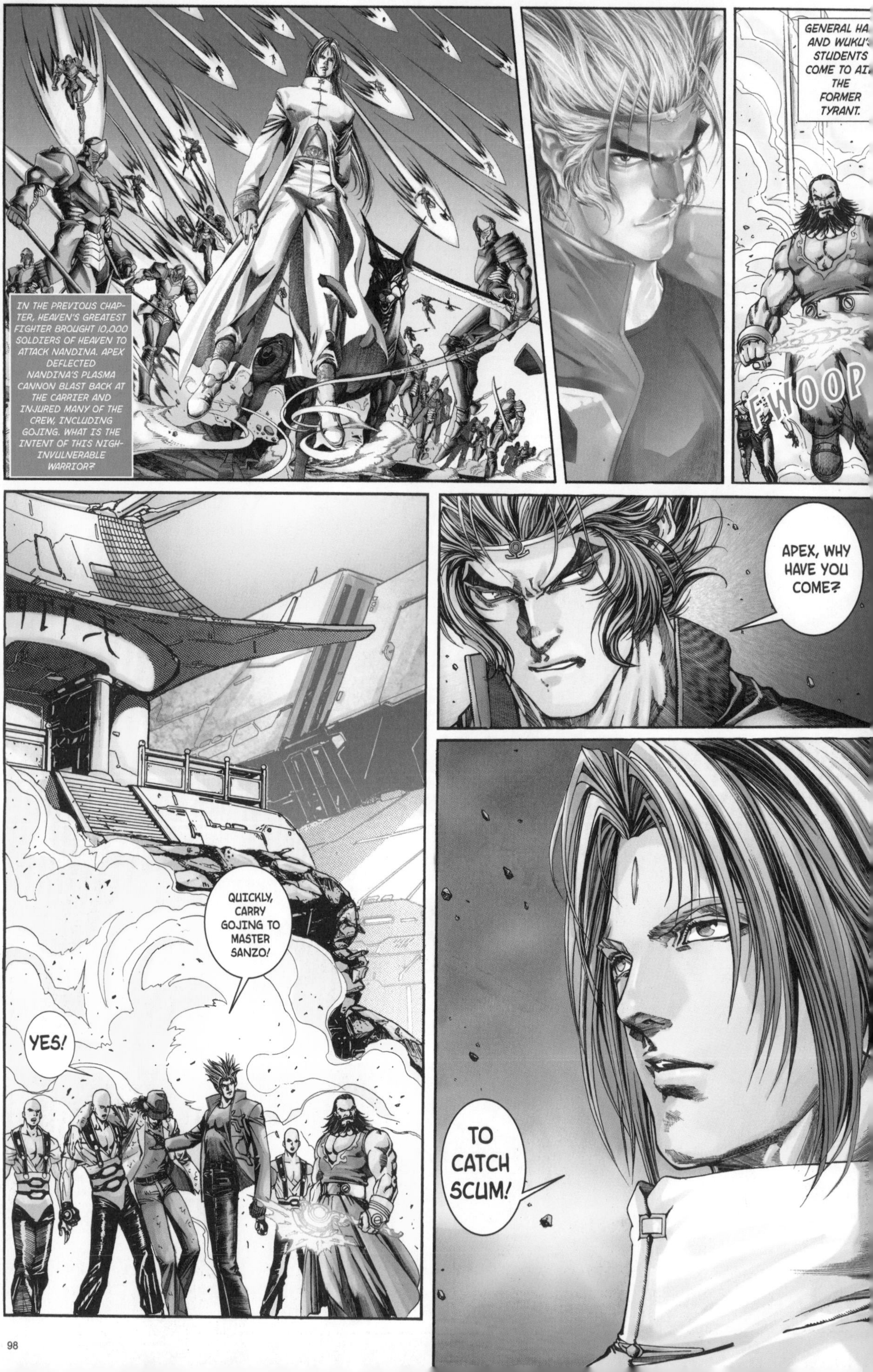

IN THE PREVIOUS CHAPTER, HEAVEN'S GREATEST FIGHTER BROUGHT 10,000 SOLDIERS OF HEAVEN TO ATTACK NANDINA. APEX DEFLECTED NANDINA'S PLASMA CANNON BLAST BACK AT THE CARRIER AND INJURED MANY OF THE CREW, INCLUDING GOJING. WHAT IS THE INTENT OF THIS NIGH-INVULNERABLE WARRIOR?
GENERAL HA AND WUKU'S STUDENTS COME TO AI THE FORMER TYRANT.
FWOOP
APEX, WHY HAVE YOU COME?
QUICKLY, CARRY GOJING TO MASTER SANZO!
YES!
TO CATCH SCUM!

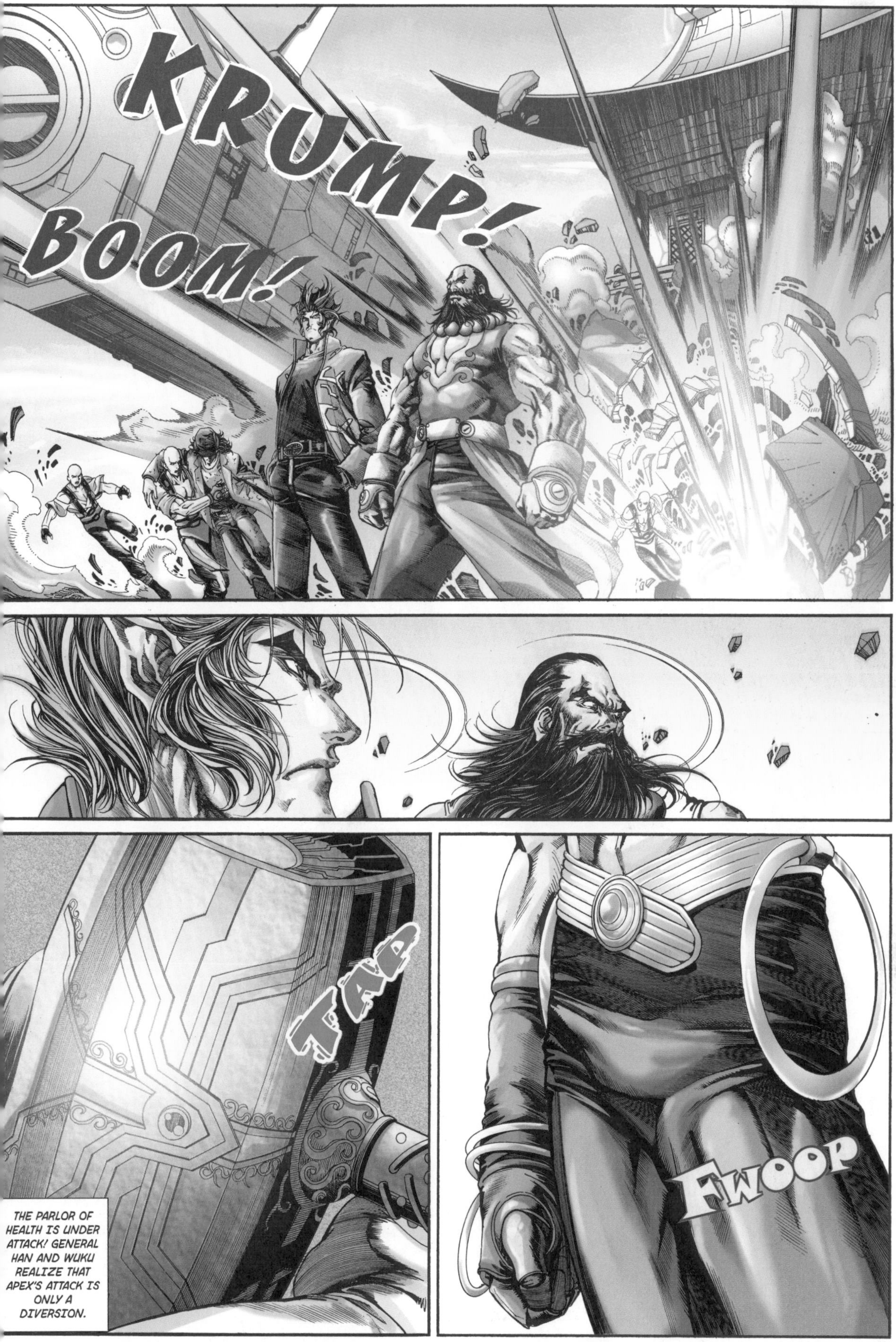
KRUMP!
BOOM!
TAP
THE PARLOR OF HEALTH IS UNDER ATTACK! GENERAL HAN AND WUKU REALIZE THAT APEX'S ATTACK IS ONLY A DIVERSION.
FWOOP

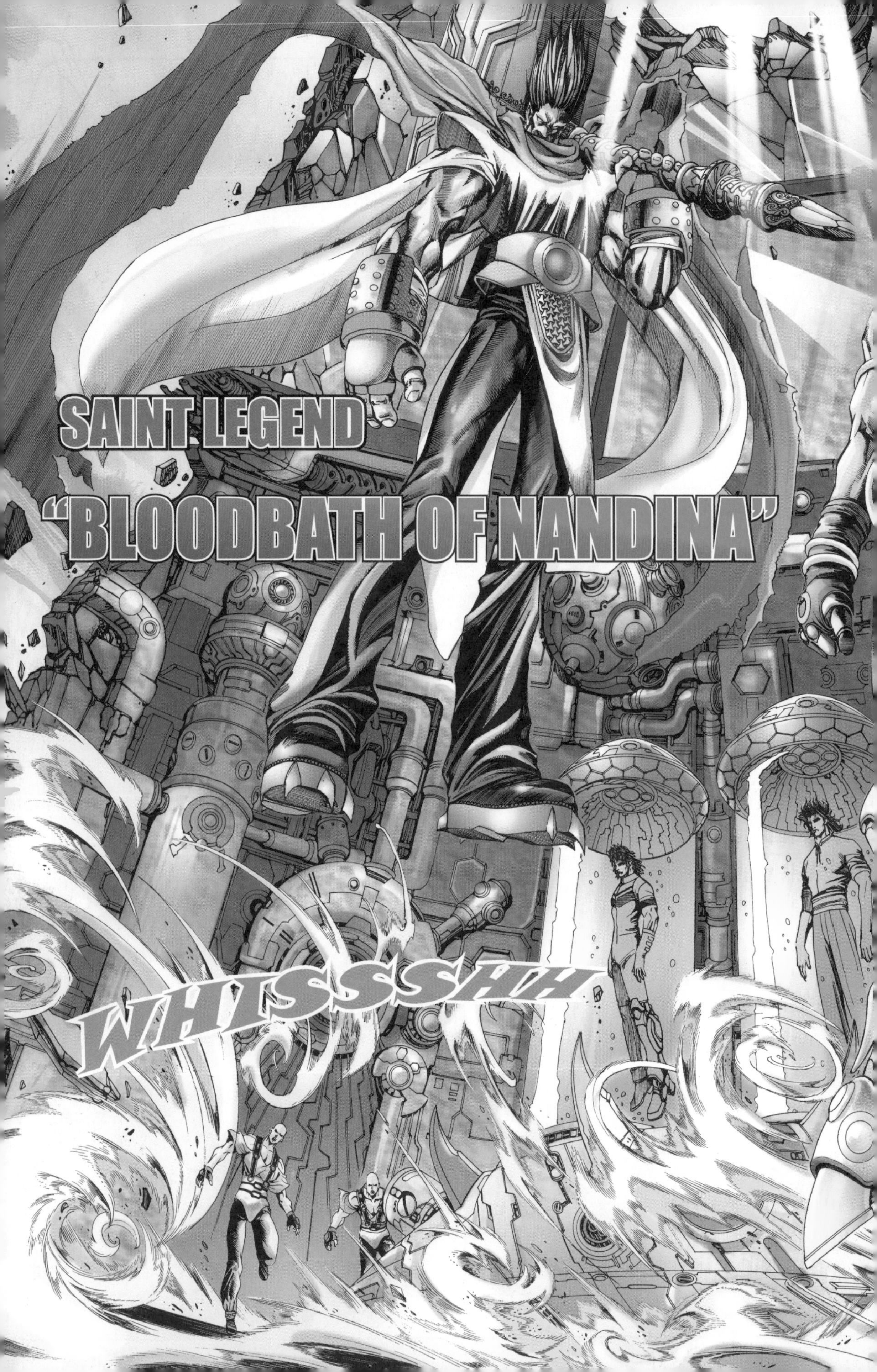
SAINT LEGEND
"BLOODBATH OF NANDINA"
WHISSSHH

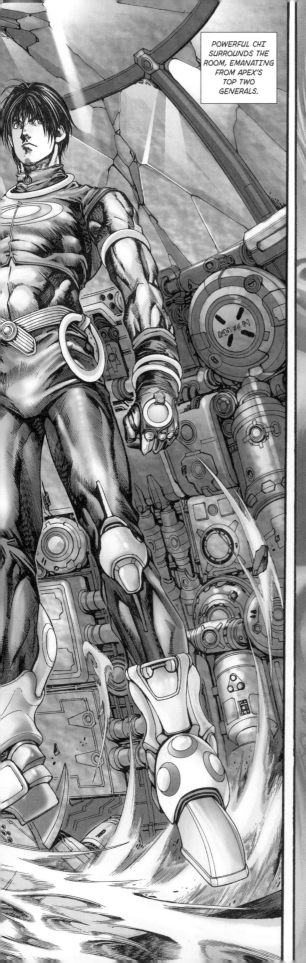

POWERFUL CHI SURROUNDS THE ROOM, EMANATING FROM APEX'S TOP TWO GENERALS.

JUSTICE ENFORCER: MAELSTROM

HAND OVER IRON-CRUTCH LI AND PIG OR BE EXECUTED!

JUSTICE EXECUTOR: NORTEL

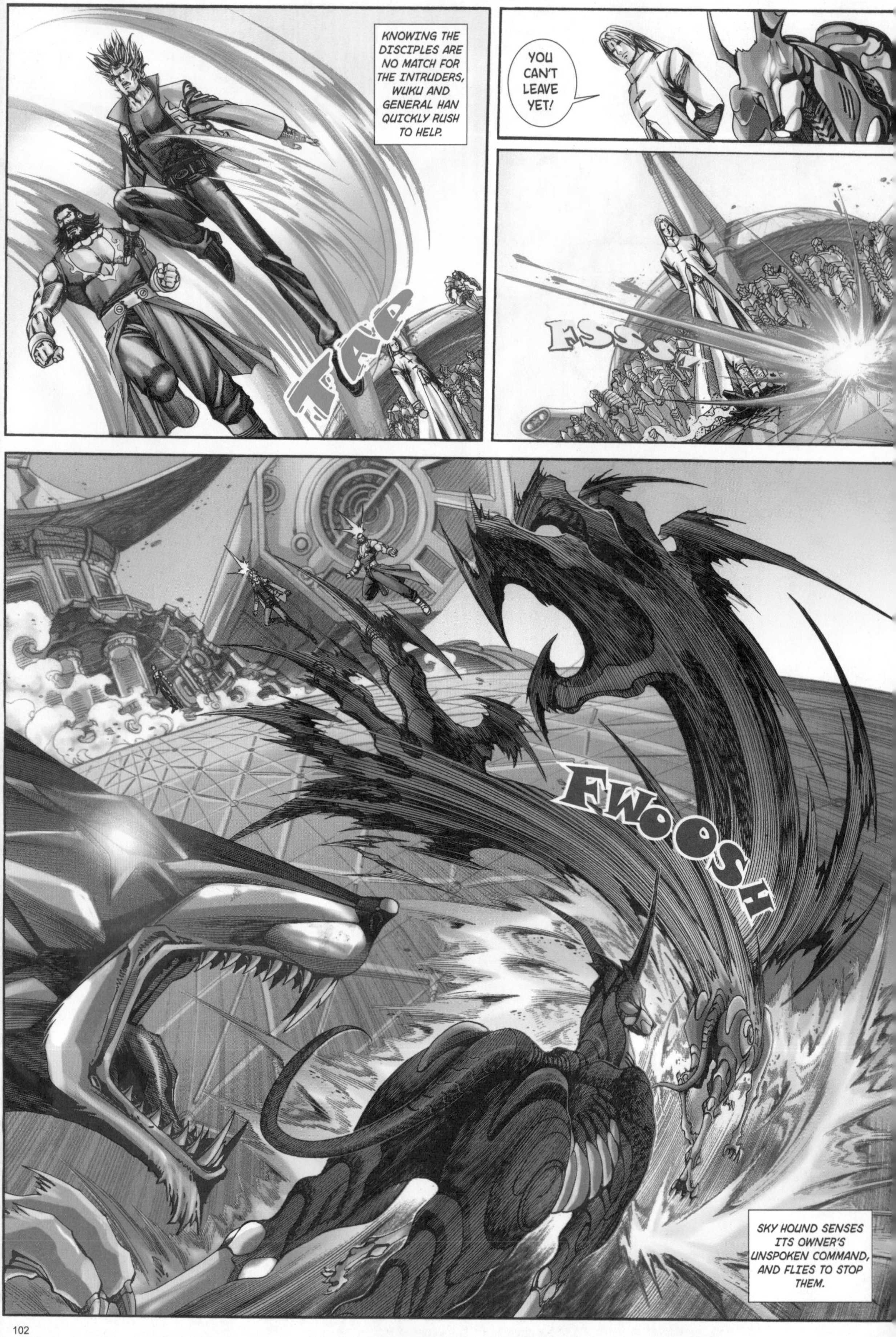
KNOWING THE DISCIPLES ARE NO MATCH FOR THE INTRUDERS, WUKU AND GENERAL HAN QUICKLY RUSH TO HELP.
TAP
YOU CAN'T LEAVE YET!
FSSSH
FWOOSH
SKY HOUND SENSES ITS OWNER'S UNSPOKEN COMMAND, AND FLIES TO STOP THEM.

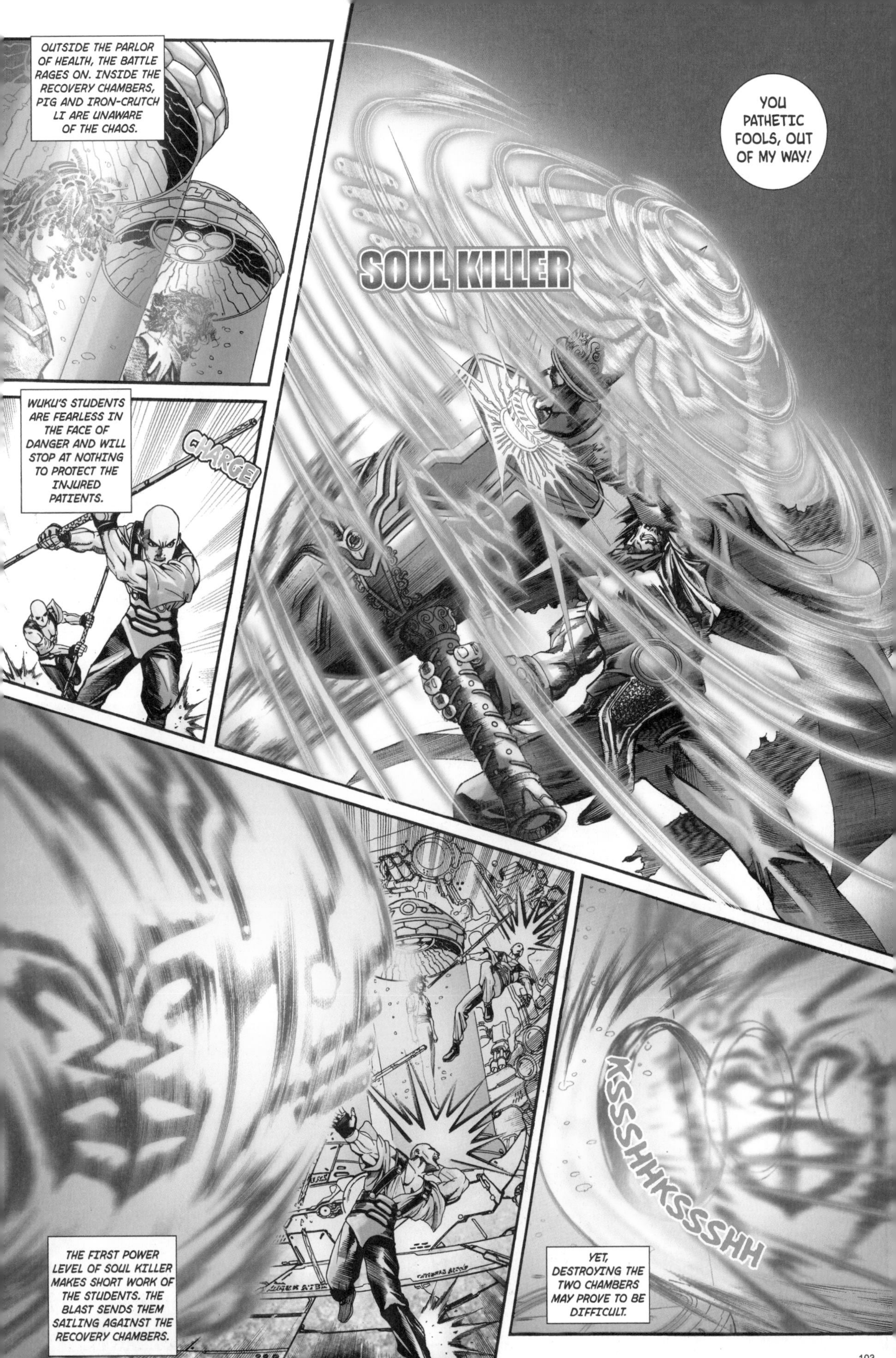

OUTSIDE THE PARLOR OF HEALTH, THE BATTLE RAGES ON. INSIDE THE RECOVERY CHAMBERS, PIG AND IRON-CRUTCH LI ARE UNAWARE OF THE CHAOS.
YOU PATHETIC FOOLS, OUT OF MY WAY!
SOUL KILLER
WUKU'S STUDENTS ARE FEARLESS IN THE FACE OF DANGER AND WILL STOP AT NOTHING TO PROTECT THE INJURED PATIENTS.
CHARGE!
THE FIRST POWER LEVEL OF SOUL KILLER MAKES SHORT WORK OF THE STUDENTS. THE BLAST SENDS THEM SAILING AGAINST THE RECOVERY CHAMBERS.
KSSSHHKSSSSHH
YET, DESTROYING THE TWO CHAMBERS MAY PROVE TO BE DIFFICULT.

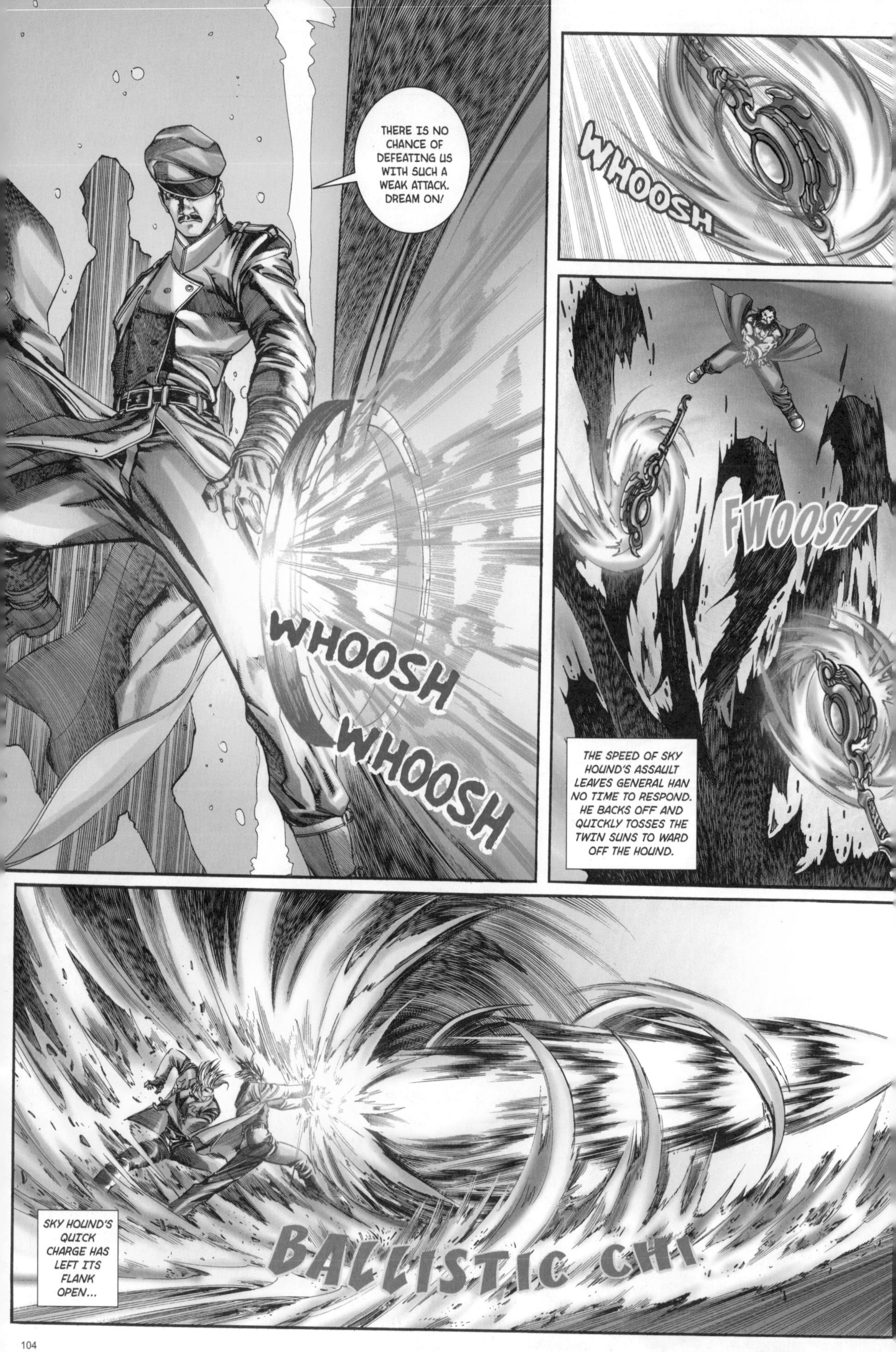
THERE IS NO CHANCE OF DEFEATING US WITH SUCH A WEAK ATTACK. DREAM ON!
WHOOSH
WHOOSH
WHOOSH
FWOOSH
THE SPEED OF SKY HOUND'S ASSAULT LEAVES GENERAL HAN NO TIME TO RESPOND. HE BACKS OFF AND QUICKLY TOSSES THE TWIN SUNS TO WARD OFF THE HOUND.
SKY HOUND'S QUICK CHARGE HAS LEFT ITS FLANK OPEN...
BALLISTIC CHI

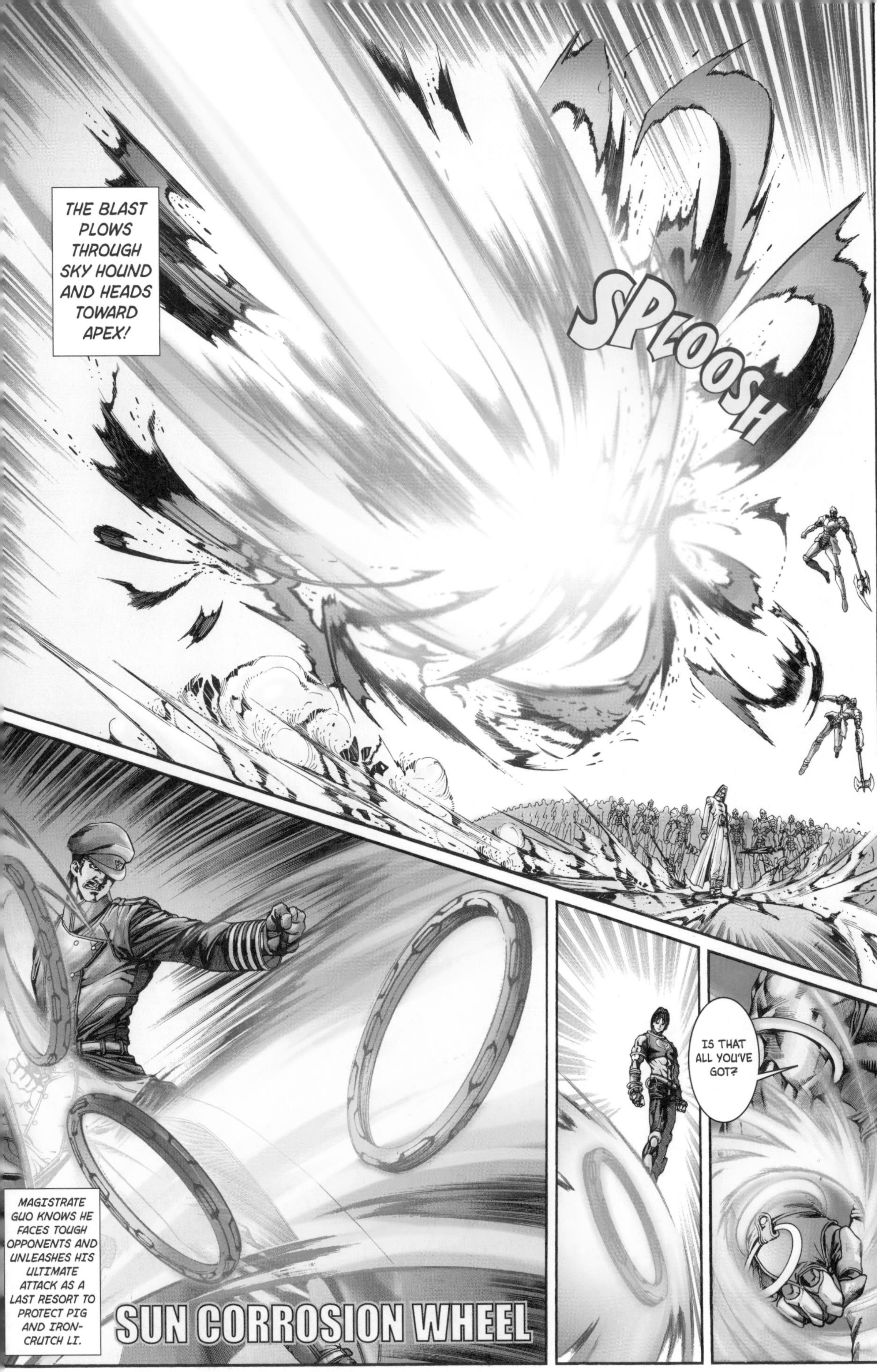

THE BLAST PLOWS THROUGH SKY HOUND AND HEADS TOWARD APEX!
SPLOOSH
MAGISTRATE GUO KNOWS HE FACES TOUGH OPPONENTS AND UNLEASHES HIS ULTIMATE ATTACK AS A LAST RESORT TO PROTECT PIG AND IRON-CRUTCH LI.
SUN CORROSION WHEEL
IS THAT ALL YOU'VE GOT?

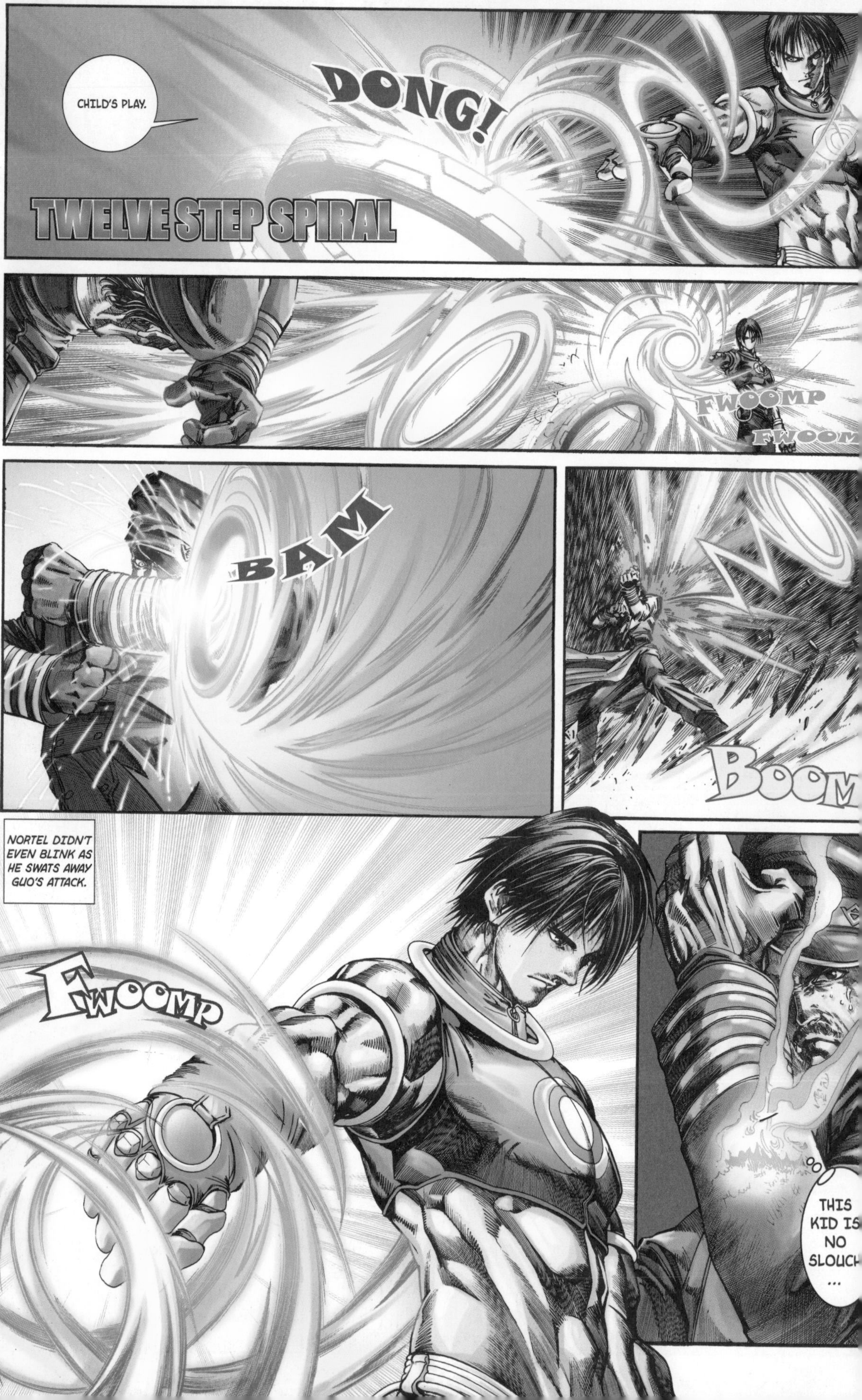
CHILD'S PLAY.
DONG!
TWELVE STEP SPIRAL
FWOOMP
FWOOM
BAM
BOOM
NORTEL DIDN'T EVEN BLINK AS HE SWATS AWAY GUO'S ATTACK.
FWOOMP
THIS KID IS NO SLOUCH ...

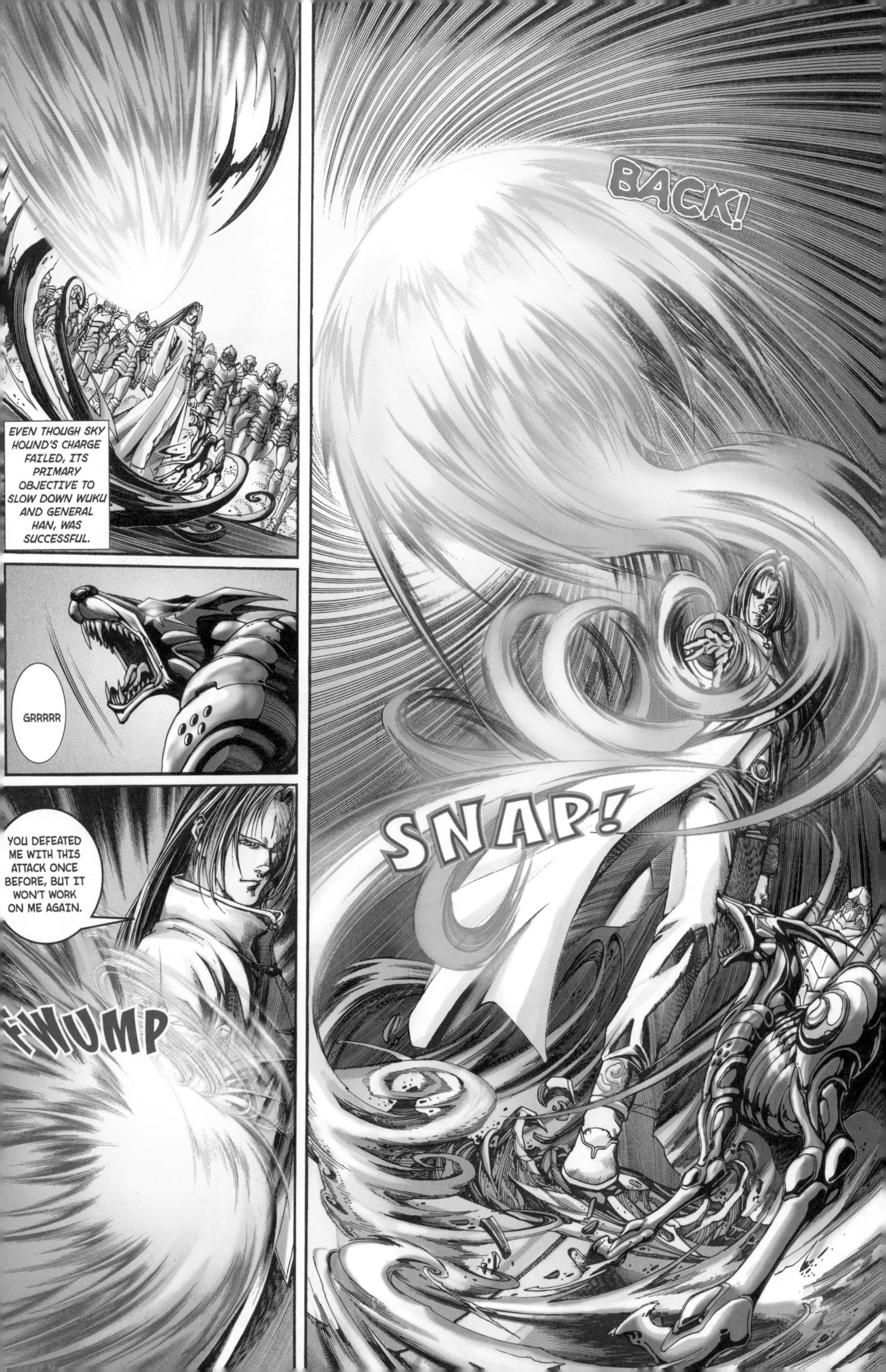
EVEN THOUGH SKY HOUND'S CHARGE FAILED, ITS PRIMARY OBJECTIVE TO SLOW DOWN WUKU AND GENERAL HAN, WAS SUCCESSFUL.
GRRRRR
YOU DEFEATED ME WITH THIS ATTACK ONCE BEFORE, BUT IT WON'T WORK ON ME AGAIN.
WUMP
BACK!
SNAP!

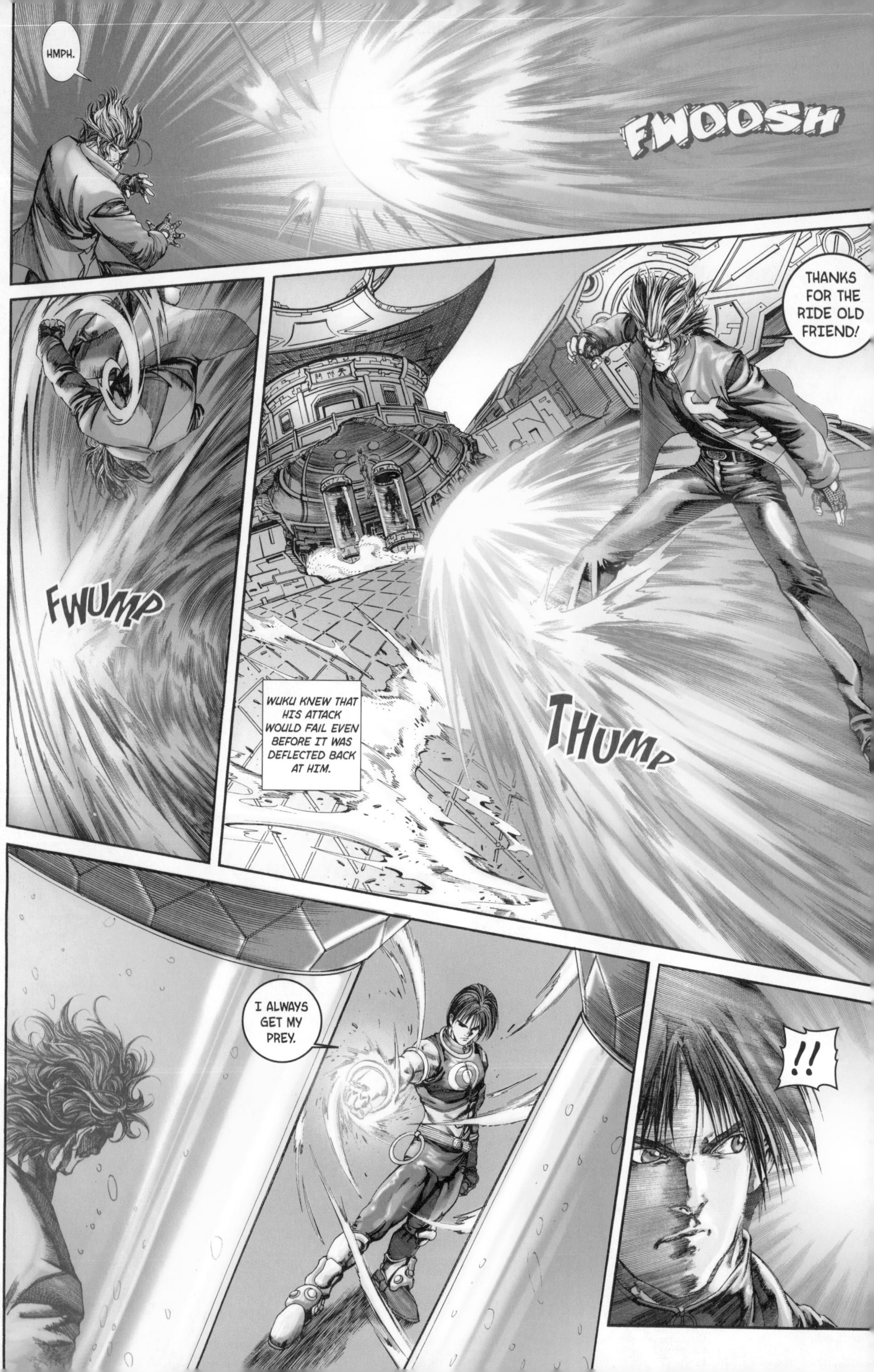
HMPH.
FWOOSH
FWUMP
THANKS FOR THE RIDE OLD FRIEND!
WUKU KNEW THAT HIS ATTACK WOULD FAIL EVEN BEFORE IT WAS DEFLECTED BACK AT HIM.
THUMP
I ALWAYS GET MY PREY.
!!

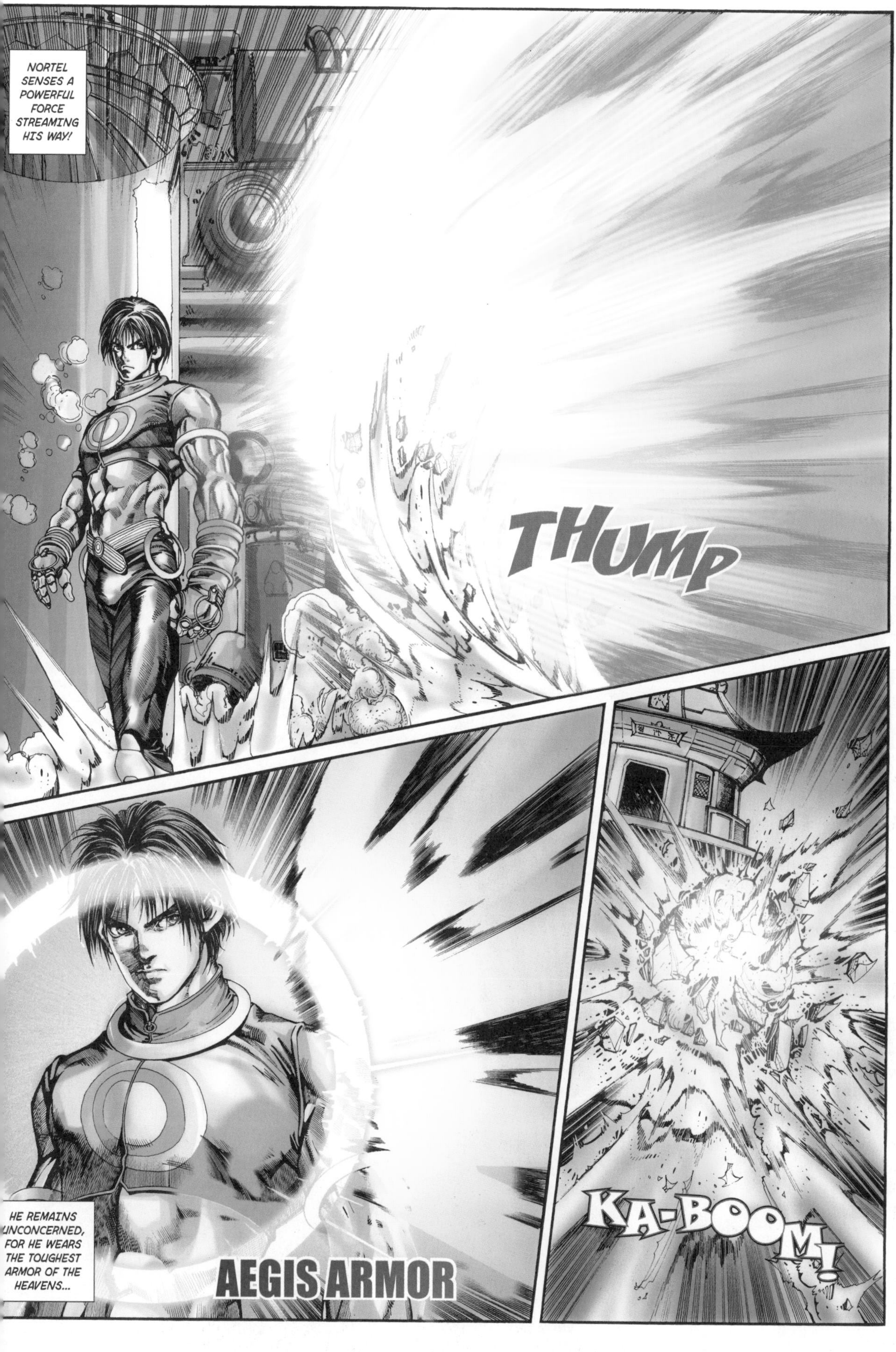
NORTEL SENSES A POWERFUL FORCE STREAMING HIS WAY!
THUMP
HE REMAINS UNCONCERNED, FOR HE WEARS THE TOUGHEST ARMOR OF THE HEAVENS...
AEGIS ARMOR
KA-BOOM!

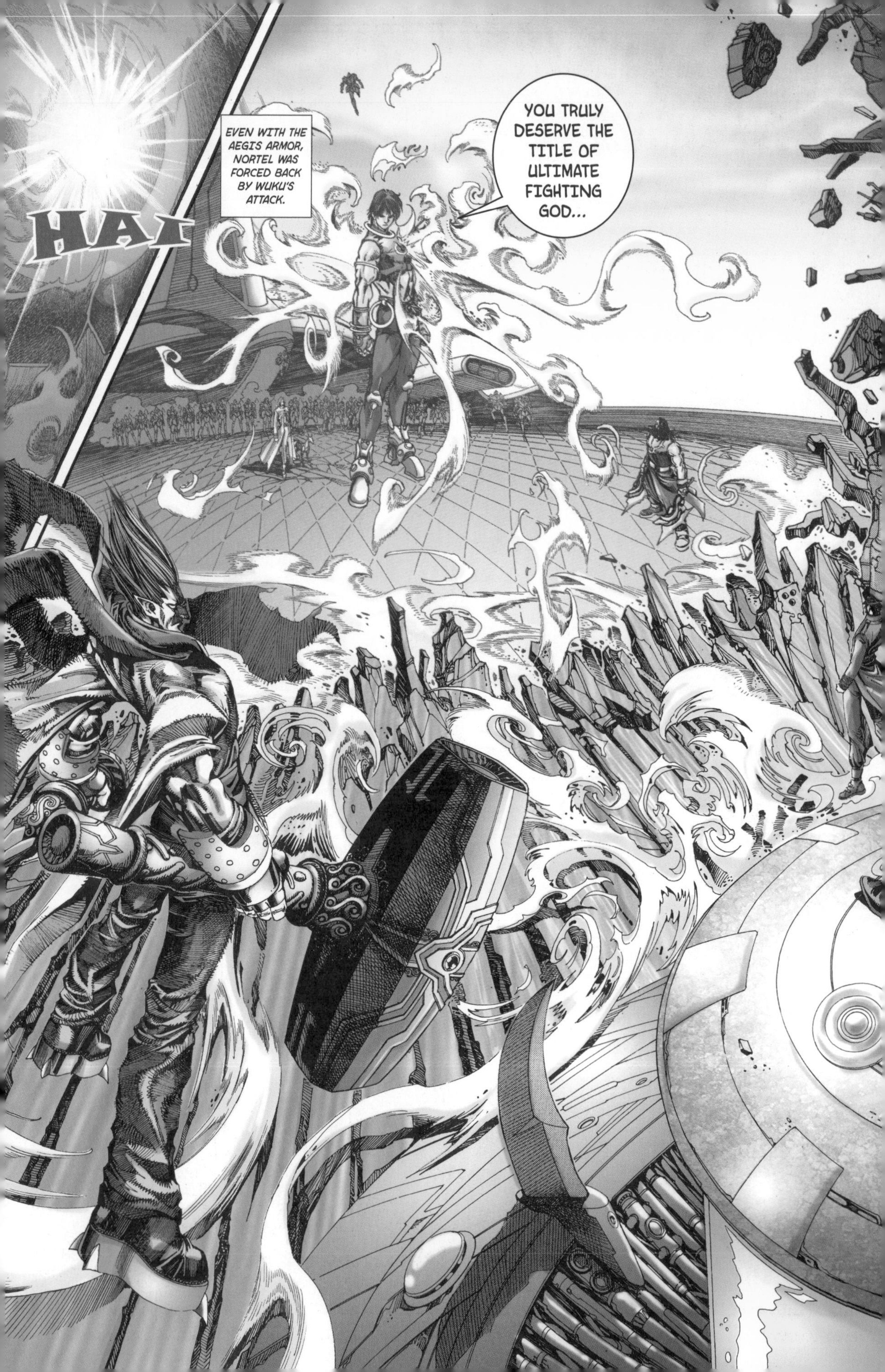
HAI
EVEN WITH THE AEGIS ARMOR, NORTEL WAS FORCED BACK BY WUKU'S ATTACK.
YOU TRULY DESERVE THE TITLE OF ULTIMATE FIGHTING GOD...

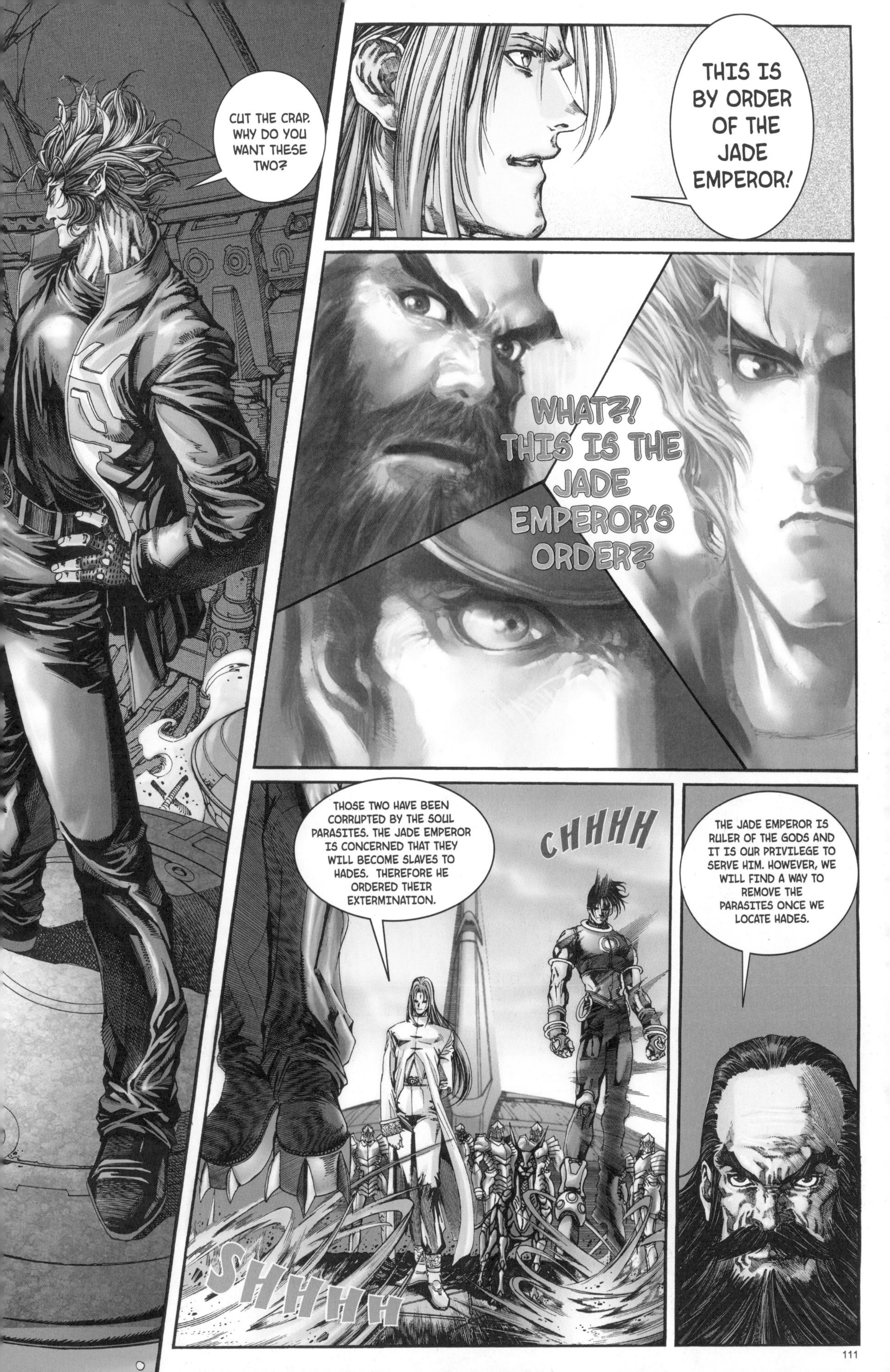
CUT THE CRAP. WHY DO YOU WANT THESE TWO?
THIS IS BY ORDER OF THE JADE EMPEROR!
WHAT?! THIS IS THE JADE EMPEROR'S ORDER?
THOSE TWO HAVE BEEN CORRUPTED BY THE SOUL PARASITES. THE JADE EMPEROR IS CONCERNED THAT THEY WILL BECOME SLAVES TO HADES. THEREFORE HE ORDERED THEIR EXTERMINATION.
CHHHH
SHHHH
THE JADE EMPEROR IS RULER OF THE GODS AND IT IS OUR PRIVILEGE TO SERVE HIM. HOWEVER, WE WILL FIND A WAY TO REMOVE THE PARASITES ONCE WE LOCATE HADES.

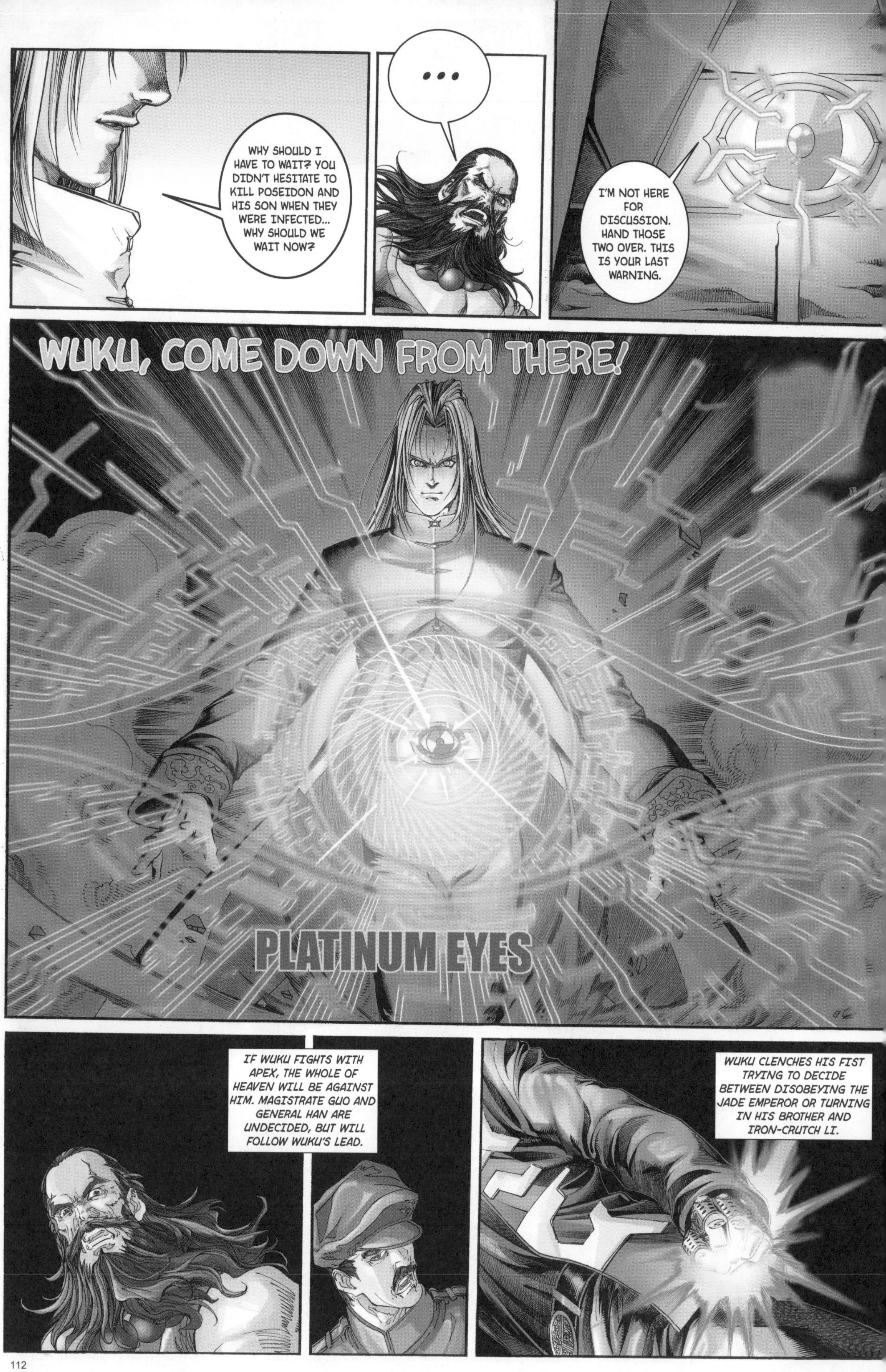
WHY SHOULD I HAVE TO WAIT? YOU DIDN'T HESITATE TO KILL POSEIDON AND HIS SON WHEN THEY WERE INFECTED... WHY SHOULD WE WAIT NOW?
...
I'M NOT HERE FOR DISCUSSION. HAND THOSE TWO OVER. THIS IS YOUR LAST WARNING.
WUKU, COME DOWN FROM THERE!
PLATINUM EYES
IF WUKU FIGHTS WITH APEX, THE WHOLE OF HEAVEN WILL BE AGAINST HIM. MAGISTRATE GUO AND GENERAL HAN ARE UNDECIDED, BUT WILL FOLLOW WUKU'S LEAD.
WUKU CLENCHES HIS FIST TRYING TO DECIDE BETWEEN DISOBEYING THE JADE EMPEROR OR TURNING IN HIS BROTHER AND IRON-CRUTCH LI.

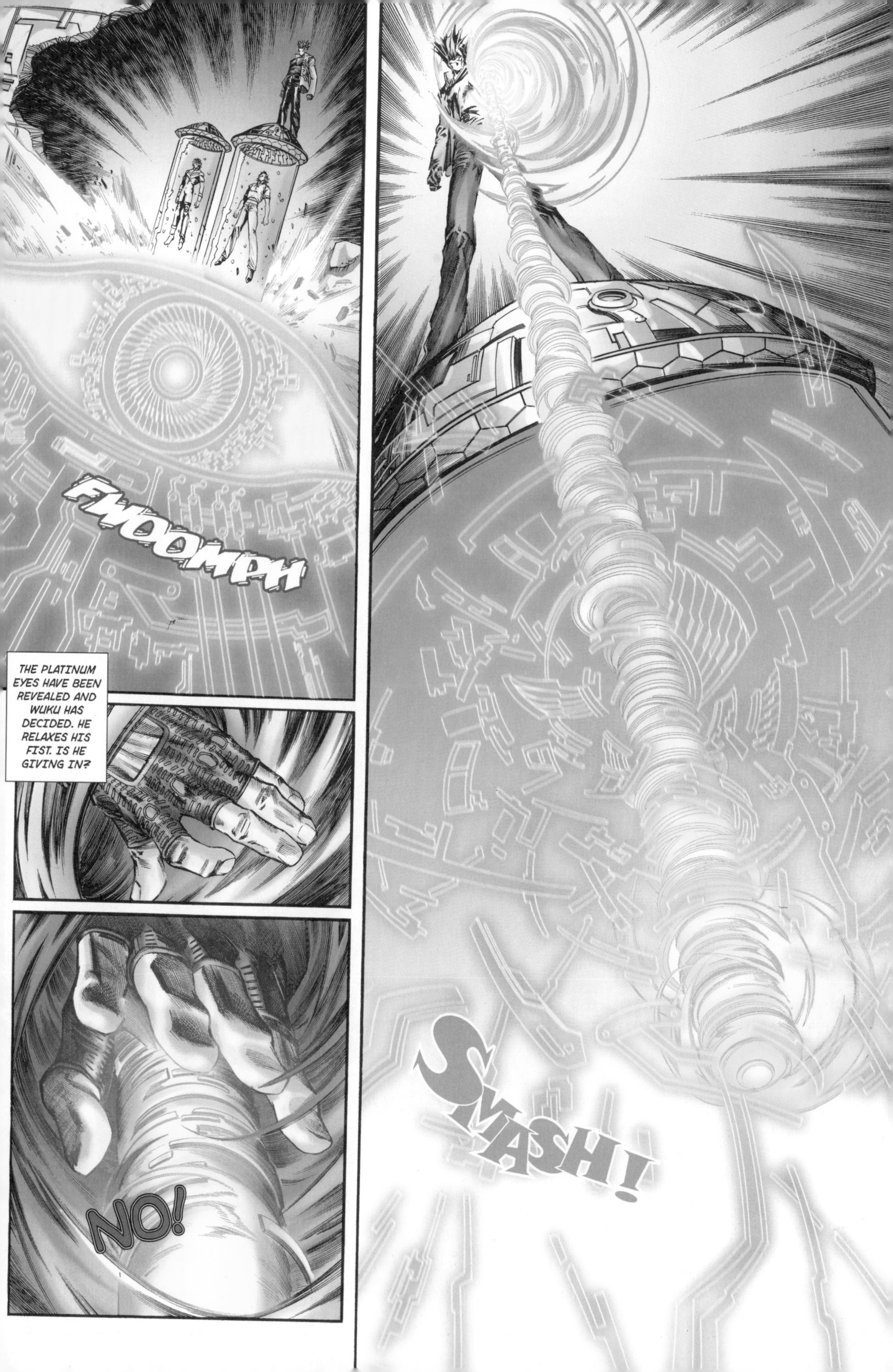
FWOOMPH
THE PLATINUM EYES HAVE BEEN REVEALED AND WUKU HAS DECIDED. HE RELAXES HIS FIST. IS HE GIVING IN?
NO!
SMASH!

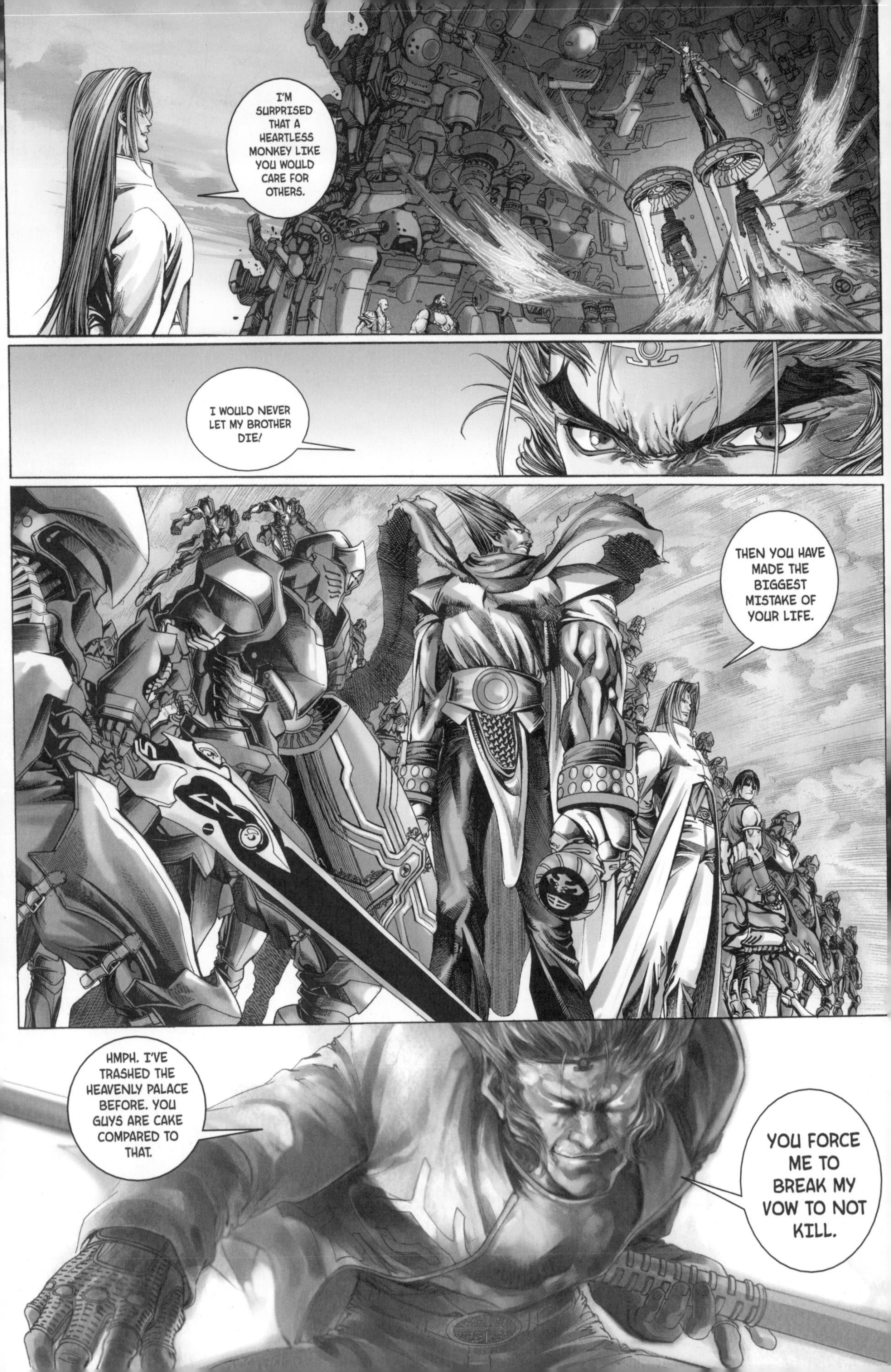
I'M SURPRISED THAT A HEARTLESS MONKEY LIKE YOU WOULD CARE FOR OTHERS.
I WOULD NEVER LET MY BROTHER DIE!
THEN YOU HAVE MADE THE BIGGEST MISTAKE OF YOUR LIFE.
HMPH. I'VE TRASHED THE HEAVENLY PALACE BEFORE. YOU GUYS ARE CAKE COMPARED TO THAT.
YOU FORCE ME TO BREAK MY VOW TO NOT KILL.

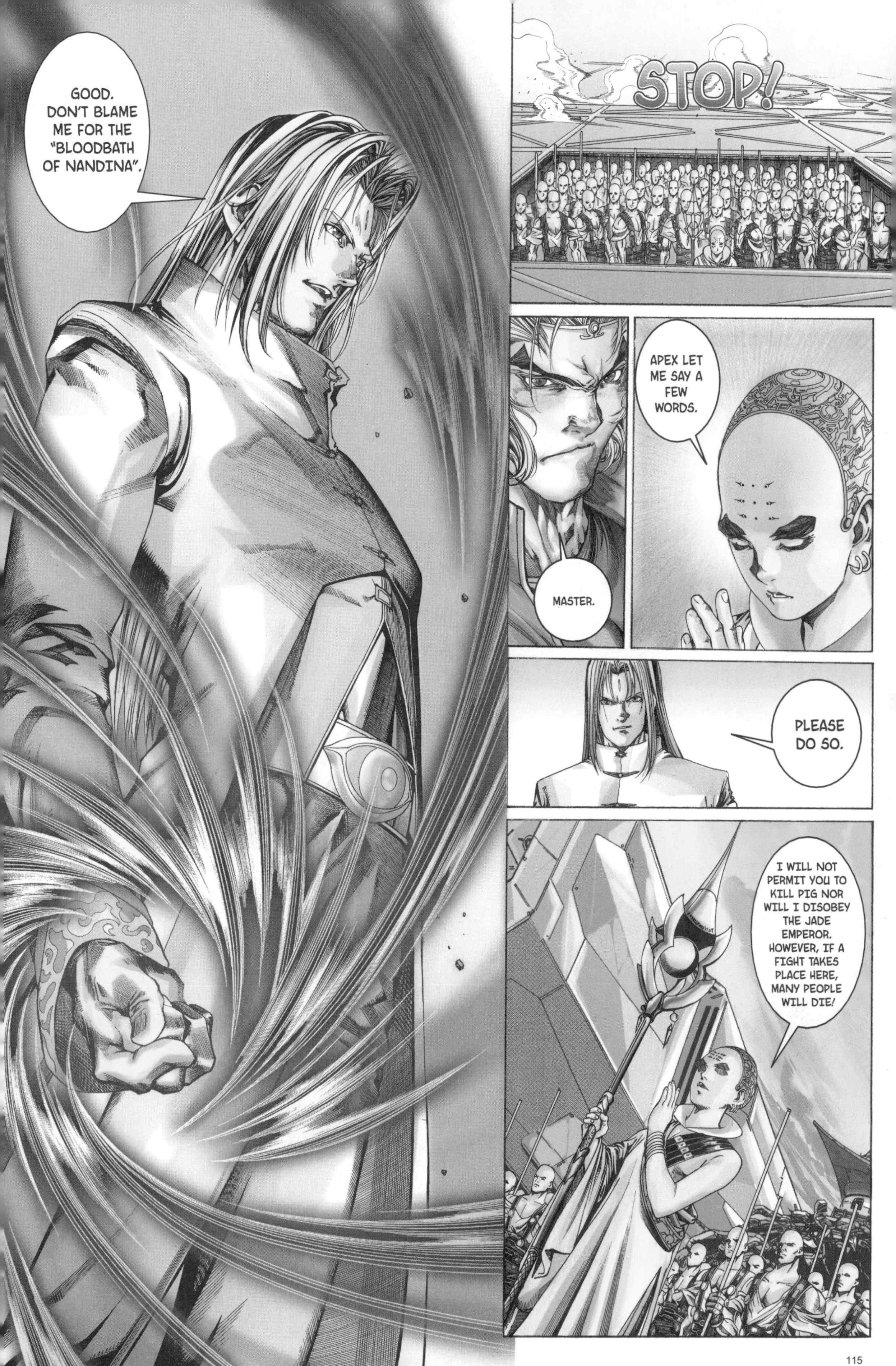
GOOD. DON'T BLAME ME FOR THE "BLOODBATH OF NANDINA".
STOP!
MASTER.
APEX LET ME SAY A FEW WORDS.
PLEASE DO SO.
I WILL NOT PERMIT YOU TO KILL PIG NOR WILL I DISOBEY THE JADE EMPEROR. HOWEVER, IF A FIGHT TAKES PLACE HERE, MANY PEOPLE WILL DIE!

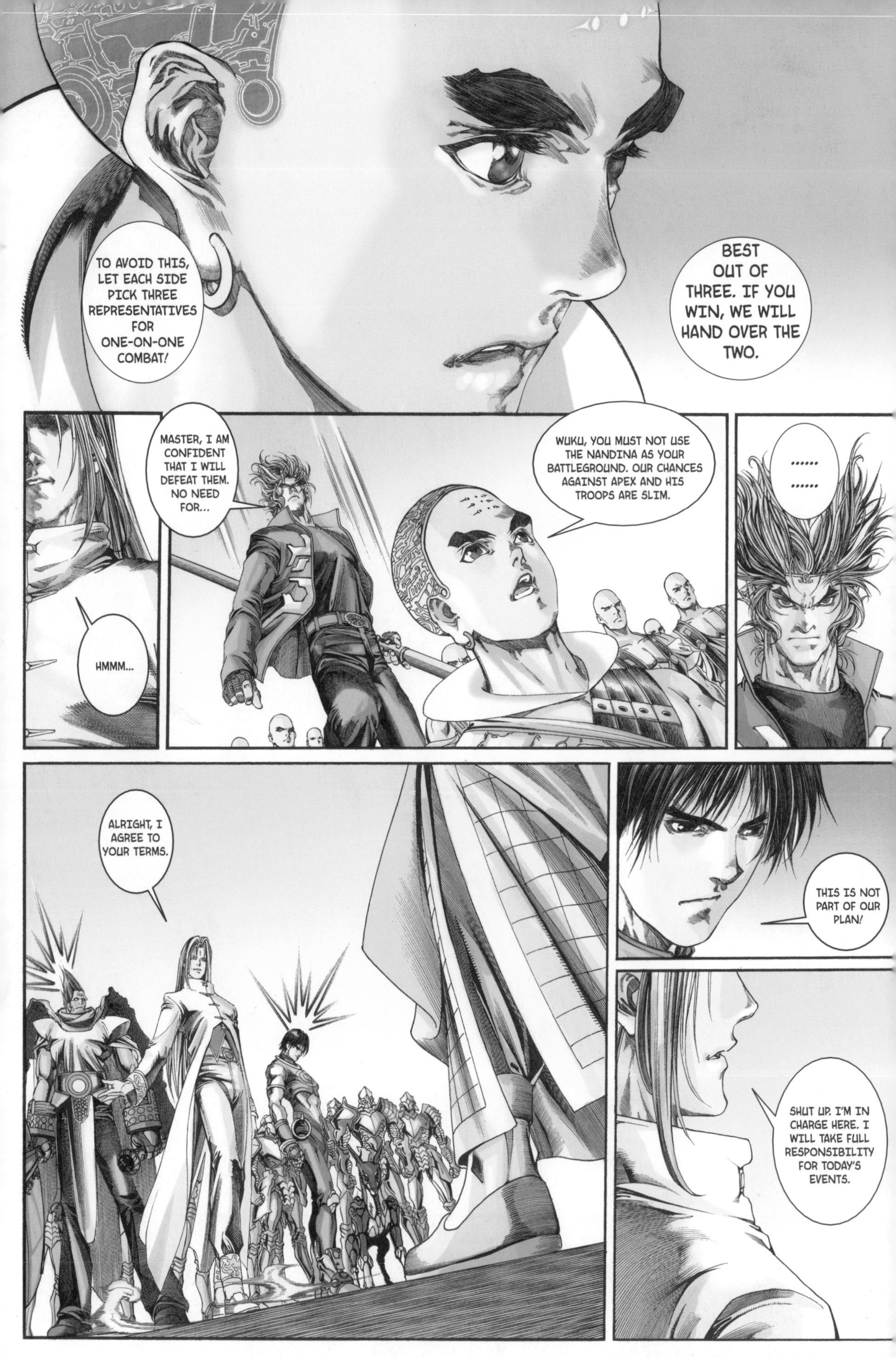

TO AVOID THIS, LET EACH SIDE PICK THREE REPRESENTATIVES FOR ONE-ON-ONE COMBAT!
BEST OUT OF THREE. IF YOU WIN, WE WILL HAND OVER THE TWO.
HMMM...
MASTER, I AM CONFIDENT THAT I WILL DEFEAT THEM. NO NEED FOR...
WUKU, YOU MUST NOT USE THE NANDINA AS YOUR BATTLEGROUND. OUR CHANCES AGAINST APEX AND HIS TROOPS ARE SLIM.
....
ALRIGHT, I AGREE TO YOUR TERMS.
THIS IS NOT PART OF OUR PLAN!
SHUT UP. I'M IN CHARGE HERE. I WILL TAKE FULL RESPONSIBILITY FOR TODAY'S EVENTS.

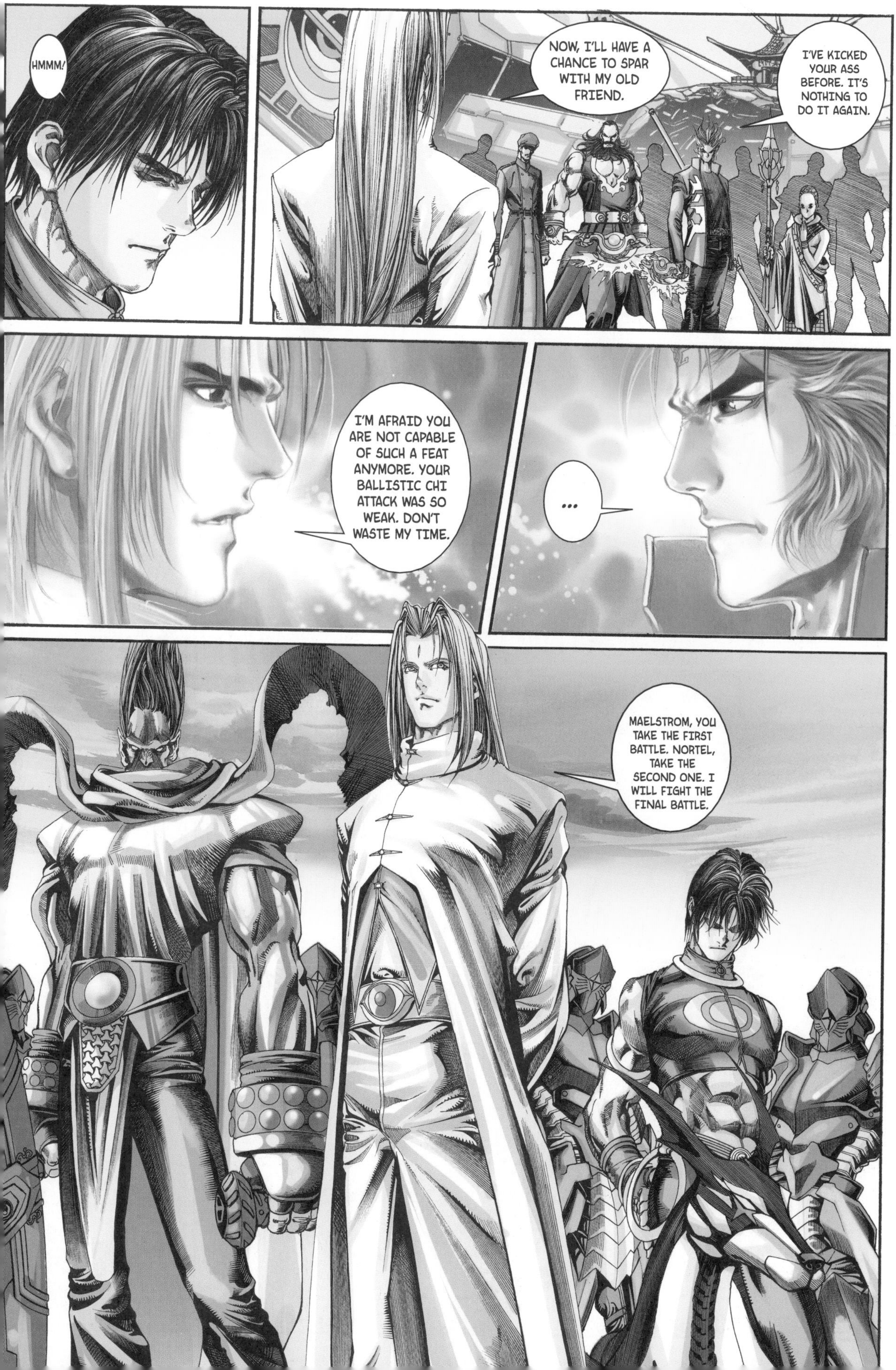
HMMM!
NOW, I'LL HAVE A CHANCE TO SPAR WITH MY OLD FRIEND.
I'VE KICKED YOUR ASS BEFORE. IT'S NOTHING TO DO IT AGAIN.
I'M AFRAID YOU ARE NOT CAPABLE OF SUCH A FEAT ANYMORE. YOUR BALLISTIC CHI ATTACK WAS SO WEAK. DON'T WASTE MY TIME.
...
MAELSTROM, YOU TAKE THE FIRST BATTLE. NORTEL, TAKE THE SECOND ONE. I WILL FIGHT THE FINAL BATTLE.

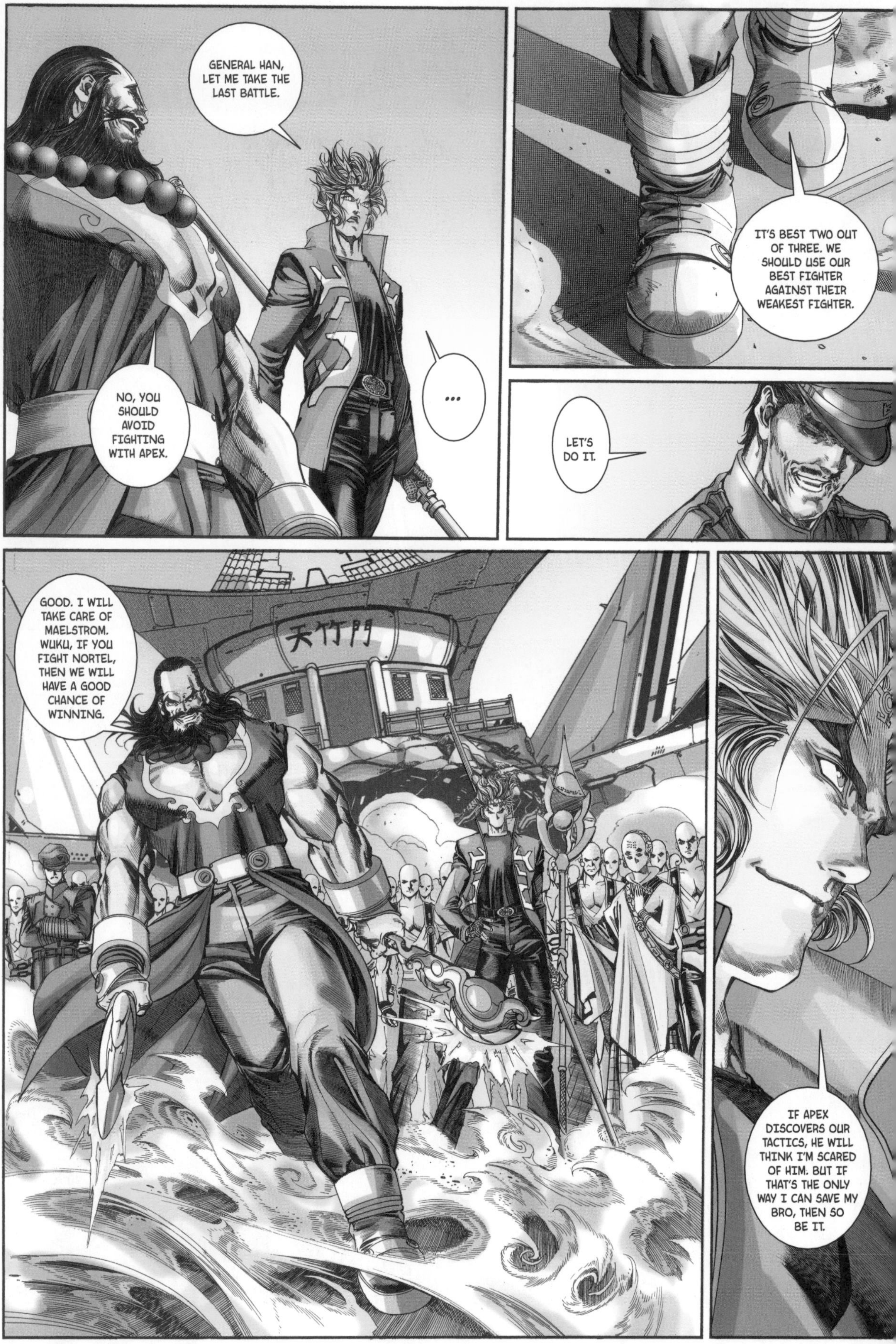
GENERAL HAN, LET ME TAKE THE LAST BATTLE.
NO, YOU SHOULD AVOID FIGHTING WITH APEX.
...
IT'S BEST TWO OUT OF THREE. WE SHOULD USE OUR BEST FIGHTER AGAINST THEIR WEAKEST FIGHTER.
LET'S DO IT.
GOOD. I WILL TAKE CARE OF MAELSTROM. WUKU, IF YOU FIGHT NORTEL, THEN WE WILL HAVE A GOOD CHANCE OF WINNING.
天竹門
IF APEX DISCOVERS OUR TACTICS, HE WILL THINK I'M SCARED OF HIM. BUT IF THAT'S THE ONLY WAY I CAN SAVE MY BRO, THEN SO BE IT.

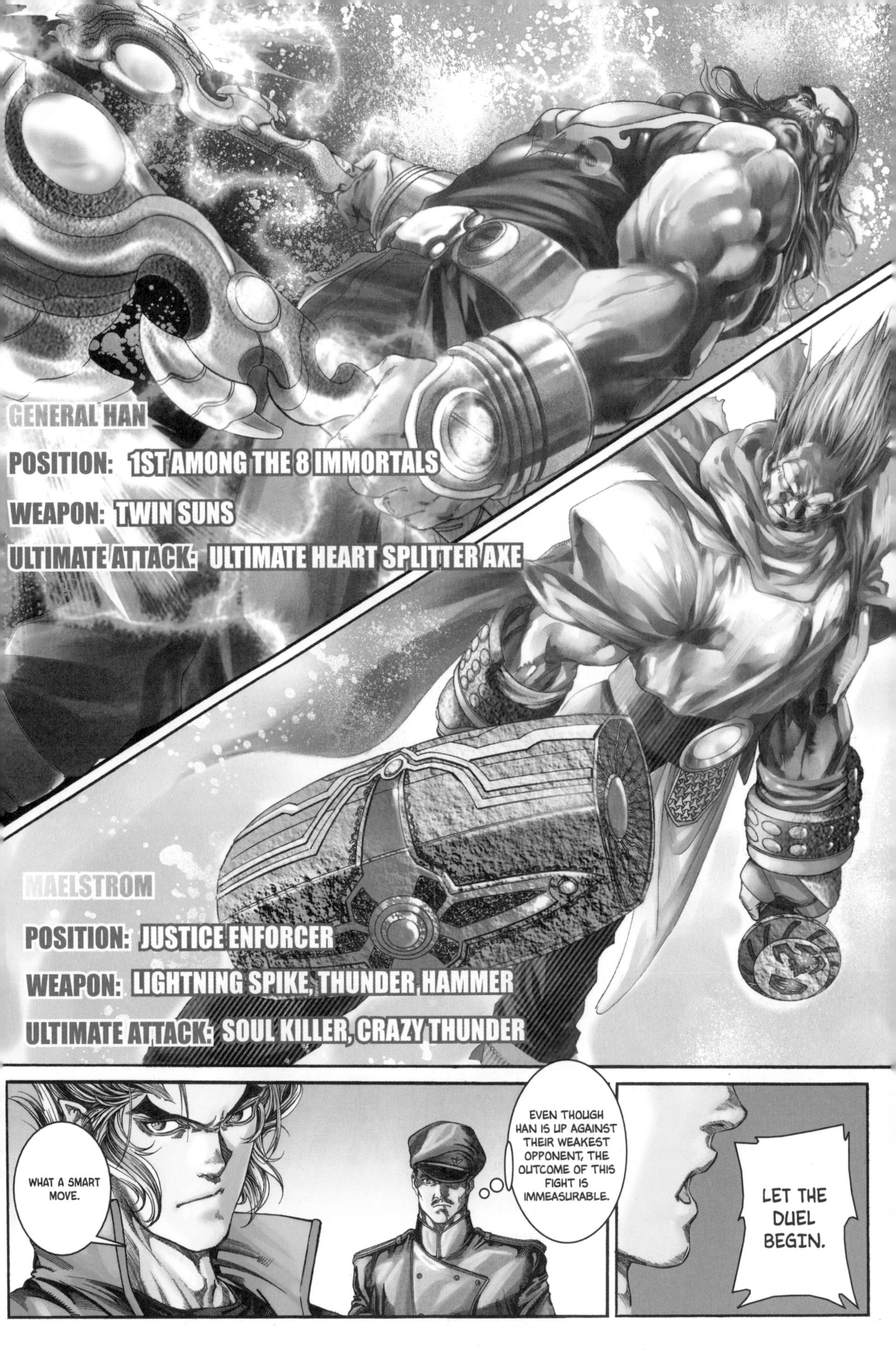
GENERAL HAN
POSITION: 1ST AMONG THE 8 IMMORTALS
WEAPON: TWIN SUNS
ULTIMATE ATTACK: ULTIMATE HEART SPLITTER AXE
MAELSTROM
POSITION: JUSTICE ENFORCER
WEAPON: LIGHTNING SPIKE, THUNDER HAMMER
ULTIMATE ATTACK: SOUL KILLER, CRAZY THUNDER
WHAT A SMART MOVE.
EVEN THOUGH HAN IS UP AGAINST THEIR WEAKEST OPPONENT, THE OUTCOME OF THIS FIGHT IS IMMEASURABLE.
LET THE DUEL BEGIN.

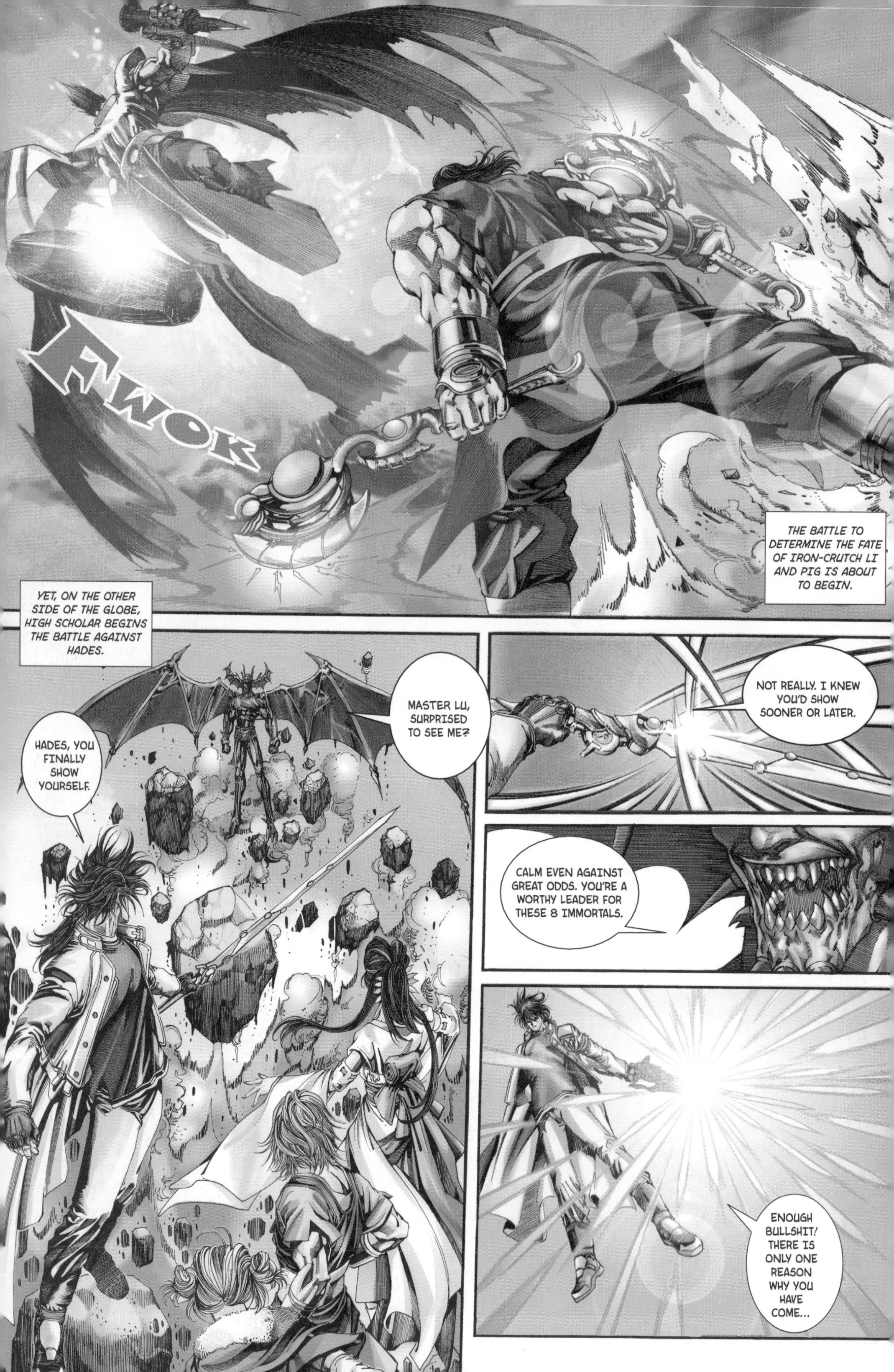
FWOK
THE BATTLE TO DETERMINE THE FATE OF IRON-CRUTCH LI AND PIG IS ABOUT TO BEGIN.
YET, ON THE OTHER SIDE OF THE GLOBE, HIGH SCHOLAR BEGINS THE BATTLE AGAINST HADES.
HADES, YOU FINALLY SHOW YOURSELF.
MASTER LU, SURPRISED TO SEE ME?
NOT REALLY. I KNEW YOU'D SHOW SOONER OR LATER.
CALM EVEN AGAINST GREAT ODDS. YOU'RE A WORTHY LEADER FOR THESE 8 IMMORTALS.
ENOUGH BULLSHIT! THERE IS ONLY ONE REASON WHY YOU HAVE COME...

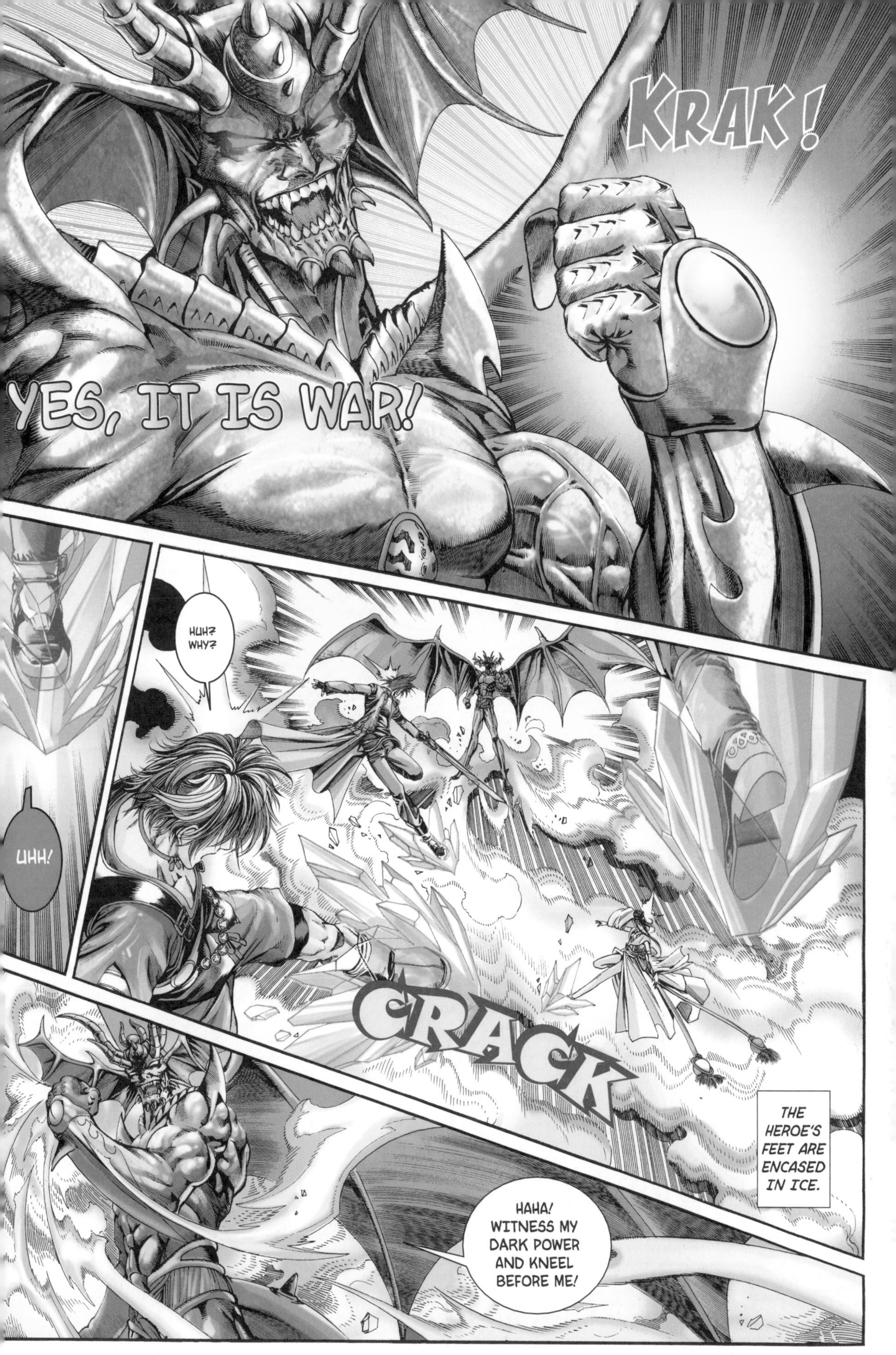

KRAK!
YES, IT IS WAR!
HUH? WHY?
UHH!
CRACK
THE HEROE'S FEET ARE ENCASED IN ICE.
HAHA! WITNESS MY DARK POWER AND KNEEL BEFORE ME!

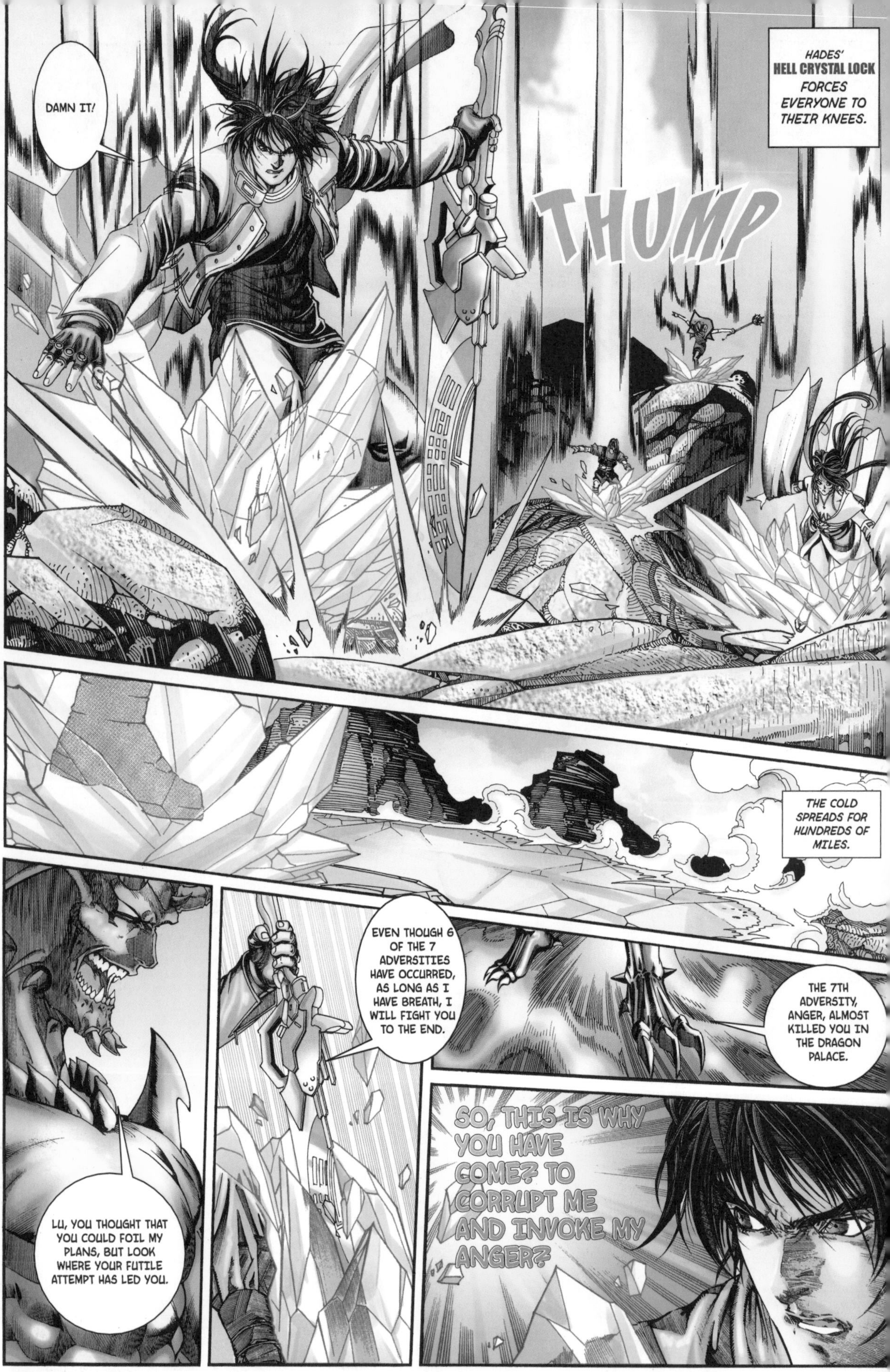
HADES' HELL CRYSTAL LOCK FORCES EVERYONE TO THEIR KNEES.
DAMN IT!
THUMP
THE COLD SPREADS FOR HUNDREDS OF MILES.
THE 7TH ADVERSITY, ANGER, ALMOST KILLED YOU IN THE DRAGON PALACE.
EVEN THOUGH 6 OF THE 7 ADVERSITIES HAVE OCCURRED, AS LONG AS I HAVE BREATH, I WILL FIGHT YOU TO THE END.
LU, YOU THOUGHT THAT YOU COULD FOIL MY PLANS, BUT LOOK WHERE YOUR FUTILE ATTEMPT HAS LED YOU.
SO, THIS IS WHY YOU HAVE COME? TO CORRUPT ME AND INVOKE MY ANGER?

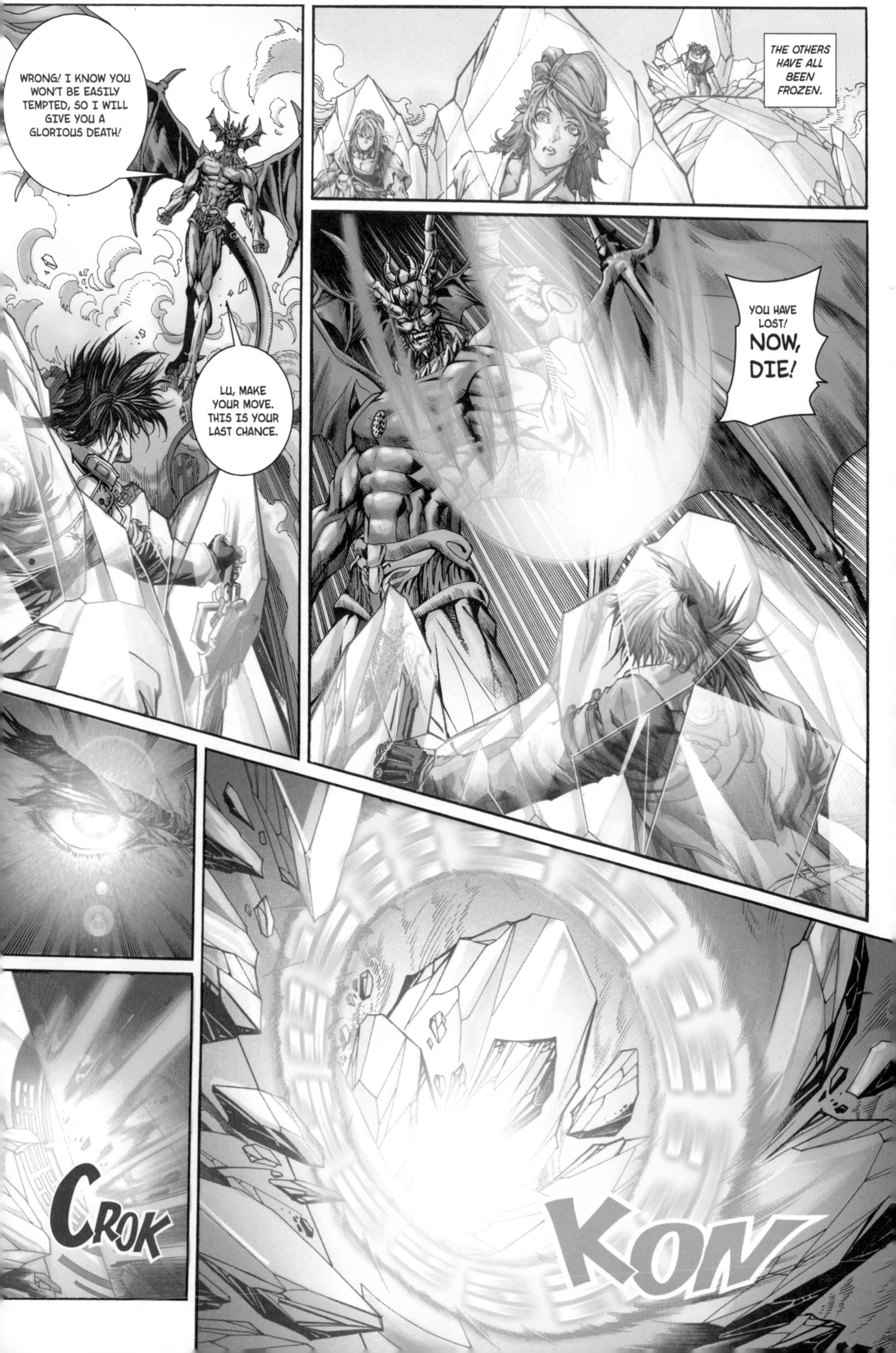
WRONG! I KNOW YOU WON'T BE EASILY TEMPTED, SO I WILL GIVE YOU A GLORIOUS DEATH!
THE OTHERS HAVE ALL BEEN FROZEN.
LU, MAKE YOUR MOVE. THIS IS YOUR LAST CHANCE.
YOU HAVE LOST! NOW, DIE!
CROK
KON

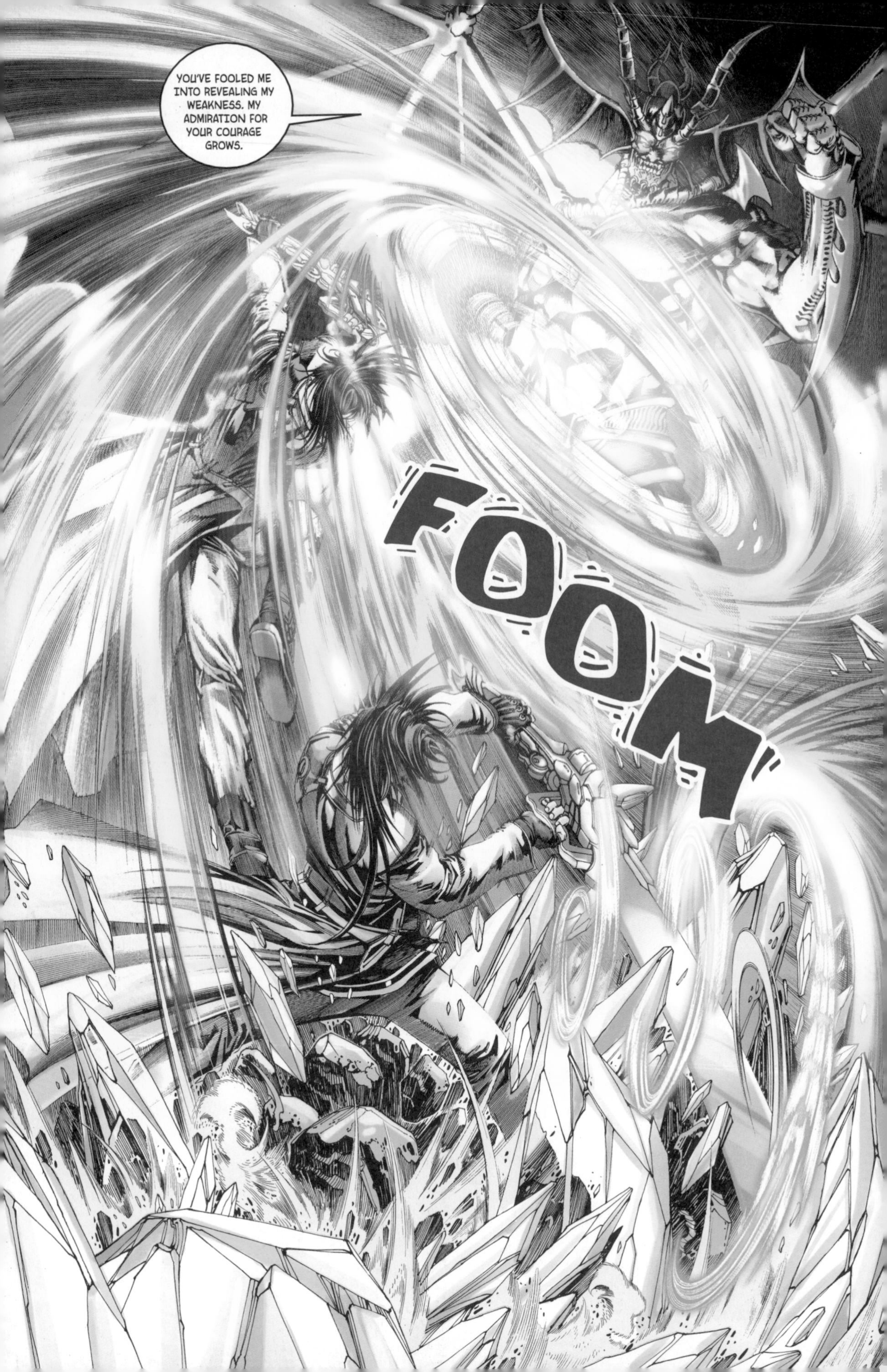
YOU'VE FOOLED ME INTO REVEALING MY WEAKNESS. MY ADMIRATION FOR YOUR COURAGE GROWS.
FOOM

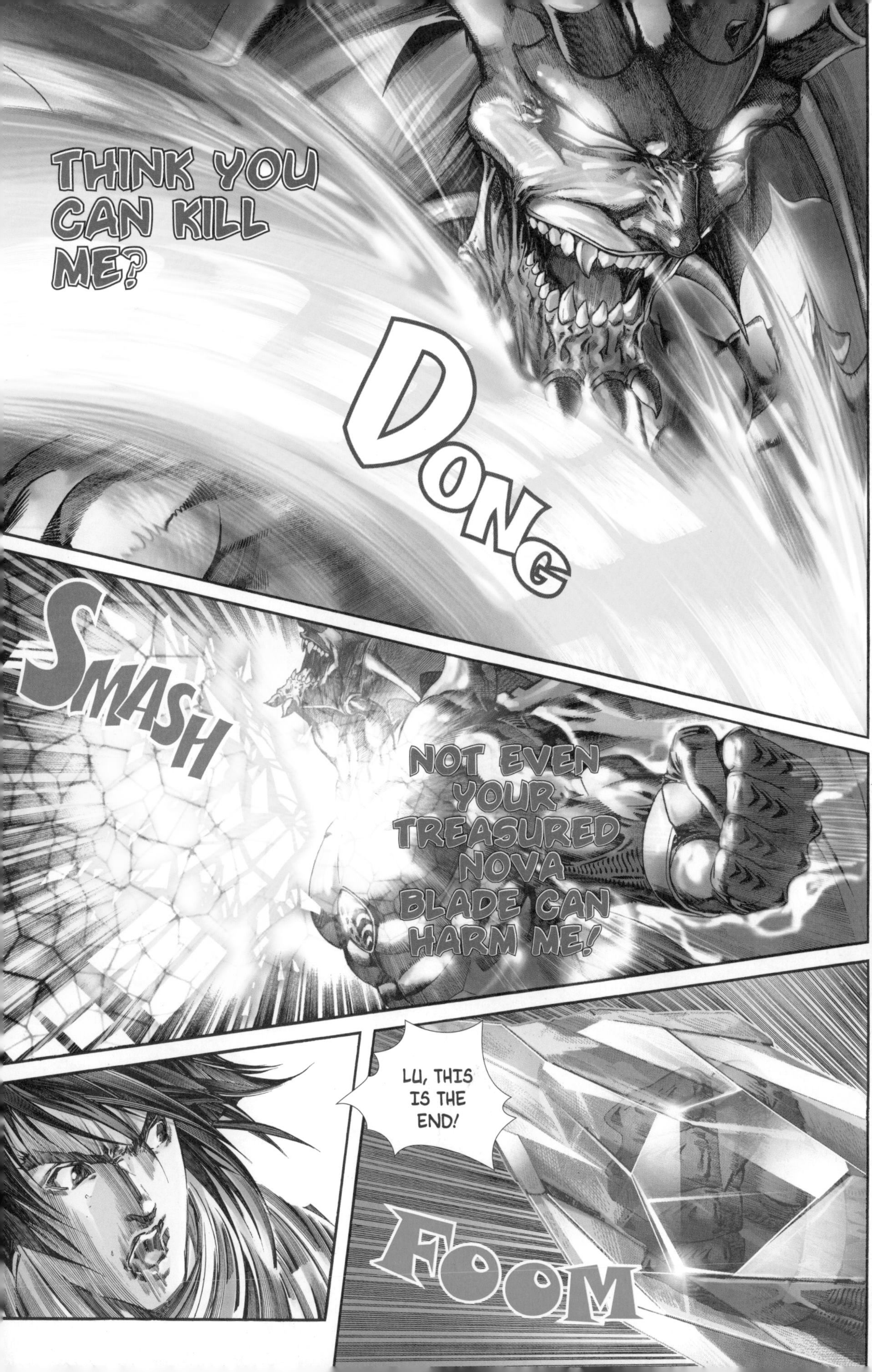
THINK YOU CAN KILL ME?
DONG
SMASH
NOT EVEN YOUR TREASURED NOVA BLADE CAN HARM ME!
LU, THIS IS THE END!
FOOM

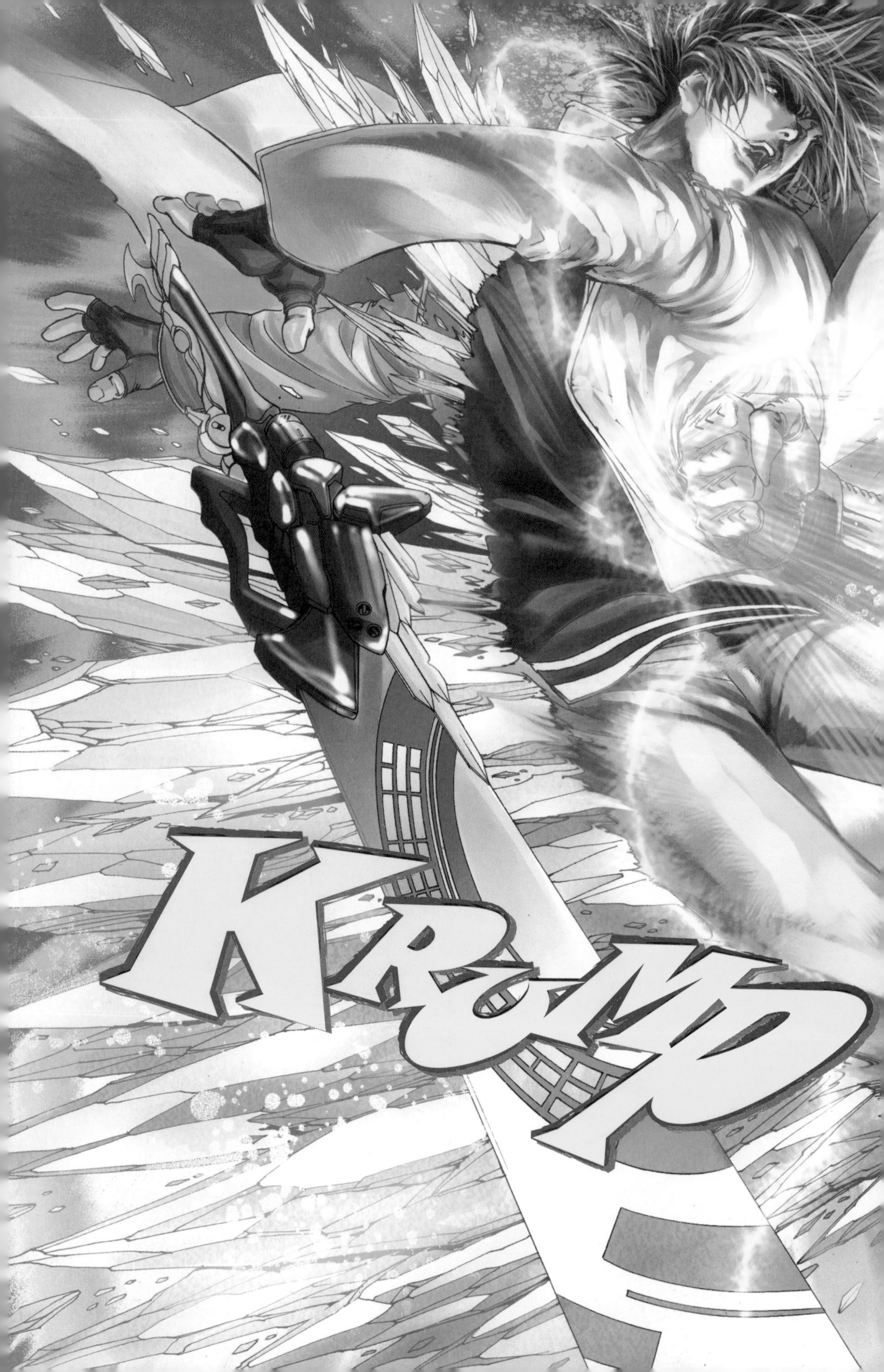
KRUMP

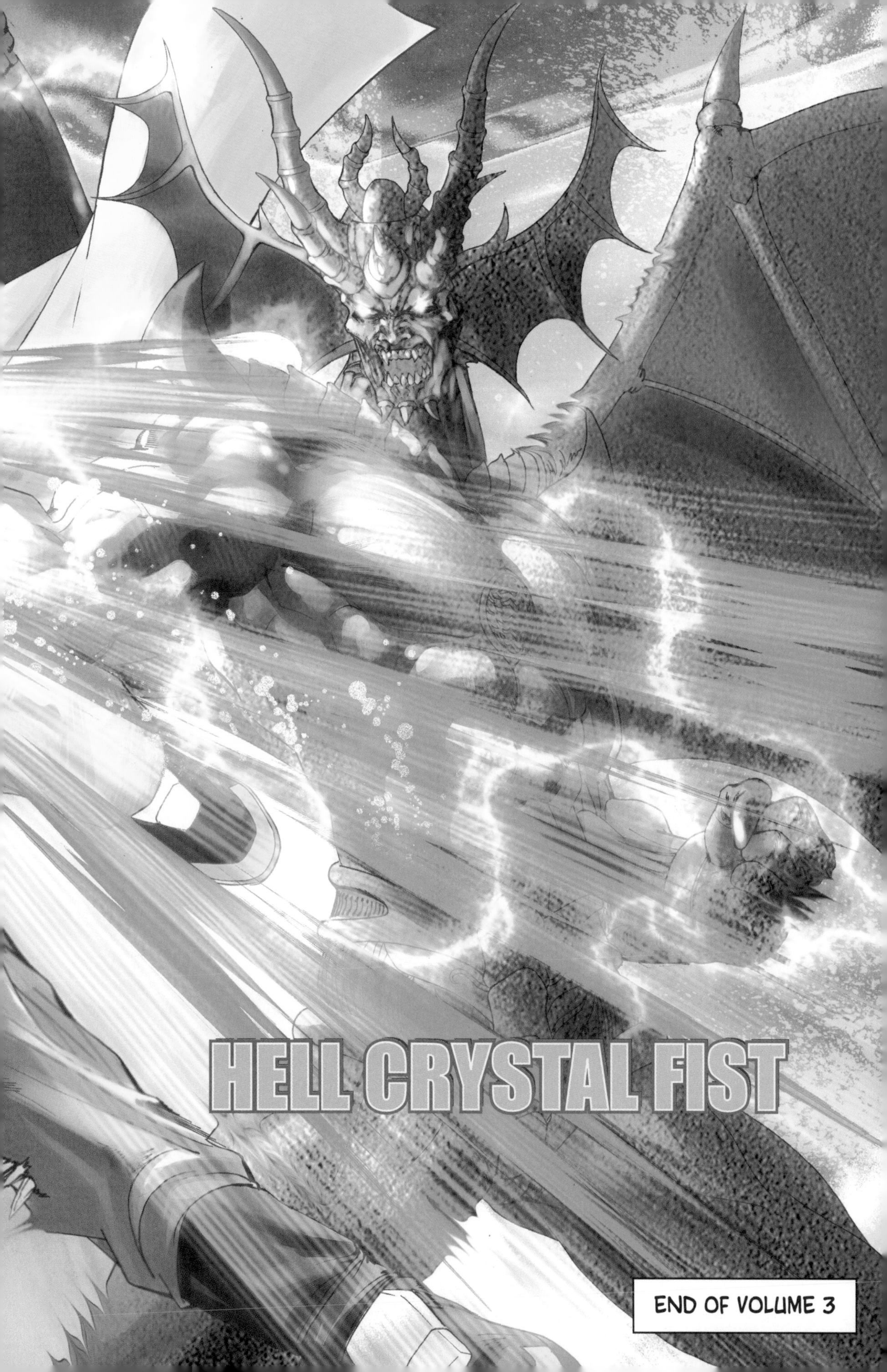
HELL CRYSTAL FIST
END OF VOLUME 3

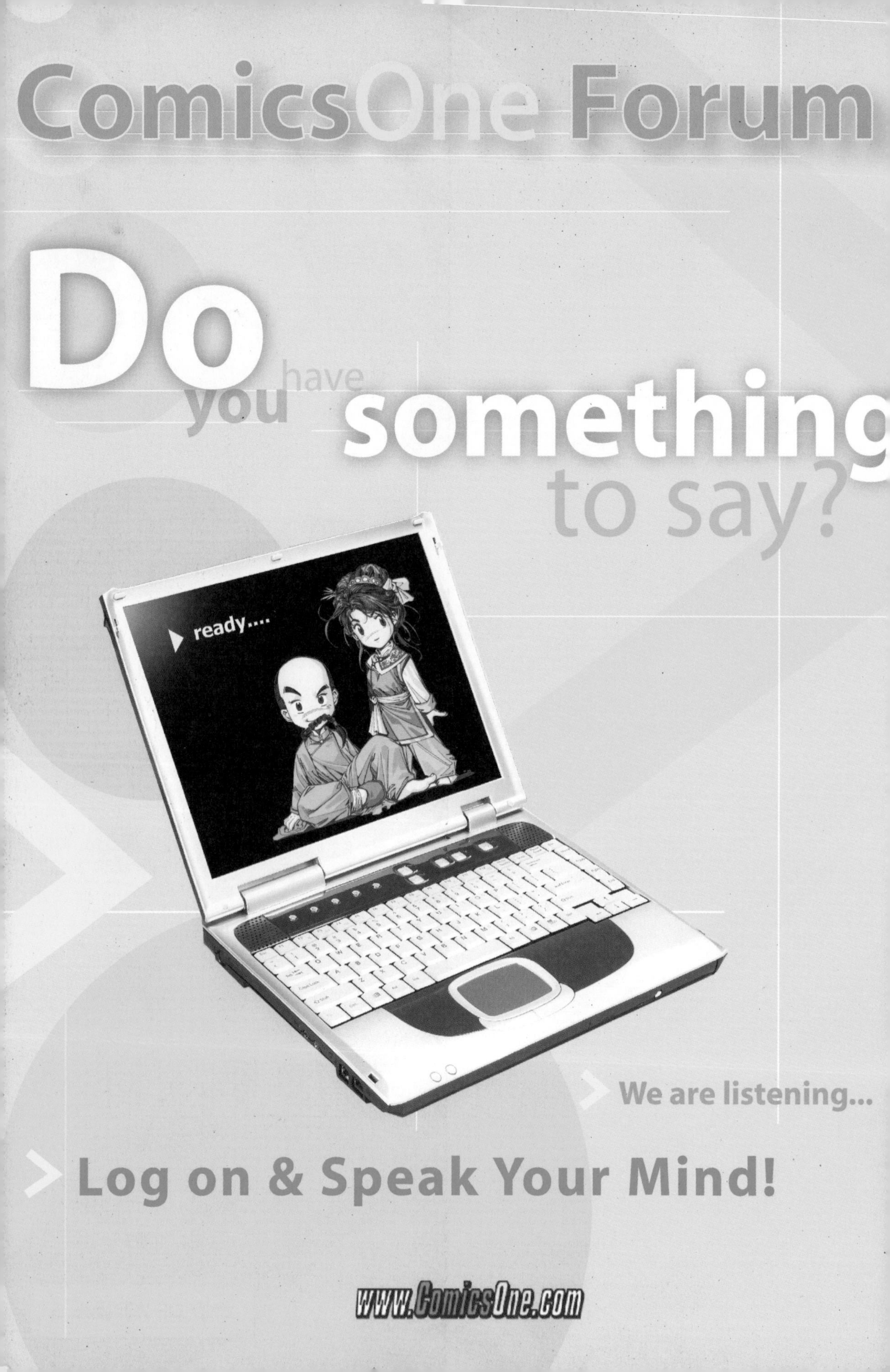
ComicsOne Forum
Do you have something to say?
ready....
We are listening...
Log on & Speak Your Mind!
www.ComicsOne.com